DRAWINGS BY JOSHUA TOLFORD

Music edited with the assistance of
Raymond Kane McLain,
Annabel Morris Buchanan,
and John Powell

Guitar chord accompaniment by
John E. Curtiss

American Folk Tales and Songs

AND OTHER EXAMPLES OF
ENGLISH-AMERICAN TRADITION
AS PRESERVED IN THE APPALACHIAN MOUNTAINS
AND ELSEWHERE IN THE UNITED STATES

Compiled
With Introduction and Notes
by RICHARD CHASE

Dover Publications, Inc.
New York

Published in Canada by General Publishing Company, Ltd., 30 Lesmill Road, Don Mills, Toronto, Ontario.
Published in the United Kingdom by Constable and Company, Ltd., 10 Orange Street, London WC 2.

This Dover edition, first published in 1971, is an unabridged republication, with minor corrections, of the work originally published by the New American Library of World Literature, Inc., New York, in 1956. New guitar chords have been prepared by John E. Curtiss especially for the Dover edition.

Acknowledgments are gratefully made to:
Annabel Morris Buchanan for permission to include the following traditional tunes, recorded by her and in her manuscript collection: OH LORD, HOW LONG? AT THE FOOT OF YONDER MOUNTAIN, THE DEVIL'S QUESTIONS, LADY GAY, NICKETY NACKETY, THE RICH OLD LADY, LOLLY TOO DUM, PADDY O'DOYLE, DEVILISH MARY, JOHNNY'S GONE TO HILO, WONDROUS LOVE, JESUS WALKED IN GALILEE.
The Dickensonian for permission to reprint OLD HIDE AND TALLER from H. M. Sutherland's column, TALES OF THE TALL TIMBER, Copyright, 1956, by H. M. Sutherland.
Houghton Mifflin Company for permission to reprint JACK AND THE OLD RICH MAN from *The Jack Tales*, Copyright, 1943, by Richard Chase, and WICKED JOHN AND THE DEVIL from *Grandfather Tales*, Copyright, 1948, by Richard Chase.

International Standard Book Number: 0-486-22692-1
Library of Congress Catalog Card Number: 72-140231

Manufactured in the United States of America
Dover Publications, Inc.
180 Varick Street
New York, N. Y. 10014

To Bill
and all his kindred
at
Pine Mountain and Hindman Settlements
and
Berea College

Acknowledgments

It would be difficult to list all the people who have had a hand one way or another in the making of this book. I am beholden to many whose names I did not record, and to many chance conversations which have turned up new and interesting information concerning things included here. Special thanks are due to: Annabel Morris Buchanan who gave me invaluable help with all the tunes; to Raymond Kane McLain who prepared the music for the printer; to Shelton Applegate and Anne Chase Applegate who had many good suggestions to offer; to Cratis Williams and James Still who both had a hand in improving the Introduction; to Alton C. Morris, Edwin C. Kirkland, Adele Clark, Willoughby Ions, Hilton Rufty, Louis C. Jones, Marjorie Loomis and Kathleen Garis Bolger who helped with the songs from Miss Ora Canter; Mrs. Pearl Wallace Chappell, George Steinman, Mrs. Willard Brooks, Mrs. George Biggs, Fletcher Collins, Jr., William Stephenson, Mrs. Homer Grandstaff, and The Council of Southern Mountain Workers' office at Berea College. Mr. and Mrs. Smith Harman, my host and hostess here at Beech Creek, North Carolina, gave me much good advice as well as actual tales and other information about the old ways. John Powell's counsel and encouragement have again helped me in many ways. I am grateful also to John E. Curtiss, who added the guitar chord accompaniment for the second edition.

Contents

"Tradition tells of King Alfred's genial good nature . . . and above all of his love for song. In his busiest days Alfred found time to learn the old songs of his race by heart and bade them be taught in the palace school. As he translated the tales of the heathen mythology he lingered fondly over and expanded them."

John Richard Green
A Short History of the English People

"A genuine carol [or folk ballad, folk song] may have faults of grammar, logic, and prosody; but one fault it never has—that of sham antiquity. . . . [It is] spontaneous and direct . . . rich in true folk poetry . . . fresh and buoyant . . . gives voice to the common emotions of healthy people in a language that can be understood and music that can be shared by all."

The Oxford Book of Carols
(Edited by Percy Dearmer, R. Vaughan
Williams and Martin Shaw)

INTRODUCTION

What is folklore?

Webster says: "Traditional tales, songs, dances, customs, beliefs, sayings, preserved unreflectively among a people . . . hence, the science which investigates the life and spirit of a people as revealed in such lore."

Who then are the "folk"?

Again let's consult Webster: "A group of kindred people . . . bound together by ties of race, language, religion, etc., and that great proportion of its number which determines the group character and tends to preserve its civilization."

American civilization stems from Old World sources. Our ideas of religion come from Hebraic traditions and from Christianity as it developed in the Greco-Roman world. Parts of the Bible are Jewish folklore. Much of Christianity is based on lore that preceded it in Egyptian, Hellenic, Alexandrian, and Roman civilizations. Many of our ideas of drama, poetry, architecture and sculpture come from the ancient Greeks. Greek art and literature developed from Mediterranean folklore.

Our American uses of the English language, literature, music, and folklore stem from the North of Europe. Other groups of kindred people in the United States speak French, Spanish, German, Scandanavian, and other languages—as well as English—and each tends to preserve here in our nation a great variety of Old World lore. Celtic tale-tellers (*sheenacnies*) can be found in New York and Chicago. Basques in Montana and Washington perform their ancient ritual dances regularly. Folklorists have difficulty collecting Armenian songs and dances in Armenia but find them readily in Detroit!

Each "group of kindred people" coming across the Atlantic brought its own lore—things of the mind and spirit—and often "unreflectively," sometimes deliberately, have kept the identity of each individual set of folk traditions. The use of the word "American" (especially "native American") can lead to confusion in the field of folklore. The only truly

11

American folk are the Indians, and individual tribes have to this day kept their own separate group character and civilization.

It is strange that the English-American heritage of folk tales, folk songs, and folk dances should have been so neglected by scholars and folklorists. When a certain scholar, the first to collect "The Jack Tales," approached the English Department of her university with a project for further work in the field of British folk tales in America she was told that such things did not exist.

Indian lore has been thoroughly collected. The Negro's songs and tales are widely known. Today there is an increasing interest in the folklore of many traditions, with an emphasis on Anglo-American materials, throughout the country. Our English-American folkways are still too often connected, in the minds of some, with a vulgarized idea of things "hillbilly." This is unfortunate. For there are many Americans who keep, unreflectively, these folkways: a store of traditions which they call, not "folklore," but simply the old songs, the old tales, the old ways. And those of us who know this heritage are not just mountain people, nor are we only country folk. We live in every state, and we can be found in large cities as well as out on the land.

This lore is not confined to any one geographical location —little pockets of Elizabethan culture isolated in remote mountain hollows. Such traditions are loved and remembered wherever tale-telling grandfathers and singing grandmothers are close to their children and grandchildren. For the genuine thing, carried on through generations and acquiring lively local and individual variations, always has strength, beauty, and a sort of quietness that make it convincing. Its power often resides in understatement. It does not flare into sudden "popularity" and then die out. Many of our English-American folk songs have been "popular" for seven hundred years! Our folkways are as solid, as lasting, and as adaptable as the language we use. This lore is organic, not static, and changes with each generation of singers and tale-tellers.

This book, then, presents samples of the lore of a kindred people—those of us here in America who, whatever our origins across the Atlantic, are bound together by a common use of the English language.

One of the first to deal with British folklore as preserved

12

here in the United States was the English scholar and musician, Cecil J. Sharp. From 1914 to 1918 he collected English folk ballads and folk songs (and one form of the English Country Dance) in the Southern Appalachians. In the years since Mr. Sharp's work was published (1932) a flood of Anglo-American folklore books has appeared, presenting such lore as found in twenty-four states and two Canadian provinces, and covering every kind of tradition, secular and sacred, from children's skip-rope rhymes to witchcraft. Folklore courses are now being taught in many colleges and schools, and The American Folklore Society, which publishes *The Journal of American Folklore,* is an active organization. The Country Dance Society of America, which developed from The English Folk Dance and Song Society in England, sponsors the social uses of all these lively traditions throughout the United States.

In this volume each song, tale, dance, or riddle will speak for itself. Notes are given telling where I learned each item. Some are well-known; some are rare. I have collated and edited the material to try to present the best and most universally usable versions, except where stated as given verbatim from the informant. Headnotes to individual songs and tales give details of my editing "for popular use."

Many of the tunes are printed in shape-notes because about twenty years ago a singer in the mountains asked me:

"You going to put these old songs in a book?"

"I hope to, some day."

"Then you be sure to get the music set down in shape-notes so we can sing it."

And I promised I would.

Shape-notes are simply an aid to sight-singing. They are in use all over the South. This device is much like the "tonic sol-fa" system used in England, but in our case the notes are in their usual places on the staff.

Since nearly every school child can sing the syllabus do-re-me-fa-sol-la-ti-do, once the shapes are learned, and the major scale sung by them a few times, the shape of the note head helps the singer locate the syllable and the tone. *Do* is keynote, of course, for all major tunes (Ionian mode). *Do* is movable in position but fixed in shape. In folk music there are primitive minor tunes (normal minor, pure minor, or Aeolian mode) that are sung with the keynote *la*. We might call this "*la* mode." Our folk singers never heard of the modes, however much they use them in their singing. There are six

13

such modes, or scales: *do* to *do*, *sol* to *sol* (Mixolydian mode), *la* to *la*, *re* to *re* (Dorian mode), *mi* to *mi* (Phrygian mode), and *fa* to *fa* (Lydian mode). *Do* scale, of course, predominates. *Sol*, *la* and *re* scales are fairly common. *Mi* scale is infrequent, and *fa* scale rare. *Note*: In all these modes the half-steps always stand exactly where they are in the major (*do*) scale, between *mi* and *fa*, and between *ti* and *do*.

Major scales.

do re mi fa sol la ti do

do re mi fa sol la ti do

do re mi fa sol la ti do

La scale. (Aeolian Mode.)

la ti do re mi fa sol la

Re scale. (Dorian Mode.)

re mi fa sol la ti do re

Five-tone scales. (All black keys.)

do re fa sol la do

la do re mi sol la

And what of the creative uses of our folk traditions?

"Great art," wrote John Jay Chapman, "does not come on call, and when it comes it is always shy." And when in the intellectual and spiritual development of a nation it does come, "it is always based on folklore, tradition, and a reverence for the past."

And Ralph Vaughan Williams says, "An art must be the reflection of the whole life of a community. Any direct and unforced expression of our common life may be the nucleus from which a great art will spring; of such expressions the folk song is the most genuine and unadulterated, besides being in itself a complete form of art."

Our nation is seeing a revival, a restoration, of various folk arts. If these traditions are kept straight and simple, and are enjoyed with the unself-conscious dignity which is their chief characteristic, then our folkways can play an important and constructive role in the work of both schools and churches. When country dancing, for example, is offered as social recreation in a community it welds any group into a highly spirited fellowship activated by an enjoyment that carries its own self-discipline, and it is self-perpetuating.

The genuine folk heritage has an immediate appeal for all ages, and as it becomes known to more and more individuals in the community it spreads naturally, toning up the whole cultural outlook. There is a living force in these old games and dances, tales and songs, that cannot be duplicated through mechanized and commercialized forms of recreation; their living social use, if thoughtfully planned and carefully taught, often results in an awakened attitude that relates to more basic concerns of life and of art in the broadest and best sense.

A great cultural development took place in Greece just after Athens and her allies conquered the Persian armies. The Elizabethan Age followed the defeat of the Spanish Armada. We and our allies have only recently gained a victory over forces that threatened our way of life.

There are signs that a great American art may be on its way. The outdoor dramas now being produced across the nation are full of "folklore, tradition, and a reverence for the past."[1] Symphonic works based on Anglo-American folk music are being written. The movements of John Powell's

[1] Such as "The Horn in the West" in Boone, North Carolina, and "Wilderness Road" at Berea, Kentucky.

15

Symphony in A are built around 1) country dance tunes, 2) "a love song," 3) two dramatic ballad tunes, and 4) a great triumphant march based on an ancient English ritual morris dance tune—which tune also appears in the 1835 edition of THE SOUTHERN HARMONY as "Mississippi," a Judgment Day hymn still sung in Kentucky. Stage plays based on folk ballads and tales have been attempted. Folk festivals are cropping up everywhere. And all this current interest in the word "folk" may be truly significant. Through a rediscovery of our genuine living folkways a great cultural rebirth could begin to work its leaven. It will happen slowly and quietly. Genuine culture is always shy.

A true folk singer sings "by heart" and not out of books. He never tries to impress an audience, because at his best he is a real artist. Sincerely he shares his love and knowledge of these things *with* you rather than performing them *for* you. He sings "unthoughtedly," without self-consciousness. He makes his points without overdoing. He never shows his tonsils! Folk arts lose all their magic the instant they are exploited sensationally.

"It is a small demand that these things make," wrote Cecil Sharp, "—that of being known, to be loved." And wherever the work of this man[2] has become known a restoration of these traditions has flourished: in England, and, through the Mountain Folk Festival at Berea College, throughout the southern mountains. The Berea Festival is never a "show." We meet to enjoy the old dances, to sing together, and this meeting is just another "party" to culminate the fun we have been having all winter singing and doing country dances in our own schools and communities.

In her book *The Ballad Tree*, Evelyn Wells writes: ". . . in the mountains where there was no recognition as yet [about 1918] of the value and beauty of our native songs, Cecil Sharp was able to stir a spark that has never died. Today, all over the southern mountains, a folk recreation program has developed [of which the spring festival at Berea is a part], largely because for three years a man traveled through these mountains with a divining rod which tapped the wellsprings of native music . . . nobody possesses this divining rod who does not have insight into the intrinsic fineness of human nature."

We might try to see clearly what Grundtvig did for Den-

[2]Mr. Sharp established The English Folk Dance and Song Society in England, and The Country Dance Society in America.

16

mark through her folk traditions, and what Elias Lonnrot (who collected the *Kalevala* from Finnish folk singers) and Sibelius have done for Finland. Douglas Hyde, Padraic Colum, John M. Synge, and The Abbey Theatre, working with Irish tradition helped established the New Eire. Our own cultural reawakening will follow surely, when more and more Americans discover what Cecil Sharp, Ralph Vaughan Williams, and John Powell have done for England and for us.

A fuller knowledge of the folk arts of our people—traditions we all share without always being conscious of it—will stir our minds and spirits as nothing else can by bringing us closer to our Old World origins—predominantly English but with delightful overlappings from other cultures and lores.

An immediate and direct awareness of our own rich heritage can most certainly inspire our makers of plays, novels, and poems toward more lasting "success," and give a fresh delight to those of us who are creative only in being alive and doing our daily work. This experience will restore in us a cultural sincerity that can help us see the living values in all fine art in a free society like ours. Furthermore, folk arts can give coming generations a solid basis of judgment for reading good books, listening to good music, and choosing good, more really pleasurable forms of social recreation. And these traditions are not "good" because they are "old." It's the other way around! Such things last, once we have opportunities to know them, because they excite an immediate response, particularly with young people.

John Powell has said, ". . . it is for all English-speaking people . . . that this tradition has the greatest significance, for it is a vital part of that culture without which art is impossible and education can so easily become a lifeless and useless burden."

Discovery of the spontaneous "unreflective" folkways of our nation will come to many as a welcome breath of fresh air. Our ears and eyes are becoming saturated with cheap, commercialized "cultural" products consciously designed to force on us something called "amusement." And this fare is often put forth, by design, on an almost moronic level, "because that's what the public wants."

A knowledge of our folkways will open up lively and rich experiences for many who have never been moved by symphonies and other forms of art music. The inherent qualities of folk tradition do away with sham and pretense. Folk music is a sure steppingstone to a sincere understanding of the world's other music. Ralph Vaughan Williams has stated the case quite clearly: "When . . . Cecil Sharp collected and published his new discoveries in English folk songs (discoveries made on both sides of the Atlantic) he had in mind the ordinary man, the 'divine average' of Whitman. And it is the ordinary man for whose musical salvation the folk song will be responsible. For here is an ideal music . . . neither popular nor classical, highbrow nor lowbrow, but an art in which all can take part . . . a music which has for generations voiced the spiritual longings of our race."

And this current "folk movement," in England and in America, is indeed contagious. It proves, wherever it is based on actual tradition, an enlivening spiritual experience. It puts us in touch with our own individual sources, whatever they are: Anglo-American, French-American, Spanish-American, Hebrew, Negro, Indian—all. Barriers of race, language, region, fall only when one understands deeply his own individual heritage. Only then can we truly share the folkways of others, and understand that there are no "foreign" Americans. These facts give us a better understanding of the varied regions of our own nation and can play a part in creating better cultural understanding between this country and other nations of the world.

If such a movement is to become the basis for a living creative use of art in the United States, it will spread best, perhaps only, through the living word, the human touch. There can be no commercialization, no standardization, no mechanization of these things. They elude every sort of "modern sophistication." They are always "shy."

And, be it made clear: when we say "Anglo-Saxon" no kind of "superiority" is implied. (I know the beauty of Spanish folk plays of New Mexico. I know a Finn in Massachusetts whose translation into English of *The Kalevala* may prove the best ever made.) It is an awkward expression but it will have to serve. Some years ago a southern Highlander told me, "Yes, I've heard it said that here in these mountains is the best Angry-Saxon blood in the nation." And recently I heard an orator in the Appalachian region proclaim, "We are the finest Anglo-Saxon stock in the whole United States." (Much applause.) This is almost nonsensical. But the Angles, Saxons, Jutes, Danes, Vikings, Normans, all "North-men"—mixing and re-mixing with Gaels and Celts in the British Isles did develop in time certain cultural characteristics. They gave us Woden's

Day and Thor's Day, and the word "Easter." They gave us the language which is spoken here between two oceans. Traditions are found amongst us today that were already ancient in the Elizabethan Age when English civilization was at a great height and our folk traditions were well known. Shakespeare wrote a play based on an old tale which you will find in this book.

It needs to be said here, that there are no watertight compartments separating our individual American peoples. Cultural understanding transcends differences of race, and all man-made barriers, be they political or religious. Uncle Remus knew many Anglo-Celtic tales and told two versions of "Wicked John and the Devil." It is the unreflective use of such lore in our own natural environment that recreates it for each new generation.

"We in the United States," wrote the late President Franklin D. Roosevelt, "are amazingly rich in the elements from which to weave a culture. We have the best of man's past on which to draw, brought to us from all parts of the world. In binding these elements into a national fabric of strength and beauty, let us keep the original fibers so intact that the fineness of each will show in the complete handiwork."

It is the original fibers, *kept intact,* in their living uses, that are for every group of Americans the nucleus of a genuine culture. True folk traditions have the magic of all great art, whether it be a tragic ballad, a children's song, a carol, a ridiculous tall tale, a singing game, a lilting fiddle tune, a strange-sounding "minor" hymn, or a rollicking comic tale or song.

You can tell, without being "an authority," whether it is genuine or not. You know by the feel, by a tingling of your scalp, by an indefinable something inside you when you hear the song sung, or the tale told, or the tune played. It will arouse your interest, command your respect, and finally win and hold your love.

To find your own "original fibers" you need but seek them out in your own region, your own neighborhood, or even from the older members of your own family. Here amongst my people in the Southern mountains, it is fiddlers, banjo players, the older people and the families who delight in "making music," who know these things. Often the songs and tales are buried deep in the old folks' memories and you must be patient. Sometimes the person who can tell you the most about "the old ways" will at first disclaim any knowledge of such things. But if you can tell a tale yourself, or sing some real folk song that you know, he (or she) will very likely recollect something for you sooner or later.

You might like to try it! So we have included here a brief "Amateur Collector's Guide." If you do try collecting folklore you may not only find something very important that has never been recorded, but you may also have opportunities to rediscover for yourself certain basic human values—traditions that lead us all to a better realization of lasting things in a changing world. For many of us are, as Gilbert Murray has put it, ". . . under the power of the enemy . . ."

This enemy is "he who always puts the letter before the spirit, cheapness and triviality before beauty. It is he who makes things only in order to sell them; who has forgotten that there is such a thing as truth and measures the world by advertisement or by profit; who daily defiles the beauty that surrounds him and makes vulgar the tragedy . . . the smart, the clever, *the counterfeiter of spiritual values*[3]—he is all about us, and worse, he has wormed his way inside so many of us . . . persecuting our peace, spoiling our insight, confusing our highest values. . . ."

Yes, our folk traditions—the hilarity and rich dry humor of our folk tales, the beauty and gaiety of our folk music, the deep sincerity of our old hymns—these are only one expression of an American culture. It is not the old songs and tales that are so important in themselves; it is a way of life, the essence of ourselves and of our kindred, and knowledge of a higher set of values in the realm of the mind and spirit, that my people here in America have taught me.

[3] Italics mine.

1. Tales

ANCIENT TALES

Wicked John and the Devil

According to William Butler Yeats, a similar story, about a man named Will Dawson, is told in Ireland as "The Three Wishes." Someone told me once that, in another version, Will stuck his wisp of a beard through the bars at Hell Gate and the Devil set it on fire— and that is how the swamp light got its name. Uncle Remus has two versions: "Jacky-My-Lantern" and "Impty Umpty." Dr. Stith Thompson, the great authority on folk tales, reports this tale from Germany, Estonia, Finland, Denmark, Norway, Flanders, Lapland, Russia, and Latvia. And in *A Treasury of French Tales*, published early in 1954, this same tale—without the will-o'-the-wisp ending—is given as told in France.

As printed here it is based on the way I heard it from Mrs. Jenning L. Yowell of Charlottesville, Virginia. Her name for the blacksmith was "Wicked Jack." I changed it to "John" to avoid confusion with the boy "Jack" of *The Jack Tales,* who appears also in other Irish, English, and Scotch folk tales.

My first knowledge of the Devil's "curtain line" (". . . and start you a Hell of your own!") came from *Mules and Men,* a collection of Negro folklore from Florida, by Zora Neal Hurston. From Peck Daniel of Bristol, Virginia, I learned of a radio broadcast of this tale, in which it was Saint Patrick who granted the three wishes, and the old man wound up haunting the waterfront under Brooklyn Bridge. Another variation of the "mean"- mortal-being-denied-entrance-to-Hell was told on Hitler here in the mountains: "And the Devil wouldn't let him in. He was too mean for Hell, having people mommicked and gaumed up the way he did." A dramatization of this story proves great fun. I saw junior high school students do it once in Evanston, Illinois.

Appalachian State Teachers College in Boone, North Carolina, did it in the fall of 1953. And in the spring of 1954 a mountain high school performed it several times. In my own dramatization I retained John's wife, and had her raise the Devil against John because he "pulled a rusty on her" by putting salt in her skin when she left it behind in changing into a black cat hide "to go do her witchin'."

One time there was an old blacksmith named John. He was so mean they called him Wicked John. Mean? Aa-aa Lord! He didn't wait till Saturday night for *his* dram. He'd just as soon start in drinkin' of a Sunday . . . Monday . . . Tuesday. It didn't differ. He stayed lit-up all week anyhow. Talked mean. Acted mean. Independent minded. He wasn't afraid of nothin' nor nobody.

One thing about him though: he always did treat a stranger right. And one mornin' Wicked John was workin' there in his shop when an old beggar came to the door: crippled-up with rheumatism, all bent over and walkin' on two sticks. Looked right tired and hungry-like. Stood there till fin'lly Old John hollered at him, says, "Well come in! Confound! Come on in and sit down! Rest yourself."

The old beggar he heaved over the sill, stumbled to where there was a nail-keg turned up, sat down. John kept right on workin', talkin' big; but seemed like the old man was so give-out he couldn't talk much. So directly old John throwed his hammer down and headed for the house. "You wait now. Just sit right there."

Came back with a plate full of vittles: boiled sweet tater, big chunk of ham-meat, beans, greens, slice of cake—and he'd even gone to the spring-house and fetched a pitcher of sweet milk. "Here, old man! Try these rations. I hope you can find something here you can eat."

"Thank ye. Thank ye."

"Oh hit ain't much. If I can eat it three times a day every day, you can stomach it once I reckon."

Wicked John he went on back to work a-hammerin' and a-poundin'. Watched the old beggar out the corner of his eye: saw him lay the plate and glass to one side directly and start to get up. He let his two walkin' sticks fall to the ground. Commenced straightenin' up, straightenin' up, all the kinks comin' out of him. There was a flash of light all at once. And the next thing old John knew—there, r'ared up in the door,

22

was a fine stout-like old man: had a white beard and white hair, long white robe right down to his feet, and a big gold key swingin' in his hand.

Old John stood there with his jaw hangin', and his eyes popped open.

"Well John, I don't reckon you know me, do ye?"

"Why—now, what happened to that old beggar? And where-in-the-nation did you come from—where folks dress like that?"

"I don't see you've got any way of knowin' me, John, since you never have been inside a church-house your whole life. I'm Saint Peter."

"Aw-w-w, now! You expect me to believe that?"

"It don't differ whether you believe it or not. I'll just tell you how-come I'm down here. Once a year I walk the earth to see can I find any decent folks left on it. And the first man I run across that treats me right I always give him three wishes. So you go ahead, John. Wish for anything you've a mind to, and hit'll be that-a-way. Take your three wishes, and be careful now."

Well, Old John he was grinnin' at Saint Peter like he didn't believe none of it. He was already pretty high that mornin', so he looked around: started wishin' on the first thing would pop into his head.

"Three wishes, huh? Well now—see that old high-back rockin chair yonder? I keep it there so I can sit and rest everwhen I get done with ar' job-of-work. But—don't you know!—these dad-blame loafers that hang around in here of an evenin'! Nearly every time I go to sit down, there sits one of them lazy no-'count fellers a-wearin' out the seat of his britches in *my* rocker. Hit makes me mad! And I just wish that anybody sits there will stick to the chair-bottom and that old rocker rock 'em till they holler! Hold 'em stuck fast—till I let 'em go."

Saint Peter was writin' it down with a gold pencil in a little gold notebook. "That's one, John."

"Aa-aa Lord! Lemme see now. Well, take my big sledge hammer there. Every day after school these blame school kids come by here and get to messin' with my tools: slip that sledge out and take it across the road. Play pitch-hammer, or see how big a rock they can bust. And—confound!—every time I need it I have to go and hunt the dad-blame thing where them feisty boys have dropped it in the grass. Blame take it! I wish: that *any*body teches that hammer will stick to the

23

handle and hit pound right on—shake 'em! Shake the day-lights out of 'em, till I let 'em go."

Saint Peter was scowlin' and shakin' his head like he thought old John was wastin' his wishes pretty bad.

But John was mean, like I said. *He* didn't care! Looked at Saint Peter mischievous-like, grinned sort of devilish, says, "One more wish, huh, Peter? All right. Now: There's that big firebush just outside the door. Gets full of all them red blooms real early in the spring-of-the-year. I like my old thornbush but hit's been mommicked up right bad here lately: folks backin' their wagons over it, horses tromplin' it—and these here highfalutin' folks comin' over the mountain a-fox-huntin'. Humph! Go gallopin' all around these pasture-fields fox-huntin' on horseback—their little red coats flappin' out behind. Looks like they got to stop and break ridin' switches off that bush every time they pass here. I wish that *any*body teches that firebush, it will grab 'em and pull 'em headfore-most right down in the middle where them stickers are the thickest—hold 'em there till *I* let 'em out."

Saint Peter quit writin', shut his little book, put hit and the gold pencil back inside his white robe, says, "Mighty sorry wishes, John. Looks like you might have made one wish for the good of your soul. You've sure wasted your chance. But that's what you've wished for and hit'll be that-a-way just like I said. Well, I got to go now."

"Oh, just stay the night, Peter."

"Can't stay."

And Saint Peter stepped over the doorsill and he was gone from there, and Wicked John couldn't tell which-a-way he went nor nothin'.

II

Well you'd a-thought old John might have done a little better one way or another after havin' a saint right there in his shop, but it didn't have no effect on *him*. Aa-aa Lord! He got meaner than ever. Somebody 'uld come and John would tell 'em, "Sit down." He'd trick a man into helpin' him hammer somethin' with that big sledge—and let it shake 'em a while 'fore he'd make it turn loose. And if anybody hap-pened to brush against that firebush hit would grab 'em and they'd get scratched up right pityful, but old John he 'uld just laugh and let 'em stay stuck till he got ready to let 'em go.

So, one way or another, Wicked John turned so cussed he

got to be the meanest man in the world. And The Devil—he keeps pretty good track of what's goin' on up here, you know —he got worried. Decided that wouldn't do: havin' anybody out-do him in meanness. So he sent for old John. Wouldn't wait for him to die. Sent one of the little devils to fetch him right now.

Old John looked up one mornin' and there, standin' in the door, was a little horn-ed devil—about a fifth-grade-size devil —little horns just startin' to bump up on his forehead.

"Come on, old man. Daddy sent me to get ye. Said for me to bring ye right on back."

Old John had his hammer raised up, starin' at that little devil—started in hammerin' again. Says, "All right, son. I'll be ready to go with ye in just a few more licks. Got to finish this one horseshoe. Come on in. Hit won't take me but a minute."

"No. Daddy said not to wait."

"All right! All right! Come on in. I'll be as quick as I can."

The little devil he came on inside, frettin'. Watched old John pound a few licks. Looked around the shop—and made for that old rockin' chair. Eased down in it, r'ared back and started rockin'. Says, "You hurry up now. Daddy'll sure get mad if we take too long."

John finished that shoe, soused it in the coolin' tub, throwed it on the ground. The little devil started to get up. Heaved a time or two. And directly the poor little devil's head was goin' *whammity-bang!* against the chairback.

"Oh, mister, I'm stuck!"

"Now! Hain't that too bad!"

"Ow! Please mister! Let me up!"

"I'll let you go if you get out of here and not bother me no more."

"Yes, sir! I'll leave right now! And I'll not *never* come back."

"All right. Away with ye!"

And the rockin' chair throwed him out on the ground and—*rippity-tuck!*—out the door, and down the road!

John went on with his work, and in a few minutes there was another'n—a little devil about high-school-size, little horns spike-in' up. Stood there in the door actin' biggity. Says, "You come on here, old man."

"Why hello, son. Come on in." John kept right on workin'.

"You stop that poundin' and come on with me. Ye hear?"

"Why I can't stop now. This thing's red-hot and I'm bound to finish it 'fore we leave."

"No now! You quit right where you're at. Daddy said if I didn't fetch you back in five minutes he'd roast me good."

John kept right on—bam! bam! bam!

"Huh? Can't hear ye. I can't talk till I get done with this wagon tire."

Well that little devil saw old John was havin' it kind of awkward the way he had to hold up that big iron wagon tire and beat it one-handed. So he lumbered right on inside the shop.

"Stand back then, old man. You hold that thing and let me pound it. We got to hurry."

Leaned over and picked up the big sledge hammer, started swingin' it. Wicked John, he held the tire up and turned it this-a-way and that-a-way. Pulled it out from under the hammer directly, cooled it in the big tub, and leaned it against the wall.

26

"Much obliged. Hit's finished. What ye poundin' so hard for?" And old John went to laughin'.

Well, the way that hammer was swingin' that little devil around, jerkin' him up and down with his legs a-flyin' ever' which-a-way—hit was a sight-in-this-world!

"Ow! My hands is stuck! O please mister! Make this thing turn me loose!"

"You promise to leave here?"

"Shore I promise!"

"And not come back?"

"Yes, sir! No, sir! You won't never catch *me* here again!"

"Then away with ye!"

When the hammer let go, it slung that little devil up in the rafters. He hit the ground, and when he got his legs untangled he streaked out the door and went dustin' down the road.

Then it wasn't hardly no time at all till Wicked John looked up and there standin' in the door—with his old goat horns roached back over his head, and his forked tail a-swishin', and that big cow's foot of his'n propped up on the sill—was The Old Boy. His eyes were just a-blazin'. Old John kept right on with his work. "Howdy do! Come on in."

"YOU COME ON HERE, OLD MAN! AND I AIN'T GOIN' TO TAKE NO FOOLISHNESS OFF YE NEITHER!"

"All right sir. Just as soon as I get done. Promised a man I'd sharpen this mattick head 'fore twelve. Hit won't take but a few more licks. Come on in, confound it, and sit down!"

"NO! I'LL NOT SIT IN NO CHAIR OF YOUR'N!"

"Suit yourself. But we'll be ready to go quicker'n you can waste time arguc-in', if *you'll* hit this mattick a lick or two while I hold it with the tongs here. Just grab the big sledge leanin' there on the door jam and . . . "

"NO! I AIN'T GOIN' TO TECH NO SLEDGE HAMMER NEITHER! YOU DONE MADE ME MAD ENOUGH ALREADY, OLD MAN, THE WAY YOU DONE MY BOYS. AND I'M TAKIN' YOU OFF FROM HERE RIGHT NOW!"

Old John r'ared up, says, "You and who else? Jest tech me! I dare ye!"

The Devil made for him and old John let him have it. And such a punchin', knockin', beatin', you never did see! Poundin', scratchin', kickin', buttin', like two horses fightin'. Wicked John was mean, like I said. He wasn't goin' to take nothin' off nobody, not even the Devil himself. They had a round or two there by the door and fin'lly The Devil grabbed old John by the seat of his britches and heaved him outside. John twisted around some way or other and got hold of The Devil's tail—kinked it up, you know, like tryin' to make an unruly cow go in the barn—yanked right hard. Well that really made The Devil mad.

"BLAST YE, OLD MAN! I'M GOIN' TO LICK THE HIDE OFF YOU RIGHT NOW. JUST SEE IF I DON'T. WHERE'LL I GET ME A SWITCH?"

And the Devil reached to break him a switch off that firebush. Time he touched it, hit wropped all around him and jerked him headforemost right down in the middle of all them long stickers. The old Devil he tried to get loose but the more he thrashed around in there the more he got scratched, till fin'lly he had to give up: his legs hangin' limp out the top of the bush and his head 'way down in there.

"Mister?"

Old John was laughin' so hard he had to lean against the shop. "What ye want now?"

"Please sir. Let me out."

"Who was that you was goin' to whip? Huh?"

"Nobody.—Now will you let me out of here?"

"I'll let you out of there on one condition: you, nor none of your boys, don't ye never—none of ye—ever come back up here botherin' me no more. You promise me that and I might let ye go."

"Hell yes, I promise.—Now please will you make this bush turn loose of me?"

The bush let go, and when the old Devil crawled out he had leaves and trash caught on his horns, and his old long black coat torn to rags. He turned around and when he got his legs to workin', such a kickin' up dust you never did see! They tell me that when The Old Boy left there he wasn't moseyin'.

III

So Wicked John he never was bothered by any more devils after that. Just kept on blacksmithin' there in his shop. Lived on till he was an old old man. Stayed mean, too—just as mean as ever right to the day he died. And when fin'lly he *did* die, he didn't do a thing but go right straight to The Pearly Gates. Bam! Bam! Bam!

Saint Peter cracked the door, and when he saw who it was, he backed off a little, says, "*Uh*—oh!" Looked out. "Er—Hello, John. Just what did you want?"

"Well Peter—seein' as you knowed me, I thought that maybe . . ."

"Why John, you can't come in here."

"Oh I know I can't *stay*, Peter. But I'd sort of like to take me one look around: see them golden streets, hear me a little harp music, and then I'll go."

"Can't do it, John. Can't do it. You wait a minute. I'm just goin' to show you your accounts here on the record. Hand out the book, one of ye."

Saint Peter reached and took the big book, licked his thumb and turned the pages.

"Here you are.—Now here's your two pages in the ledger, John. Look there on the good-deed side. All the ninety-two years you've lived, three entries, 'way up at the top of the page. But over here on the *other* side—Why!—hit's black, clean to the bottom line. And all the meanness you've done the past twelve years, you can see for yourself, it had to be writ in sideways."

Saint Peter shut the book and took off his spectacles, says, "I'm sorry, John, but you can't put one foot inside here. So if you'll excuse me now———" And Saint Peter backed through the gates and reached and shut 'em to.

Well old John he just shuffled around and headed back down the stairsteps.

IV

That day several devils was there in front of the gate to Hell, playin' catch with a ball of fire. And one of 'em happened to be that first 'un was sent to fetch Wicked John. He chanced to look off down the road directly. His eyes popped open and he missed his catch. Turned and ran through the gates just a-squallin', "Daddy! O Daddy! Run here quick!"

The old Devil came and looked out. And there, headed right that way, with his hands in his pockets, a-whistlin', and just a-weavin' down the road—was Wicked John. The Devil turned around, says, "Bar the door, boys! Bar the door."

So when old John got there, there was the gates to Hell shut and padlocked: the little devils peepin' out from behind the mine-props and coal piles scared to death, and the old Devil standin' 'way back, says, "Un-*unh!* You ain't comin' in *here* now. Don't ye come no closeter. You just turn around right where you're at and put off! I done had enough of you. Now git!"

Old John stood there scratchin' his head, says, "Confound!" Turned to the Devil, says, "Look-a-here. I went up yonder and Saint Peter told me I couldn't get in up *there,* and here *you've* gone and locked me out. Why! I don't know where to go to, now."

The Devil studied a minute, grabbed up some tongs, reached in one of his furnaces and got hold of a hot coal. Edged over 'side the gate and handed the tong-handles out the bars, says, "Here, old man. You just take this chunk of fire and go on off somewhere else—and start you a hell of your own."

Old John took it and put off.

And right to this day, they say that in The Great Dismal Swamps—somewhere over yonder between Virginia and Carolina—you can look out of a night and see a little bob of light movin' around out there.

One old-time name for it is the Will-o'-the-wisp, and some old folks call it the Jacky-my-lantern. Now some people that don't know any better—these schoolteachers and college professors—they'll try to tell you it's nothin' but some kind of marsh gas a-lightin' up out in the swamps.

But you'uns know better now, don't ye?

Here, from a disc recording, is Mrs. Yowell's actual ending of the tale, as told August 5, 1945.

And the years went on by; and Jack really, finally, died. After so many years—lived longer'n most anybody else—he *died.* And of course he was so wicked there wasn't nowhere else for him to go but right on to Hell, was it? Well, when he got down to the gates—just before he got there, some of the boys was dancin', makin' merry around the fire, and they peeped out, says, "Dad! Look out yonder! Who is that staggerin' down the hill?"

"Great goodness alive![1] That looks like Wicked Jack!—Bar the door, boys! Bar the door!"

So they put a big iron bar across the door.

Jack came: Thump! Thump!

"You can't come in! . . . We don't want you!"

"Well, if I can't come in, will you just give me a torch so I can see how to get back up to the flats?"

So they said Yes. Just to get rid of him they gave a torch.

[1] Hardly a remark the Devil would make!

30

So he took his torch, and the last they ever saw of him was goin' up the swampy flats.

And *ever* since then we've been seein' Jack-a-lanterns.[2]

R. CHASE: Been seein' what?

MRS. YOWELL: Jack-a-lanterns.

R. C.: Is that the little bob of flame that goes along in the swamps?

MR. Y.: In swamps! You see these lights, you know, they call Jack-a-lanterns. That's what you *call* 'em!

MRS. Y.: That's right.

Rush Cape

This is one of the three world-wide types of the Cinderella tale. English-American variants of all three types exist: "Catskins," "Ashpet," and "Like Meat Loves Salt," as given in *Grandfather Tales*. In the United States the tale has been reported from Nova Scotia, New York, Tennessee, Missouri, the Sea Islands of South Carolina, Virginia, and Kentucky. The version printed here is based on information from Mrs. Milton F. Hears of Abingdon, Virginia, and on Kentucky and Tennessee versions received through Lois Fenn of Kansas. The old king's madness as an integral part of the tale seems to be traditional in only three versions: 1) "as told to J. B. Ortoli, in 1881, by Adelade de Alam, Porto Vecchio, Corsica," 2) in the Virginia version, and 3) in Shakespeare's *King Lear*. Joseph Jacobs calls attention to the King Lear parallel in his "Cap o' Rushes."

It would be interesting to see what some young American playwright might do in creating a "folk" play from these sources.

[2] This throws another light on our Hallowe'en customs. I have a clipping from an unidentified Star newspaper headed "A Legend of the Jack-o'-Lantern," by John J. Doohan (a member of the *Star's* staff). It reads, in part: "Jack-o'-Lanterns are said to be of Irish origin, although no pumpkins were raised on the Old Sod. The children hollowed out large potatoes, turnips, and rutabagas as lanterns at Hallowe'en festivities." Then follows a version of this tale: "A Boy Called Jack Who Would Not Obey His Parents." "Jack traps the Devil with a sign of the cross, and after catching him in a wallet, and then up an apple tree, makes the Devil promise never to bother him again."

Mr. Doohan's version ends as follows:

"When Jack died he was turned away from heaven for his misdeeds, and having nowhere to go, knocked at the gates of Hell. The devil said Jack could not enter.

" 'Where will I go?' Jack asked.

"The devil threw him a lighted coal. Jack put it into a large potato he was carrying, cut some holes so that the glow might escape to light his way, and wandered the earth with his Jack-o'-Lantern."

31

One time there was a King had three girls. He was getting very old, so he called his daughters one day and told them, says, "There's a question I want answered and I want the truth."

Looked at the oldest, says, "How much do you love me?"

The oldest she spoke right up, says, "I love you more than all the gold and silver in the world."

Then he asked the second one and she put-on even more than the first. "Why," she says, "I love you more than all the gold and silver and diamonds and fine jewelry there is in the world."

That's what she had on *her* mind.

Now his youngest, she was his baby and his pet, and she really thought the world of her old father, so she made up her mind she'd try to tell the truth the best way she could. So when the old King turned to her and asked her that, she looked at him right straight, says, "I love you, father, like bread loves salt."

The old man r'ared back, and threw up his head.

"Is *that* all you can answer?"—Talked hateful.

"Yes," she says. "I love you but I know that someday there'll be a young man I'm bound to love better. I love you all my duty can allow me, and that's the dyin' truth."

So he turned his back on her and the two oldest girls took the old King's arms and off they went. He settled a lot of land on them and they married rich.

The youngest she went to a swamp and wove herself a cape out of rushes. Put on that cape and covered her fine clothes, and hid her pretty hair in a rush bonnet. Then she went to seek her fortune.

She traveled on, traveled on until she came to England. Hired out to a King there, and went to work in the kitchen. They called her Rush Cape.

Then one night there was a dance and she decided she'd go. So she slipped out and took off her rush bonnet and cape and hung them on a tree. Shook out her pretty yellow hair and went to the dance in her fine clothes.

When she got there the King's son he took her for his partner every set they danced. Wouldn't even look at any other girl. But Rush Cape she slipped out and went back ahead of the others. Put on her rush bonnet and cape, and when they came in there she was asleep on the hearthrock.

The next night there was another dance.

"You goin' to the dance tonight, Rush Cape? You can stand by the door and watch us."

"No. I'm too tired."

"You ought to come. There was the prettiest girl there last night. Nobody knows who she is or where she came from. And the King's boy wouldn't dance with anybody else but her."

But Rush Cape said No, she didn't see how she could go tired as she was with all her work. Then after they all left she went out and took off her rush things, and when she came in there at the dance everybody looked at her—and the King's son wouldn't let go her hand. But when they were doin' a Grand-Right-and-Left he *had* to turn her hand loose, so she slipped out the ring, and back she went. That boy didn't know what to do when he couldn't find his partner.

The others came home and there she was curled up before the fire with her old rush bonnet on and that rush cape tucked around her feet.

She worked hard the next day scouring the pots and doing all the washing and mopping. And then after supper the other girls came to her, said, "Why don't you go with us tonight? This is the last dance and everybody is wonderin' if that beautiful woman will come again."

But Rush Cape she stayed there by the fire till they'd all left.

And when she finally walked in where they were dancing they all stopped. Started whisperin'—"There she is!" "Who is she?" "Isn't she beautiful!" "Where does she live?" "What's her name?"

The King's boy took her hand and after they danced a while he sat down with her by the fireplace and slipped a ring on her finger. She had a hard time getting away from him that night, but when they did

Wave of the Ocean! Wave of the Sea!
Turn my pretty girl back to me!——

the King's son reached for her and she wasn't there!

Well, after that the boy got his father to send all over the country lookin' for that girl, and when the King's men kept coming back saying they couldn't find her, the boy finally got so love-sick he wouldn't get up: just lay there like he would die. He wouldn't hardly eat. Then one day Rush Cape she fixed him a bowl of soup, and the boy's mother started feedin' it to him. She spooned it in his mouth and directly something clinked against the spoon.

"Why what's this? Look, son, here's a ring in the bottom of the bowl."

And she wiped it on her apron and showed it to him. He took it and when he saw it he raised up off the pillows, says, "Who made this soup?"

"Why I don't know. One of the kitchen girls I reckon."

"Go find out which one," he says, and he reached for his clothes.

They finally brought Rush Cape in, and the boy looked at her, says, "Why it was you!"

So she let her rush cape fall and took off that rush bonnet, and the King's son he took both her hands, says, "Now I'll never let go of you as long as I live."

And they got married.

34

Some time after that, her two oldest sisters they had used up all the old King's gold and silver, everything he had, and they finally turned the old man out of his own house.—That hurt him.

Then one dark night there was somebody called out at the King of England's door. The King's son went to see who it was. Opened the door, and there stood an old beggar. The boy told him to come in. The girl looked up and saw it was her father. He was ragged and his hair was all tangled, but he looked at everybody right proud-like. He had wythed him some briars and weeds and had that on his head for his crown.—His daughter came to him but he didn't know her.

Well, they took him and helped him get clean and dressed him in good clothes. Combed his hair and fed him, but he hardly spoke a word, and no matter what his girl said to him he still didn't know her at all.

The next day she told the cook, says, "When you fix dinner today don't put a speck of salt in anything."

"That'll sure taste bad."

"It don't differ. You do what I say."

So when the old King started eating he laid his fork back on the plate, and reached for some bread. Tasted it. Put it down and then he looked up sort of puzzled-like. Then his girl brought the salt and set it there by the old King's place. He looked at the salt, and then he dropped his head and the tears started falling.

The King's boy asked him what was the matter, and the old man spoke right out clear and told about his three daughters.

"And I can remember now," he told them, "how my youngest girl said she loved me like bread loves salt. She was the only one that really loved me." And he dropped his head down again.

His girl came right to him and took his hand and raised him up. Then he looked at her and he knew who she was, and his mind came back to him clear.

And after that they all lived happy.

Jesus to Supper

This is told in the Southern Mountains. I heard it, most recently, from my neighbors in Watauga County, North Carolina. Tolstoy has a tale, somewhat similar, about a cobbler.

Two old people had invited The Lord to supper, and he was late coming. They kept the supper hot and waited and waited, but still he didn't come.

Directly an old beggar came to the door and asked for something to eat. The old woman thought, "Well, I'll let him have my part." They were so poor they hardly had enough for the three of 'em. She went ahead and fed the beggar, and he thanked her and left.

They still waited and waited and kept looking out the door. Then a little ragged boy came along. He looked cold and sort of starved, so they took him in. The old man told his wife, says, "I'm not much hungry. He can have my supper."

So they fed the boy and let him sit and get warm. Tried to get him to stay the night but he said he couldn't, and when he left the old man got a coat for him so he'd keep warm.

They kept the fire going and kept Jesus' supper ready. And finally they looked out and saw him coming. They went to meet him at the gate, said, "We waited so long! We were afraid you'd never come."

The Lord took their hands, says, "I've already been here twice."

Mister Fox

This murder-mystery was known to Shakespeare: *Scene 1, Act 1,* of *Much Ado About Nothing,* where Benedick remarks, "Like the old tale, my lord, 'It is not so, nor 'twas not so, but, indeed, God forbid it should be so!' "

As told here, it has been put together from tellings by R. M. Ward[8] of Beech Creek, North Carolina, and by Polly Johnson of Norton, Virginia. The German version is called "The Robber Bridegroom," and Joseph Jacobs' "Mr. Fox," from England, is close to the American tale. Mr. Ward called the villain "Old Foister." I have never actually heard the "Fox Riddle" told with the tale. It is my own guess that it must have once been part of the story. This tale, as in the case of "Wicked John," is known all over northwestern Europe, as reported by Dr. Stith Thompson.

One time there was a young woman named Polly. They called her Pretty Polly. She wasn't married and she lived by herself. All her folks were dead. And one day a stranger came into that settle-ment. Said his name was Fox. Slick-lookin' feller, and he went to courtin' Pretty Polly right off. He'd come to see her of a Saturday night, and they'd talk. Then one day he asked her would she meet him the next Saturday night under a big pine out on a ridge there. So she told him she would. But when he left, she got to studyin' about him askin' her to meet him away off like that and she decided she didn't like it much.

Well that Saturday night came and she didn't feel like goin', but she fixed up and went on anyhow. Hit was cold and the wind was blowin' something awful when she got out on that ridge. She got to the pine tree but he wasn't there. She thought first she'd wait, then she thought she'd run back; and before she could make up her mind she heard him comin' up the holler. Then she thought she'd hide but there wasn't any place to hide. She happened to look up in that tree, and it had a few low branches to it, so she caught hold on them and cloomb right on up till she was in the thickest part of that big pine.

[8] Chief source of *The Jack Tales.*

She could see down through the branches a little, see what was right under the tree. And directly here came Mr. Fox carryin' a lantern. She saw him put the lantern on a big rock and sit down to wait. He waited and waited. Then, after a right long time, he reached over behind a rock and she saw him lift out a mattick and shovel. He started diggin'. She watched. He kept on diggin' and Polly saw the place he dug was about six-foot long and three-foot wide. She kept watchin', and then she knew it was a grave, and that he was diggin' it for her.

Mr. Fox got the grave started and then he sat down again. He 'uld look and listen, turn his head up this way and that. Then he'd act restless-like: jump in that grave and just dig and dig. He kept on diggin' and waitin' and diggin' till 'way up in the night.

Pretty Polly nearly froze up there. The wind kept blowin' the top of the tree way over to one side, and the branches 'uld creak and rattle, but she kept holdin' on. And fin'lly she heard a rooster crow 'way off in the settle-ments somewhere, so she knew it must be close to midnight. Well, pretty soon after that she saw Mr. Fox pick up his tools and throw 'em across his shoulder, and he picked up his lantern and left. Polly she waited till he was good-and-gone, and then she got down from there in a hurry and struck out for home by all the near cuts she could figger.

Well, Mr. Fox he quit comin' to see her after that.

Then hit wasn't long till Pretty Polly heard folks talkin' about how three young women had disappeared from around the settle-ment. Some said Mr. Fox had been courtin' all three of 'em. He'd not come to any of their houses: met 'em out somewhere. But nobody had any evi-dence on him, so they couldn't do nothing about it. They'd tried to find out where he lived but nobody had any notion where his house was at.

Then one day he came to Pretty Polly's place again. She didn't let on like she knowed a thing, and they got to talkin' and directly he asked her would she come with him to his house. She told him, "Well I might, sometime."

"Come on and go with me now. Hit's not far."

"No," she says. "I can't go today."

"Can you come next Saturday?"

"I don't know where you live at."

"I'll come after you."

"No," she says to him. "If I come, I'll come by myself."

Mr. Fox he studied about that a minute, says, "If you'll give me a poke of flour I'll lay you a trail."

Polly went and got him a little sack of flour and he took it and went on off. He 'uld sift out a little of that flour every few steps.

Well—Polly she didn't go that next Saturday. It was the one after that she decided what she 'uld do. She was brave. It hadn't rained nor been very windy that two weeks, so she found the trail all right. She followed it on and on till fin'lly she came to an old rickety house awa-a-ay out in the woods. She hid and watched. Then she saw Mr. Fox come out of the house and go off. And when he was out of sight she went to the house and went on in.

Now there was a parrot in there and hit talked to her. Polly looked around, and when she went up the stairs and started to open a door, the parrot hollered at her, says,

Don't go in, pretty lady!
You'll lose your heart's blood!

But she opened the door anyhow, and looked in. It was like a slaughter room in there: women hung up all around the walls with their heads cut off. Polly shut the door right quick, and started runnin' down the stair-steps. Then she heard a racket sounded like a woman screamin'. Slipped to the window and peeked out, and there came Mr. Fox a-draggin' a woman by the arm. "Law me! What'll I do now!"

Hide! Pretty lady!
Hide! Hide!

"Don't tell him I'm here!"

No, pretty lady!
No! No!

Polly ran and hid under the old rickety stair-steps.

Mr. Fox came on in the house jerkin' that girl along and dragged her on up the stairs. She reached out and caught the stair-rail a-tryin' to hold back. Mr. Fox took out his sword and hacked her hand off and it fell through the cracks in the stair steps, landed right at Pretty Polly's feet.

Mr. Fox stopped, and asked that bird, "Has anybody been here?"

No, sir!
No! Oh no!

So he pushed the girl in his slaughter room and went on in after her and shut the door. Pretty Polly she reached and grabbed up that girl's hand, and slipped out the door and ran for life.

Well, in about a week or two after that there was a play-party in the settle-ment. Everybody went, and when Pretty Polly got there she saw Mr. Fox in the crowd. So all of 'em were havin' a good time dancin' and playin' kissin' games and first one thing and then another, and 'way up late in the night they all sat down close to the fireplace where the old folks were at, and they got to tellin' tales, and tellin' dreams, and singin', and askin' riddles.

Pretty Polly slipped out and got that hand: brought it back wropped up in a piece of cloth. She sat down again and unwropped that hand under her apron where nobody could see. Sat right on listenin' to what somebody was tellin',

didn't say a thing. Then directly she says, "I've got a riddle."
"What is it? Tell us!"
So she told 'em, says,

> Riddle to my riddle to my right!
> Where was I that Saturday night?
> All that time in a lonesome pine.
> I was high and he was low.
> The cock did crow, the wind did blow.
> The tree did shake and my heart did ache
> to see what a hole that fox did make.

They all tried to guess. Mr. Fox sat right still.
"What's the answer?" they all asked her. "Tell us the answer."
"Not now," she told 'em. "I'll tell you directly." Says, "I dreamt me a quare dream the other night. You might like to hear that."
"Ain't nothin' in dreams," says Mr. Fox.
They all begged her to tell her dream. Polly folded her hands under her apron and she told 'em, says, "I dreamed that I went to Mr. Fox's house. He wasn't at home, but I went on in to wait for him. There was a bird there and when I went to look in one of the rooms hit told me, says,

> Don't go in, pretty lady!
> You'll lose your heart's blood.

But I cracked the door just a little anyhow, and I saw a lot of dead women in there—hangin' on the walls."
"Not so! Not so!" says Mr. Fox. And the young men there all looked at him. Pretty Polly kept right on. "Then I dreamed I heard a woman screamin' and cryin', and I looked out and there came Mr. Fox a-draggin' a woman after him."
"Not so! Not so!" says Mr. Fox. "It couldn't 'a been me!"
And a couple of the men there moved back against the wall.
"That bird told me to hide and I ran and hid under the stair-steps. Then I dreamed that girl grabbed hold on the rail and Mr. Fox took out his sword and hacked her hand off, and it fell through the stairs and landed right where I was at."
Old Mr. Fox jumped up, says,

41

But it was not so,
and it is not so,
and God forbid it ever should be so!

And several young men moved over between Mr. Fox and the door. Polly paid Mr. Fox no mind.

"Then I dreamed he shoved the girl in his slaughter room and went on in and shut the door. And I grabbed up that hand and ran away from there fast."

Old Mr. Fox hollered out again,

But it was not so!
And it is not so!
And God forbid it ever should be so!

Then Pretty Polly answered him back, says,

But it was so!
And it is so!
For here's the very hand to show!

And she took that hand out from under her apron and held it up right in Mr. Fox's face. Then all the men there they took hold on Mr. Fox and they sure did handle him.

And after they took Mr. Fox out, everybody recollected Pretty Polly's riddle and asked her about it, and she told 'em about that grave and all.

They took Mr. Fox on to town, and they tried him on Pretty Polly's evi-dence and he was hung.

Pack Down the Big Chest

The existence of Chaucer's "The Miller's Tale" in oral tradition in America comes as a surprise to many people. After seven hundred years it is still, in certain lively company, a good tale to tell! Where did Chaucer get it? Where did American tale-tellers get it? Answers to these two questions would give keys to the question, "What is Anglo-American folklore?"

42

R. M. Ward could tell this tale well and with no touch of crudity. I heard it once while riding with a truck-driver between Mountain City, Tennessee, and Damascus, Virginia. Recently, I have been told of an English professor in Alabama who, when he presented "The Miller's Tale" to a class, had one of his students remark, "Why! I've heard my grandfather tell that tale lots of times!"

Some of Mr. Ward's neighbors here on Beech Mountain (in western North Carolina) tell it with the Chaucerian hot iron (*coulter*)—"got that poker red-hot"—instead of the pot of scalding water.

This is one of them step-husband tales. The step-husband, you know: he's the one that steps in when the real husband steps out.

One time there was a woman and she did have her a man, but they were pretty sorry kind of folks—*she* was anyhow. And one day her husband had to go off somewhere. Told her he'd be gone several days. So time he was good-and-gone —that very night, here come a step-husband. That woman she let him in the house, and they went to playin' around and one thing and another. But in a little while they heard somebody walk up on the porch. "Lord-'a-mercy! There's my man!"

That feller jumped out on the floor, says, "What'll I do? Where'll I get? Where'll I hide at?"

She ran up the stairs and he headed right in behind her. She opened a big chest and he rolled in it quick. She let the lid down on him and mashed it shut. Latched it fast. That old chest was half full of quilts and that feller nearly smothered.

So she went traipsin' down again and unbuttoned the door. But it wasn't her man. Hit was another feller had heard her husband was off from home. He was younger and stouter than the first one; so she let him in. Just left that poor feller up there in the chest. And she and the other man they went to playin' around and one thing and another. The one in the chest he kept right quiet. He didn't know no different and he was scared to death it *was* her husband.

Well, there was a window there right at the bed. And the next thing they knew somebody went to tappin' easy-like on a window-light. That man pulled the covers up over his head and laid right still. She opened the window a little crack. Hit was, you might say, step-husband number three.

But she didn't care much for this one. He was snag-toothed and baldheaded. "What ye want?"

"I want in."

"Oh law me, no! My man'll be back in tonight."

He kept on beggin' her to let him in and she kept on tellin' him No, till directly he asked her, says, "Well just stick your face out the winder and let me have a big kiss."

That feller inside poked her like he wanted to tell her somethin'. So she told the one outside, says, "Wait just a minute then."

And shut the window to.

The other man whispered to her, says, "Let me over there by the winder. I'll fix him."

Now it was awful thick-dark that night and there was a shade tree had a lot of branches right over that window. So that feller he slipped over there and backed up against the

window-sill, pulled up his shirt-tail. Then she opened the window right wide, and he got fixed there. "All right," she says. "Kiss me quick now."

So he did.—And the man inside hopped off the sill and she slammed down the window.

The man outside he went off just a-spittin'—and he was mad as time.

Well he went and hunted him up an old pot. Built a fire there just out of sight of the house, and it wasn't long till he had him a pot full of boilin' water. Then he got hold of it with a piece of thick rag and back he went. Tapped on the window again. "What ye want now?"

"I just got to have me another kiss."

"No. Go on now or my man'll be liable to catch you here."

"Aw just give me one more big kiss."

Well that other feller had eased over by the window. He was plumb tickled about makin' a fool of him twice. So he got fixed again and then she says, "All right, honey."

And—Kerslosh!—he let that scaldin' water fly.

That poor feller inside he went to jumpin' up and down and tearin' around knockin' over chairs and a-hollerin', "Fire! I'm on FIRE!"

The man upstairs heard all the racket, and he thought the house had caught on fire. So he hollered out, "Pack down the big chest! Don't forget the big chest! Some of ye run up here and pack down the big chest!"

The man that got burnt he thought it was a ha'nt and he left there in his shirt-tail a-goin' *whippity-cut!*

Number three he went on about his business I reckon. And after that woman had got done laughin' she went and unlocked the big chest. She told that'un what-'n-all had happened, and they both had to sit there on the loft floor and laugh some more.

Well, they fin'lly went back downstairs and got to playin' around and one thing and another—and they're at it yet, I reckon.

The Man in the Kraut Tub

This comes from Smith Harmon, my host here at Beech Creek, North Carolina. It is another "step-husband" tale. Soon after I had learned it, I happened to tell it to some friends in Richmond, Virginia, and one of them remarked, "That's in Boccaccio!" It is the Second Story of The Seventh Day.

One time a man went to see a woman. She was married, but this feller he knew that, and he had a pretty good notion, too, that her husband wasn't at home that night.

She let him in the house but he hadn't hardly sat down before somebody stepped up on the porch and made for the door. That feller headed for a big kraut tub was there in one corner and jumped in it. Scrouged down out of sight.

But it wasn't her husband. It was another feller had heard her man had gone off for the night. So he came on in and

46

sat down by the fire. Talked a while, but right then they heard somebody else stompin' across the porch. The woman jumped up, whispered, "That's my man for sure!"

That second feller he didn't have time to hide. He slipped over and grabbed hold on that kraut tub, tilted it and started rollin' it out just as the woman's husband walked in the house. "Thank ye, ma'm, for makin' my wife the loan of your kraut tub."

And the man of the house held the door open for him while he rolled it out.

He edged it down the steps and rolled it on down the road. Set it up when he got out of sight of the house and started wipin' the sweat. Went to mumblin' to himself, says, "Well, I got out of that snap mighty damned easy."

The other man poked his head up out of the tub, says, "By dad, you didn't get out of it half as slick as I did."

The Wicked Stepmother

This tale has been reported from northern England, Australia, Ireland, the Magyar country, Germany, and countries in northwest Europe. It is widely known in the Southern Mountains.

In Joseph Jacobs' "The Rose Tree" the little boy does not come back to life. The bird's song, in one German form, is sung by Marguerite in the mad scene of Goethe's *Faust*. The tune given here is from Annabel Morris Buchanan's collection.

One time there was a man and his wife, and they had two children, a boy and a girl. And the man's wife died and he married again. He didn't know it, but it was a witch he married that time. Well, one day the man killed a rabbit for supper and the witch-woman put it in the big pot, and when it began to cook she started tastin' it to see was it done. She kept on tastin' it, tastin' it, till she tasted it all up.

So she hollered for the little boy, told him to come help her look for eggs. Took him out in the woods, and then she went to liftin' up big rocks. "Peep under, and see if you can fine any eggs."

So the little boy peeped under.

"See any?"

"No, ma'am."

"Let's try that big rock yonder." The witch-woman she went and lifted the big rock. "Peep under."

The little boy hunkered down and looked.

"See any?"

"No, ma'am."

"Crawl under it and look 'way back."

And time he'd crawled under the rock she let it fall on him. Killed him. Then the wicked stepmother she throwed the rock back, and grabbed him and took him back to the house. Chopped off one arm and fixed it like a rabbit, and put it in the big pot. Then she put him in a sack and called the little girl. "Here, take this sack and bury it under them stones in the ivy thicket."

Well, the man came home that evenin' and the wicked stepmother set the meat on the table and they all went to eatin'. "Does your rabbit taste all right?"

"It's too sweet."

They eat right on. And the little girl she cracked the bones so she could suck the marrer.

"Where's my little boy?"

"He's gone over to his uncle's to stay the night."

And just about that time they heard somethin' rattlin' on top of the house and a little bird started singin'——

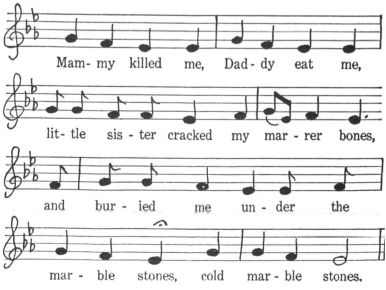

Mam-my killed me, Dad-dy eat me,

lit-tle sis-ter cracked my mar-rer bones,

and bur-ied me un-der the

mar-ble stones, cold mar-ble stones.

The stepmother told the little girl, "Go shoo that bird off the house."

So the little girl went out.

> Shoo off! Shoo off!
> You bless-ed little birdie!

And when it flew off it dropped the little girl a gold necklace. She ran back in the house and showed it to her daddy.

Then the little bird flew over again and lit on the house. It rattled up there—sounded louder that time. Went to singin'——

> Mammy killed me!
> Daddy eat me!
> Little sister cracked my mar-r-rer bones
>   and buried me under the marble stones!
> Cold marble stones!

The witch-woman told the man, says, "You go shoo that bird off. Throw a rock at it."

So the man went out.

> Shoo off! Shoo off!
> You bless-ed bird!

It flew off and dropped him down a bag full of gold and silver money. So he took it in the house and showed it to the little girl.

Then the bird flew back over, lit on the house, and that time it rattled like thunder.

> Mammy killed me!
> Daddy eat me!
> Little sister cracked my mar-r-rer bones
>   and buried me under the marble stones!
> Cold marble stones!

"Humpf!" says the old witch-woman. "Let me shoo it off. I'll go see what it'll drop down for me!" She ran out, and grabbed her up a rock.

> Shoo off, you tattlin' bird!
> Shoo off!

49

It flew off and dropped a mill-rock right on top of the wicked stepmother. Smashed her all to pieces.

Then the little bird flew down and lit on the doorsill—and there was the little boy. He didn't have but one arm, and so he picked up all the marrer bones and knocked 'em and shook 'em—and there was his arm. So he put it back on and then he was all right again.

And when they went to move that big mill-rock there wasn't a thing under it but an old dead toad-frog.

The King and Robert Hood's Horny Beast-es

This is a transcription from Gaines Kilgore of Wise County, Virginia, recorded when he was about thirty-five. Gaines was one of the most gifted of all who have ever told me "the old tales." Both Gaines and his uncle, Johnny Martin Kilgore, told "Old Roaney," one of the best tales in the American tradition. It was from his uncle that I learned "The Outlaw Boy," another oral Robin Hood tale, given in *Grandfather Tales*.

One is never sure how much the printed word may have entered into the telling of a tale such as this. But Uncle Johnny's insistence that these things happened "in this country," and the very manner of Gaines's telling of "Robin Hood and the Butcher"—even though he said it was "in a schoolbook" (perhaps to lend it a certain authority?)—indicate enough to class it in the genuine tradition.

Before the tale had been recorded on tape, we had been discussing "The Outlaw Boy." Two schoolboys, about thirteen years of age, were present. The following is an exact transcription direct from the tape, except for a few "says," "saids," and a false start or two:

GAINES: That was Uncle Johnny's. That was *his* story.
CHASE: His Robin Hood was different from yours, I reckon.
GAINES: Must 'a been. Quite a deal.—I don't know as I ever heard Uncle Johnny tell that one. He could have.
CHASE: Well, you tell your Robin Hood now, any which-a-way.
GAINES: Well, the only way I know it was:

Robin Hood was a very poor boy. He was like myself, I reckon: he just had the one father and mother.
[Boys chuckle, then laugh.]
The King shot his father and killed him—in the Shirewood Forest, for killin' the one deer. Anyhow, he had him put to death for that—for killin' one deer.
Robin was quite a kid at that time. His mother was a schoolteacher, and she took so much composure from teachin' school, and a-walkin' backwards and forwards so far, that she took pneumonia and died, at the time Robert[4] was eleven years old. So, Robert's uncle taken him, to raise him and keep him.
Robert's father had learned him to be a great shot with the bow and ar-row durin' his days before he died.
The King had put up a bull's-eye and the best shot at that would take a great crown from there that day. Robert entered that at eleven years old. He was travelin' along—had started. Had a little tiny red jacket on and all. The King and three more of his—I don't know what you might call it—his priest-es or everwhat they might have been—were takin' the air under a big tree. They laughed at little Robert as he come along and asked him where he was goin'.
Robert said, "I've started to shoot at that bull's-eye."
They laughed and made po-light of him.
King says, "Huh!" Said, "You couldn't hit my hat—ten steps." Said, "You see those three deer over yonder a-grazin'?"
Robert looked. He said, "Yes."
"Shoot at the lead one."
He drawed his bow and ar-row, and at the time his bow and ar-row landed, the lead deer fell dead.
"All right, son. I have *you* for a death punishment, too."

[4] "Robin" and "Robert" are the same name. Robin is a nickname for Robert.

51

And he invited his men to take him under arrest. Robert pulled his bow and ar-row and he killed all three of 'em, and started on his way back to the Shirewood Forest. He didn't go on, to accept the bull's-eye for a target.

Well, they appointed another King at that time.

Robin had went back in the Shirewood Forest, and they heard so much about him there was fellows come and begin to join him until he had quite a band of men.

Later days after that, the next King he put up a target of the bull's-eye, and a gold ar-row, and the one that won the gold ar-row, lay it at his daughter's feet, could marry her. And Robert he had been kind-a struck on an old country girl at that time—he had been a-goin' to see, and he didn't want the King's daughter. But he did change clothes and went in a disdress . . .

[CHASE: Disguise?

GAINES: Disguyed—that's right.]

. . . He disdressed and disguyed himself and went in to play that target shoot.

And he had joined a buddy at that time by the name of Little Black Joe, his right-hand buddy. So, at the time the target match come up, everybody else had shot but Robert and Little Black Joe. Little Joe shot and centered the bull's-eye. Robert shot and split his ar-row. [One of the boys, "Ha!"] That left it in a quartez for them to shoot the match over. And Little Joe he edged the bull's-eye the next time, and Robin Hood he centered it; he centered the ar-row in the bull's-eye. So he won the ar-row, and he taken it to this poor girl's feet and laid it, instead of to the King's daughter.

That made the King so mad he put a reward out for him, to have him caught; but still he was afraid to send his men into the Shirewood Forest. He had sent so many and lost 'em there: they'd never get back.

Well, Robert Hood stayed in the Shirewood Forest for a few years, and he decided one day he would disguard hisself and go to town.

He started out, walkin', and he met an old fellow—overtook him, on an old donkey, ridin' along. And he had an awful load of beef on it. He'd killed a cow, had it loaded.

Robert says, "Where you goin', mister?"

"I've started to market to sell this old cow."

"How much would you take for the cow, donkey, and all?"

He priced it. Said, "I believe I would take thirty dollars."

Robert bought the old cow, and the old donkey too. He got on it and rode to town. And he begin to sell the beef around at one cent a pound. That's all he wanted for it. Pretty soon the beef was all gone.

Well, the King he got a-hold of this, you know—that there was a young man in town there sellin' beef at one cent a pound: probably his father had died and left him with quite a bit of a herd of cattle and he didn't know the price of 'em: had no schoolin' and was givin' it away. He advised some of his men to go out and get in touch with him and invite him up to the Town Hall for dinner. So he did so and invited Robert up.

And Robert says, "Why yes, I have quite a bit of horny beasts back here, and they're cheap—reas'able, very reas'able. Be glad to sell 'em at almost any price."

"Well, I'll take you up on that proposition. How many head do you have?"

"Well, I have so many I've never been able to count 'em. The woods and the grazin' is full of 'em."

"Well! I'll ride over with you after we have a meal, and we'll look 'em over."

So Robert said, "O.K. I'll sell 'em reas'able. I want to get rid of 'em. I have too many." He said, "Now King, the only way I deal: I do business—business is business." Said, "You bring cash along with you and we'll trade. That's the only way we can trade."

The old King he went and filled his saddle-pockets up with greenback, you know; and him and Robin Hood started back to the Shirewood Forest.

They were ridin' along, and they got away back out near the Shirewood Forest and the old King looked over at Robin Hood and he said, "Listen: we're gettin' near the Shirewood Forest, ain't we?"

"Well, not too close."

"What about this? There's a man in this country by the name of Robin Hood that don't like me. Do you reckon there would be any danger of meetin' him here?"

"I don't think so. [Ha!]—I wouldn't think so."

So they rode on until they come up to the Robin Hood village. He blowed a horn, alarm, for his men. His men all came out, and the old King was settin' there on his horse. Robin said, "Get down. The men will take your horse and feed him and take care of him. Go up and have dinner with us: eat some wild beasts."

He taken him up and give him deer meat and bear meat and fed him a nice dinner, you know; and took his saddle-pockets off of his horse and took care of them, of course. [Chuckle.] So when the King got ready to leave, why I guess he felt good a-gettin' out.

[Gaines laughed heartily, and the two boys joined in with gleeful cackles, slapping their hands together.]

CHASE: You say you read some of that in a book?

GAINES: Un-huh.

CHASE: You boys read Robin Hood?

BOY: Yes. (To Gaines:) It was Little John instead of Little Joe.

GAINES: Little Joe, in *my* book.

Catching a Thief

I learned this tale one night recently from my good friend and host, Smith Harmon, here at Beech Creek, North Carolina.

Later I happened to buy an issue of *Ellery Queen's Mystery Magazine* and discovered that, sometime around 1900, Jack London made use of this same tale, set amongst Alaskan Indians! ". . . let all listen. With me I have brought Jelchs, the Raven, diviner of mystery. . . . Him, in his blackness, shall I place under the big black pot. . . . The slush-lamp shall cease to burn. . . . One by one shall ye go into the house, lay hand upon the pot. . . . Doubtless Jelchs will make outcry when the hand of the evildoer is nigh him."

The ending—one man with clean hands—is the same. It would be interesting to know if Jack London found this tale in Alaska.

One time dark overtook an old preacher and no way he could do but try the next house he 'uld come to and see would they let him stay the night there. So at the next house 'side the road, he went and knocked. And they said Yes, he could stay. So they cooked him something to eat, and after he'd sat by the fire and talked with 'em a while, he went on in the next room where they'd fixed him a bed. Laid down and went off to sleep.

Well these folks were pretty rough, and some more came there and they were all drinkin' and gamblin' and one-thing-and-another, till a big argument started. Seemed some money was missing. The man of the house he tried to make 'em hush. Says, "There's a preacher asleep in yonder." But they kept right on hollerin' and a fight was about to start.

55

Well that preacher had woke up and he lay there listenin'
to what-'n-all they were arguin' so loud over. And he got up,
pulled on his clothes, and went in amongst 'em. They sort of
quieted down then, and he got to talkin' with some of 'em:
told that he could find out which one it was had played the
rogue. Then they all got right still and listened to him.

"Get me a rooster," he told 'em. Somebody went out and
reached up in the tree where the chickens were roostin', and
brought him the rooster. Then he went and locked all the
doors, and put the keys in his pocket. "Now," he says, "I'll
get a pot." And he reached down and got hold of a big pot
there at the fireplace.

"Blow out the lights," he says, "and cover the fire." So they
did that.

"Now," he told 'em, "I'm going to put the rooster under
this pot, and I'll stand right here; and if everybody will come
and draw his hand across the pot, when the rogue does that
the rooster will crow, and right then whoever it is I'll grab
him for ye."

There was a lot of shufflin' around in the dark and the old
preacher kept sayin', "Now the next 'un. Let somebody else
come on and rub the pot." And finally everything got quiet
again.

"Anybody else?—Well, if any man or woman hasn't had
his go just speak up."

Nobody spoke. And the old rooster hadn't let out a single
squawk.

"Uh-oh! I reckon I've made a failure. Light the lights."

They lit the lamps and candles again and got the fire goin'
bright once more. Then the preacher spoke up, says, "Gather
around a minute here—all of ye."

They circled up around him.

"Hold out your hands, now!—all of ye!" And there was only
one man whose hands were not black from the soot on the
bottom of that pot.

The old preacher pointed at him, says, "You give back
that money, sir!"

The Big Toe

This is one of the "jump" tales—a tale which is brought to a
dramatic climax when the tale-teller *jumps* at his listeners. Joseph
Jacobs' "The Golden Arm"[5] is the same type, and that is *the*
ha'nt tale usually told at Boy Scout campfires. The story that follows is widespread. In the many mountain schools where I have
had tale-telling assemblies—and even at one high school one
hundred miles down in the lowlands of North Carolina—when I
ask "Who knows 'The Big Toe'?" there is always a great showing
of hands, often more than fifty per cent, and always, there is a
ripple of delight at this mention of a favorite tale.

We have often wondered where else in the United States, out-
side the Southern Mountain area, this tale of the big toe is known.
Can any of our readers inform us? See "Amateur Collector's
Guide."

Some fifteen years ago this was one of the first tales I heard
here near Beech Mountain in western North Carolina. I was driv-
ing an "open-air" Model A and a boy about eleven years old
flagged me to stop. I thought he wanted a ride, but, without any
preliminaries, he put one foot on the fender, grabbed the top edge
of the car door, and grinning a bit mischievously asked, "You that
man huntin' up old tales?"

"Yes, that's me I reckon."

"You ever hear that 'un about the big toe?"

"No, I don't know as I ever—."

And holding fast his grip on the car as if he feared I might not
wait long enough for him to tell it all, he plunged in, watching me
with his eyes twinkling as he neared the "jump" ending.

[5] *See also* "The Old Woman All Skin and Bones."

One time a little boy was hoein' 'taters. He was mad. He liked 'taters 'n beans for supper all right, but there wasn't any meat to put in the beans and he liked *meat* in *his* beans.

Well, he was hackin' with his hoe at a big weed when all-at-once somethin' scrambled under the dirt and went

"UR-R-R-R-R!"

—like it was hurt, and then it went off down under the ground like a big mole. The boy looked and there, lyin' in the dirt, was a big toe. He'd hacked off that somethin's' big toe. He grabbed it up and ran for life! Tore up a few bean vines, knocked down several cornstalks, and jerked the button off the gate gettin' away from there. He made it to the house. Washed that big toe with a dipperful of water and put it in his overall pocket.

And when his Mommy was cookin' supper in the fireplace he eased up the potlid when she had her back turned and slipped that big toe in with the beans. So, when they got to the table and started eatin', that boy ate three big baits° of beans—and in one of 'em his Mommy had scooped up that big toe. So he ate it.

Fin'lly his Mommy got the dishes washed and the pots scoured and out the way, and his Daddy got in a load of firewood to cook breakfast, and the boy got in his pile of kindlin' wood, and then they were all sittin' around the fireplace with a lightwood knot burnin'. The boy's Mommy she sat on one side, and his Daddy sat on the other, and that boy he was sittin' cross-legged right in the middle of the hearthrock pokin' in the ashes with the poke-stick. And—all at once they heard somethin' 'way off——

"Wha wow woo woe!"

They sat right still, listenin'. Then they heard it again. It was comin' closer.

"Where mow wow woe!"

The boy's Daddy jumped up and barred the door. They sat on sort of wonderin' and sort of scared—and then they heard it out in the road and comin' right that way!

"Where's my big toe?"

The boy's Mommy she jumped up and rolled under the bed, and his Daddy ran and crawled right in after her. They laid there a-shakin' and a-shiverin' so it rattled the bed-slats.

° baits: helpings.

That little boy was so scared he *couldn't* move! Just sat there froze to the hearthrock. Then the gate-chain rattled and he heard that thing crunchin' up the path.

"Where's my big to-o-o-o-oe?"

Heard it climbin' up on the porch roof—scratched on up the shingles till it was on top of the house.

"Where's my big to-o-o-o-o-oe?"

Then it hollered right down in the chimney.[7]

"Where's-my-big-TO-O-O-O-OE?"

The little boy saw soot fallin', and he looked up, and there, sittin' on the smoke-shelf[8] was a great-big-old-black-hairy Booger.[9] Had big red eyes, big black bushy tail, big claws, and great long sharp snag-teeth. Says, "Where's-my-big-To-O-O-O-OE?——

YOU GOT IT!"

[7] The teller hold his hands together before his mouth and "hollers down."
[8] the flat place up in the throat of a chimney, just where the smoke starts up.
[9] "Booger"—bogie.

The Haunted House

There is only one ha'nt tale and this is it. Often it ends (see below) as a "jump" tale. There are many variants but this is the basic form. In an anthology of ghost tales, once, I ran across a story set down in Roman times, 300 A.D. or earlier, which presented substantially the same situation. This is from Wise County, Virginia.

One time a preacher went to see could he lay a ha'nt at a house there in his settlement. The house had been ha'nted about ten years—and several had tried to stay there all night, but 'fore midnight they 'uld get scared out by the ha'nt.

So this preacher he took his Bible and went to the house. Went on in; built him up a good fire, and lit a lamp. Sat there readin' the Bible. Then all at once, just before midnight, he heard somethin' start up in the cellar: walking back and forth, back and forth; and then it sounded like somebody tried to scream and got choked off. Then there was a lot of thrashin' around and strugglin'—and fin'lly everything got quiet.

The old preacher took up his Bible again, but before he could start readin' he heard steps comin' up the cellar stairs. He watched the door to the cellar, and the steps kept comin' closer and closer. He saw the doorknob turn, and when the door went to open he jumped up and hollered,

"What do you want?"   Dropped his Bible.

The door shut back easy-like and there wasn't a sound.

The preacher was tremblin' a little but he fin'lly opened the Bible and read a while, got up and laid the book on the chair and went to mendin' the fire. Then the ha'nt started walkin' again and—step!—step!—step!—up the cellar stairs. The old preacher froze, watchin' the door. Saw the knob turn, and the door opened. Swung out enough for him to see—and it looked like a young woman. He backed up on the hearthrock, said, "Who are you? What do you want?"

The ha'nt sort of swayed like it didn't know what to do—and then it just faded out. The old preacher waited, waited, and when he didn't hear any more noises he fin'lly went and shut the door. He was sweatin' and tremblin' all over, but he was a brave man and thought he'd just see it over with. So he took hold of the Bible and turned his chair where he could watch. Sat down and waited.

And it wasn't long till he heard the ha'nt start up again, slow—step!—step!—step!—step!—closer, and closer—step!—step!—step!—and it was right at the door.[10]

The preacher he stood up and held his Bible out before him. Then the knob turned right slow, and the door opened wide. And that time he spoke quiet-like, says, "In the name of The Father, The Son, and The Holy Ghost—who are you and what is it you want?"

And the ha'nt came right across the room, straight to him; took hold on his coat lapels. It was a young woman about twenty years old. She smelled earthy. Her hair was torn and tangled, and the flesh was droppin' off her face so he could see bones and part of her teeth. She had no eyeballs but there was a sort of blue light 'way back in her eyesockets. And she had no nose to her face.

Then she started talkin': sounded like her voice was comin' and goin' with the wind blowin' it. She told him how her lover had killed her for her money, and had buried her in the

[10] *"Jump" ending:* The knob turned right slow and—*E-e-e-e-e-!*

61

cellar there. She said if he'd dig up her bones and give her a Christian burial she could rest.

Then she told him this: said for him to keep the end-joint of the little finger of her left hand, and lay it in the collection plate next Church meetin'—and he'd find out who it was had murdered her.

"And if you come back here once more, after that—you'll hear my voice at midnight, and I'll tell you where my money is hid, and you can give it to the church."

Then the ha'nt sobbed like it was tired and sunk down toward the floor and was gone.

That preacher found her bones and buried 'em in the grave-yard. And he prayed over her grave.

Then the next Sunday he put that fingerbone in the collection plate, and when a certain man happened to touch it—it stuck to his hand. That man jumped up, and rubbed and scraped and tore at that bone tryin' to get it off, and then he went to screamin' like he was goin' crazy. Well, they took hold on him and he confessed to the murder—and they took him on to jail.

And after he was hung, the preacher went to that house again one midnight and the ha'nt's voice told him to dig under the hearthrock. He did, and found a big sack of money. And where that ha'nt had taken hold on his coat, it looked like the print of them bony fingers was burnt right into the cloth. It never did come out.

FIVE JACK TALES

There exists in the United States a cycle of Old World tales evolved around a boy named Jack. Not counting variants of the same tale, eighteen are recorded in *The Jack Tales*, one new one is given here ("Jack and the Witches"), and five were collected in Kentucky by Leonard Roberts. The bulk of this cycle, as collected to date, comes from Beech Mountain near Boone in Western North Carolina. Three Jack Tales, not known on Beech Mountain, were found in Wise County, Virginia. There are probably more such tales somewhere in the United States, and we hope that readers of this book will inform us of the existence of Jack Tales, and other old tales, as known in their families or communities. See "Amateur Collector's Guide."

Outside the Jack Tale cycle, *Grandfather Tales* contains ten Old World tales from North Carolina, eleven from Virginia, and three from Kentucky. Three new "non-Jack" tales are given in this book. In Leonard Roberts' *South from Hell-fer-Sartin*,[1] most of the 105 tales have European parallels. Eleven of them deal with a boy named Jack. Eleven others are about the "youngest and best" type of hero but not specifically named Jack.

One of the first scholars to collect Jack Tales was Mrs. Isobel Gordon Carter who published them, as told by Mrs. Jane Gentry of Hot Springs, North Carolina, in *The Journal of American Folklore* in March, 1927. In the last thirty years British tales in America have been collected also by Emelyn E. Gardner, Bertha McKee Dobie, Ralph Steele Boggs, and Vance Randolph.

It must be remembered that these tales, as known in America, have been handed down by word-of-mouth. They have been handled freely and creatively ("unreflectively") by those who have told them and kept them alive. Thus, "Jack and the Beanstalk" becomes "Jack's Bean Tree," and, although substantially the same tale, it varies in each incident to fit pioneer American conventions, expressions, and even objects. "Jack the Giant-Killer" becomes "Jack in the Giants' Newground," and, in the North Carolina versions, this tale seems to have gathered material from many scattered sources and been "put together" into versions that are completely fresh and "new" with each teller of tales.

One indication of the age of the tradition back of our English-American variants of these old tales is the appearance, in three of the Jack Tales, of the god Woden—for whom Wednesday (Woden's Day) was named. Of course my Beech Mountain informants never heard of Woden, but he comes to help Jack in the same mysterious way he helps various heroes in the *Volsungasaga* and in the *Eddas*.

On the point of this "youngest-best" hero being called "Jack," and in regard to his appearance in a cycle-series of "little feller" (or "under-dog") tales, Martha Warren Beckwith writes: "It is the cycle form of the Jack Tales that is interesting and their appearing among the whites of this coun-

[1] Published at Lexington by the University of Kentucky Press, 1955.

try where so little European story had been collected—except among the blacks. The Jack hero is thoroughly European. Joseph Jacobs' collections of English and Irish tales has less familiar Jack stories. Jack is, in fact, an equivalent figure in European story to Br'er Rabbit; that is, he is the trickster hero who overcomes through quick wit or cunning rather than by physical force. He is often aided, in European stories, by a supernatural helper. Hans is the German form, and you will find the name in its French and Spanish forms in the "Jack Tales" of those countries. You will also find a Jack cycle in Spanish-American stories collected in the Texas Folklore Society publications. European folktales told in Jamaica make Jack the hero except when, like the Irish, they invent a fancy name."

It is clear that much of our American tradition is Irish and German as well as British.

I have not, as yet, found any *animal* tales (i.e. like the Uncle Remus tales) among English-American folk. Perhaps some of our readers can inform us of the existence of such all-animal tales in an English-American tradition. See "Amateur Collector's Guide."

Jack and the Witches

Recorded from R. M. Ward, Nancy Ward, Nora Hicks, and Kel Harmon, of Beech Mountain in western North Carolina, Sally Middleton and Rosella Boggs of eastern Kentucky, and Mrs. Hattie Kiser of southwestern Virginia, this Witches' Sabbath tale seems to be fairly widely known in the Southern Mountains. Usually the boy is not named. R. M. Ward (see Preface to *the Jack Tales*) had forgotten what must have once been a most interesting part of this story: where the Devil, evidently, used some sort of ritual to "take in new members." Mr. Ward said that Council Harmon, his grandfather ". . . had a lot of words right there. I can't recollect any of it anymore."[2] It may be that some of our readers can supply the missing parts of this tale.

There is a curious parallel to this tale in Merejkowski's *Romance of Leonardo da Vinci* (Book Four: chapters VI, VII, and VIII), in which, however, it is not The Devil but Dionysius who is being worshiped.

[2]—"anymore"—often used in the sense of "nowadays."

One time Jack was workin' for an old man, and they lived in an old-time one-room log house. The man had a wife and one girl that was just about grown. The old woman was ugly, looked like a witch, and the girl was just about as mean-turned as the old woman. The old man was nearly blind, and hard of hearin', had asthmy and was so crippled with rheumatism he couldn't straighten up. There was some suspected the old woman of bein' a witch but hadn't nobody ever proved anything on her.

Now Jack he slept up in the loft, like the kids used to do in them old houses. Had him a little pile of straw up there and an old ragged quilt or two. And every now and then Jack had been hearin' somebody get up and stir around 'way up in the night, then everything would get right quiet again. He never had paid much attention to it. But one night Jack heard the old woman talkin'. Heard her tell that girl to get up, says, "If you want to go with me tonight and j'ine, you'll have to hurry!"

Well, Jack knew the old man had a chain on the door and locked it every night, and he got to wonderin' how in the world anybody could get out of the house. So he turned over right quiet-like and looked down through the cracks and knotholes in the loft floor to see what was goin' on. The old woman and the girl were dressed. And Jack saw the old man was still in the bed asleep. Then he saw the old woman get a broom and take it over by the bed. She set that broom on the bald-headed end and turned loose of it, pulled back the covers and said somethin', and the broom humped itself and got into bed with the old man. Jack knew right then it was witchery: that the broom was witched so the old man would sleep right on as long as the broom was in the bed with him.

Jack figured they must be goin' to a witch meetin' and that the girl was goin' to j'ine that night. So he watched to see how-in-the-nation they'd get out. He heard the old woman tell the girl, says, "Now you do everything I do and say everything I say, and be sure you say it exactly like I do. And while we're out yonder don't look back the way you've come. And by no means don't you dare mention the name of The Lord."

Then the old woman reached up on the fireboard and stuck her finger in some kind of oil in a gourd, rubbed it around her eyes this-a-way and that-a-way, sort of like a figure eight, reached and got hold of a bresh broom. She got side-saddle-on that broom and hollered out,

65

Rise up, Devil, and fly!

and the broom raised her up off the hearth-rock in front of the fireplace and she was floatin' in the air. Then she squalled out,

Thick through thin!
Touch never a thing!

and that broom and the old woman sailed right up the chimney.

Then the girl she tipped her finger in that oil, ran it around her eyes, and went and got her a hickory mop. Sat on it, says,

Rise up, Devil, and fly!

and there she was ridin' her mop. Then she squealed out, says,

Thick through thin!
Touch never a thing!

and S-s-s-s-s-st! out the chimney she went, just like smoke.

Well, Jack took a notion he'd try to foller 'em. So he scrambled down out the loft. Rammed his whole hand down in that witch-oil and smeared it around his eyes. Looked around for somethin' *he* could ride. All he could find was the churn-dasher. So he straddled it and tried to think of what he had to say. Says,

R'ar up, Devil, and fly!

And that churn-dasher started r'arin' up, a-throwin' Jack every which-a-way and bumpin' his head against the rafters. Jack was sort of scared but he tried to say what came next, hollered out,

Thick through thin!
Touch ever-a-thing!

and he went out that chimney just a rattlin'! There wasn't a rock his head didn't butt. Aa law, he cleaned out the soot! That sort of addled him, but he could tell he was outside, and that he was ridin' on somethin' alive. Jack got the soot wiped out of his eyes, and saw the old woman takin' off on a cow. The girl was gallopin' off on a heifer. Jack's churn-dasher had turned into a little bull calf. And hit took off after the cow and the heifer with Jack holdin' on the best he could.

Now witches don't have to foller the roads. They can go straight on to wherever they're aimin' to go, straight across fields and everything. Come to a fence they just sail over it. Go up over briar patches, and head straight through the woods somehow or other: just go a bee line. So Jack's little bull calf and him kept right on. The old woman and the girl, of course, didn't turn their heads to look behind. They came to a big pond of water directly and when the old woman's cow went to stop she hollered out,

Up and over, Blue Bonnet!

and up she went. The heifer started slowin' up and Jack heard the girl tell it,

Up and over, Blue Bonnet!

and hit sailed up in the air.

So when Jack's little bull calf went to balkin' Jack hollered at it—and he got it right that time—says,

Up and over, Blue Bonnet!

And next thing Jack knowed he was flyin' through the air 'way up over that pond of water. About half way over Jack got to thinkin', *That's a hell of a jump for a little bull calf!*—and he turned his head and looked back. And—pow!—the bull calf went from under him, and there was Jack stuck in the mud the other side of that pond, mired up to his knees, a-straddlin' that churn-dasher. He just did make it! Didn't hurt him, much.

But Jack took notice where the woman and the girl was headed straight out before him, and so he stomped out of the mud and took out that same way, usin' his churn-dasher for a walkin' stick.

Went on, went on, and it wasn't long till Jack came on an old waste house on top of a mountain. And all around that house were cows and calves and old bulls and yearlin' bulls and rams and goats—every kind of brute there was and all of 'em just standin' there outside the house. Jack looked and he couldn't hear a thing or see nothin' either. It looked like it was just an old house with the roof about to cave in and the chimney ready to fall. He went a little closer and saw a little thin streak of light under the door. So Jack slipped up on the porch, tipped along and eased in right quick: shut the door behind him.

Well, inside that house it was all lit up, and the fastest music you ever heard was goin', and the witches were laughin' and shoutin' and dancin' up and down and around and around, circlin' first one way and then another, and swingin' and sashayin' across the middle—cuttin' all kinds of shines! Jack leaned back against the wall and had him a time watchin' all that. Then Jack noticed a lot of folks crowdin' around one corner of the big room, bowin' down and listenin' to somethin' or somebody back in that corner, and then bowin' and backin' away. Jack wondered what-in-the-nation that could be. Then all at once the music stopped and everybody started comin' off the floor and crowdin' back to the walls. And when they'd all got back Jack saw what it was: There in that corner was the old horn-ed Devil himself, sittin' r'ared back in a big chair, with his knees crossed and his old cow's foot swingin' up and down. Jack's hair started risin' up, but he kept right quiet.

The Devil fin'lly stood up and opened a big book, says,

NOW WHO ELSE WANTS TO JOIN?

And they started goin' through all kinds of services and one sort of rigamarole and another, cuttin' their fingers and writin' their names in blood in the Devil's book. Jack saw the woman take the girl over and the Devil took her in: told her, like he done the others, all about how to be a witch—boilin' a black cat at sun-up on the east side of a mountain to get the witch-bone, shootin' at the sun with a silver bullet, and washin' your hands in a spring nine times with strong lye soap and sayin' every time you rinse,

> I wish my soul as free from grace
> as my two hands are free of grease!

And Jack got so scared fin'lly he just froze.

Then the Devil shut that big book and looked around. He saw Jack, and pointed his clawed forefinger straight at him, says,

WHAT'S HE A-DOIN' HERE?

and he made for Jack.

Jack caught his breath, says, "Lord have mercy!"

And when Jack said that the top of the house blew off like a charge of dynamite. All that light went out quick, and Jack couldn't see nothin'; but it sounded like there was a hundred cats runnin' and squallin', and one old goat bawlin' and bleatin' and pawin' up the floorboards.

But Jack beat 'em all gettin' out of there! He went through the field a-goin' whippity-cut! And he could see all them brutes streakin' off in every direction, and on the back of every one of 'em, with its eyeballs just a-blazin', was a big black cat.

Jack ran for life. Then he heard a goat bleatin' mad-like close in behind him, and Jack fairly tore up the gravel. He was so scared he started sayin' his prayers and when Jack did that he didn't hear the goat any more. But he didn't slow up till he'd run about five miles.

It was still thick dark, and Jack had a time figurin' out the way back, but fin'lly he got headed right and wasn't scared so bad, so he kept goin' steady and thought he could beat his way back about daylight.

69

Well the old man got up right early and started the fire. His old woman lay there asleep in the bed and the girl snorin' in a little cot 'side the wall. Then the old man hollered up the scuttle-hole for Jack. The old woman raised up, says, "No use you hollerin' for Jack. He's took corn to get ground."

The old man got to thinkin' *That's a mighty funny thing: Jack goin' to mill 'fore daylight. Besides, he couldn't get out.* So directly he unlocked the chain on the door and went outside: locked the house again. He stood around and waited and looked up and down the road, and just the first streaks of daylight here came Jack. The old man went to meet him.

"Jack, that's not the way to the mill."

"Law, I've not been to mill."

"Where ye been, Jack?"

"Law, I've been to the awfullest place, and seen the awfullest things!"

"What did ye see, Jack?"

"You won't like it if I tell you."

"Tell it all, Jack."

So Jack told him: all about how they left the house, and how they went, and what-'n-all went on at the witch meetin'.

"And my wife was there?"

"She sure was, and that girl, too."

"You sure?"

"Yes I'm sure."

"Who else that you knowed from around this settle-ment did you see there, Jack?"

Jack named everybody he knew was there.

"Come on, Jack. We got work to do."

So Jack and the old man they went and told everybody Jack had named that the old woman was down sick and wanted them to come. Told 'em to just wait when they got there and he 'uld let 'em in. They fin'lly got every witch rounded up, and when the old man let 'em go in he locked the chain back, and he and Jack fired the house.

And such a crackin' and fryin' and poppin' and sizzlin' you never heard!

So Jack helped make an end to all the witchin' had been goin' on in that settle-ment. And in a few days that old man got his sight back, and got so he could hear as good as anybody, and he never was bothered any more with asthmy, and all that rheumatism left him . . . and the last time I was down there he was standin' as straight as you or me, and doin' well.

Jack and Old Tush

This tale was recorded in the Spring of 1942 from Eulus Kiser who was then twelve years old, and from Cecil Kiser, of Flat Gap, Virginia; also from James W. Isom at Hindman Settlement School in Kentucky.

Any connection this tale (and "Jack and Old Fire Dragaman") might have with the ancient Anglo-Saxon epic *Beowulf* may seem, at first, quite far fetched. But here also, a monster makes raids on a feast, and the hero descends into another world to fight him.

An eminent folklorist, Martha Warren Beckwith, wrote us:

"Panzer believes that the *Beowulf* epic is based on the folktale of the Bear's Son, whose story is familiar to us in Grimm . . . where Hans is youngest-best. In Kennedy's *Fiction of the Irish*

Celts . . . is a version of the same story . . . the Bear's son
. . . Beowulf—Bee-wolf—i.e. Bear, because of the bear's fond-
ness for honey . . . Panzer's . . . folktale parallels seem all well
taken. Old Fire Dragaman is certainly a variant of the same story."

Jack was off cuttin' timber one cold winter-time. Had to stay
in an old pole shack was up there where they had a new-ground
started. And one day he had just enough meal left to make
him a few ashcakes. Got one made-up and laid it in the ashes.[3]
And when it was just about done Old Tush opened the door
—old slobbery hairy man, looked like a gorilla.

"Bread most done, Jack?"

"Yes, but you're none the better by it."

Old Tush reached his long limber hairy arm in the door
and snatched up Jack's ashcake. Jack grabbed the poke-stick
and lit out after him—whippity-cut!—right down the field,
knockin' the cornstalks every which-a-way, and Jack's old
ragged clothes catchin' on the briars. Old Tush jumped down
a hole there at the foot of the field, and Jack went on back—
mad as time.

He made him another ashcake and time he'd started cookin'
it, here came Old Tush again.

"Bread most done, Jack?"

"No it ain't done! And you leave it alone!"

But Old Tush reached in right quick and grabbed it—and
there they went again—whippity-cut! whippity-cut!—Old
Tush gobblin' up Jack's ashcake and Jack right after him
tryin' to hit him with his pokin' stick, knockin' down cornstalks, and the briars a-tearin' Jack's ragged shirt and britches.
Old Tush went slidin' down his cave-of-a-place out there, and
Jack he cussed down the hole at him a time or two, and
fin'lly went on back to his pole shanty.

Jack didn't have but a little dust of meal left by then and
hit made him just a little bitty ashcake. He got it fixed in the
ashes, took that poker and slipped over by the door.

"Bread most done, Jack?"

And that time Jack didn't answer. And when Old Tush
grabbed his ashcake Jack lammed him on the head. Old Tush
ran and Jack took off right close in behind him smackin' him
over the head and shoulders—whippity-cut! whippity-cut!

[3]That's the way some folks had to do back in old times. Had nothing to
cook in. Put the dough down in cabbage leaves in the ashes. Cover it with
more leaves, and then pile more ashes over it—cold ashes first, then hot.
Made right good bread, even if you did have to blow off a few ashes.

whippity-cut! wham! wham! wham!—the cornstalks just a-
flyin' and that time the briars tore Jack's clothes plumb off
him. Old Tush took a dive down his hole-in-the-ground and
Jack he jumped down right after him—naked as he was!
He didn't care: he was mad about his ashcakes.

Down, down, down Jack went, and when he hit the bottom
it knocked him out cold. He landed on a pile of hay or it
would have killed him. He laid there addled right bad: felt
like every bone in him was broke. And when he got his senses
back he looked around, and it was like another world down
there.

There wasn't any sign of Old Tush, but here came a pretty
girl. Jack jumped behind some bushes. The girl came to him
and handed Jack a sword and a wishbone—and some clothes.
Jack he dressed. Strapped that sword around him, stuck the
wishbone in his pocket, and started courtin' that girl.

All at once she jumped up, "Look out, Jack!"

And there came Old Tush. Jack swung that sword and—
hack!—Old Tush's head rolled on the ground.

Then the girl asked Jack to let her have the wishbone. She
took hold of it, says, "I wish we were both out of here." And
there they were out on top again.

So then Jack he took the wishbone, says. "I wish we were
married, and had a pretty house and some good land, and a
thousand dollars."

They looked, and instead of that pole shack there stood a
pretty little frame house over against the hill with curtains
at every window; and in the place of all them steep fields there
was about ten acres of good bottom land with a little spring
branch leadin' through it from up above the house.

Jack took the girl by the hand and they went and opened
the door. And there on the table was a marriage license all
wrote out with their names, and a deed to the land, and a
stack of greenback money. Jack counted it and it was a
thousand dollars.

So Jack went and bought him a team and a plow and went
to farmin'. And the girl she went to house-keepin' and
washin' and ironin' and raisin' chickens. And the last time I
was down there they were doin' well.—Had three kids.

Jack and the Old Rich Man

This is a variant of "Jack and the Doctor's Girl." Its usual European name is "The Master Thief," and it is known in Germany, Norway, Scotland, and Ireland. Joseph Jacobs' "Jack the Cunning Thief" is an Irish version. Herodotus told a similar tale about a King Rampsinites around 450 B.C. The tale is given here as copied out by Anna Presnell of Beech Creek, North Carolina. I have changed some of the spelling, paragraphing, and punctuation to make the reading easier. Anna Presnell's "Jack Tale" came from Wiley Proffit as written down by his son, Frank Proffit.

Jack and his mother worked for an old rich man for their living. Jack he found out where the old rich man kept his money and he concluded he would steal it. So he got two more fellers to go with him. Jack says, "I'll go in and get the

74

money, and if they wake up and find me out, I'll whistle and you'uns can get away."

So they went to the rich man's house, and Jack he went in and opened the bureau drawer and he found so much gold and silver that he went to patting his foot and whistling. The two fellers on the outside thought he was warning them and away they ran as fast as they could go. So Jack he got all the money and slipped out and went home with it.

So then Jack didn't go down to work for two or three weeks. The old rich man went to see what had become of him. Jack had gone, and he asked his mother why Jack hadn't been to work.

She says, "We're just as independent as you are."

He says, "Why?"

"My son Jack has become a highway robber."

"He is?"

And Jack comes in.

"Jack, they say you have become a highway robber."

"Yes."

"Then there's one thing you have got to do between now and tomorrow morning or I'll have you hung or shot certain."

"What's that?"

"You got to try to steal my saddle horse tonight."

"If I do, is it mine?"

And the old rich man said, "Yes."

So that night he locked the stable door and placed two guards there. The guards built up a big fire and laid down.

About midnight an old ragged man came a-limping along. He told the guards he had traveled so far that he wanted to lie down by the fire and rest till morning. They told him he could. The guards laid awake and watched him. After a while the old man turned over and pulled out a bottle of rum, and let on like he was taking a dram, then set it there by his head. And when he went to snoring again one of the guards said, "That 'un's mine." So he got it and drank it.

After a while they saw the old man reach for his bottle of rum, and when he couldn't find it he ran his hand in his pocket, pulled out another one. Turned it up like he was taking another dram, and placed hit by his head. The other guard says, "That one is mine." And he drank that, and in a short time they didn't know nothing they were both so drunk.

So Jack he got up when he saw they were drunk. Hunted in their pockets and got the key. Unlocked the door and took the horse out, and put the saddle and bridle on. Locked the door and put the key back in the guard's pocket. Got on the horse and away he went.

The old rich man came out the next morning to the stable. "My horse is here, is he?"

"Yes. Here's the key."

The rich man unlocked the door.

"My horse is gone!—I grey Jack's got him."

He went up to see Jack.

"Jack, you got my horse, did you?"

"No sir, not yours but mine."

"There's another thing you've got to do against tomorrow morning."

"What's that?"

"You've got to steal all my Brother Dickie's money, or I'll have you hung or shot."

"If I do, is it mine?"

"Yes."

There was a meeting-house close to Brother Dickie's, and away in the night Brother Dickie heard preaching going on in the church. There wasn't no appointment of any meeting, so he went up and knocked on the door, says, "Who's in there?"

"It's the angel Gabriel."

"What can I give to be in thy place?"

"All thy money and you can be in my place."

"I'll run and get it then."

Jack he got down and slipped along behind Brother Dickie, and when he got home Jack heard his wife ask him who it was up there preaching. He told her it was the angel Gabriel.

"And he said I could be in his place for all my money."

"Just take half the money. He won't know the difference."

Jack he ran back and was up in the loft preaching away when Brother Dickie got back, "Here's all my money. Now let me be in thy place."

"Not all thy money. It's only just half. Go get the rest."

So Brother Dickie goes back, and Jack slips along to listen. Heard him tell his wife, "It is the angel Gabriel sure enough! How did he know I got just half the money?"

"Just take it all then, and go on to heaven.—A-a, Lord, I'll soon be there, too."

Jack hurried back and went to preaching again, when here came Brother Dickie.

"Here's all my money. Let me now be in thy place."

76

"All right. Go get me a big sack to take you to heaven in."
So he got it, and got in. And Jack tied it up hard and fast, and got it up on his shoulder. Throwed it in among the fattening hogs.

Bright and early the next morning the old rich man went down to his Brother Dickie's and asked his wife where Brother Dickie was.

"The angel Gabriel came last night and took him to heaven —for all his money."

He went on back home, and by that time the servants had gone out to feed the hogs. They saw the sack in there wiggling around and they got scared and ran back. They told the old man. He went out and untied the sack. Out crawled his Brother Dickie!

He went up to see Jack.

"You got my brother Dickie's money, did you?"

"Not his'n, but mine."

"Well, there's another thing you got to do."

"What's that?"

"You got to steal my five-hundred head of cattle and put 'em in your pasture, or I'll have you hung or shot tomorrow morning."

"If I get 'em, are they mine?"

"Yes."

That night the old rich man had his hands start with the cattle to another pasture. Jack killed him a sheep, and got him a bladder of blood. Ran on ahead, and stripped himself naked and put blood on his face, and hung himself over the road. The drivers came up and the cattle got scared and ran off in the woods. The drivers are scared too, but they get the cattle together again, and on they go.

Jack cuts himself down and runs ahead and hangs himself over the road again, by the heels. That time it scares the drivers so bad they run off and leave the cattle. Jack gathers the cattle up, and takes them and puts them in his pasture.

Next morning the old man looks and sees his cattle in Jack's pasture.

"Well you got my cattle last night, did you?"

"Not yours but mine."

"Well there's another thing you got to do. You've got to steal the shimmy off my wife's back before tomorrow morning or I'll have you hung or shot certain."

That night the old man sat by his bed with his gun, watching the window.

Jack he knew of a man that was buried the day before. He goes and digs him out. Goes to the old man's window and raises the dead man's face up to the window and pulls it back. Raises it up again, pulls it back. And the next time——

"KEY—BANG!"

goes the gun.

Jack drops the dead man and bust-es a bladder of blood on his face, and goes and hides. The old man comes out and sees the dead man lying there with blood on his face. He goes back and tells his wife,

"Well, I've killed him. I'll go get two of my trusted best friends to help me bury him and we'll be shet of the rascal, and no one will know nothing about it."

When the old man is gone, in a little while Jack goes and gets in bed with the old woman. Jack could talk like the old man.

"Well, we won't have to be bothered with him no more."

"I'm glad of it," says the old woman.

"I'll swear," says Jack, "if I didn't forget to wash after handling that rascal, and I've got blood all over your clean shimmy."

"That's all right. While you're washing there in the pan, I'll put me on a clean one."

Jack lets on like he's washing.

"Here, lay the shimmy over there," says the old woman.

Jack takes it and away he goes.

After a while the old man came in.

"That's a good job done," he says.

"Well! Wasn't you here a while ago?"

"Why no."

"O Law! Somebody came in and I thought it was you. He said he'd got blood on his hands and had got it all over my clean shimmy. I pulled it off, and he went away with it."

"I grey! It was Jack!"

Next morning he went over to Jack's house.

"Jack, you got my wife's shimmy last night, did you?"

Jack didn't say nothing.

"Well there's one more thing you got to do. If you do it I'll give you a deed to my farm, if not I'll have you shot and that'll be the end of it. You got to come to my house in the morning, neither riding, walking, hopping, skipping, nor jumping; neither clothed nor unclothed; neither come in nor stay out. You do that now!"

Next morning Jack tore off half his shirt and half his britches. Caught an old sow and got on her. Went from one side to the other with only one foot touching. When he got there the old man opened the gate, said, "Come in."

But Jack he just straddled the gate. Didn't come in nor stay out.

The old man gave him a deed to his farm. So Jack is now richer than the old rich man.

Jack and the Talking Crow

This is a Virginia version of "Jack's Heifer Hide." It is told also in New York, Nova Scotia, Massachusetts, Germany (Grimm's "The Little Peasant"), Denmark (Hans Christian Andersen's "Big Claus and Little Claus"), Norway, Scotland, and Ireland. Seamus O'Duilcarga calls it "One of the most widely-known and most popular of all Irish folktales." Negroes also tell it, in Florida, on the islands off South Carolina, in Jamaica, and the Bahamas. An Irish version, "Hudden and Dudden," is in Joseph Jacobs' *Celtic Fairy Tales*.

One time there was three boys, Will and Tom and Jack. Jack he was the youngest. Their daddy gave the boys a cow a-piece, and 'fore spring they got scarce of feed. Back then, if you ran out of feed you couldn't go off to town to buy hay or chop. There wasn't no feed stores. So Will and Tom they made Jack drive the cows to the woods where they could eat everwhat they could find. They always tried to make Jack do all the work. Jack he took the cattle on to the woods, and he minded their cows off ever' tree he cut down. Let his cow feed on the buds. Then he 'uld turn the other two cows to the tree and all they got was the bark and little limbs. Hit kept on that-a-way until Jack's cow was gettin' fat and Will's and Tom's cows they got skinnier and skinnier.

So they commenced jumpin' on Jack about it, and Jack told 'em, says, "I tried to get your stock to eat right but they wouldn't eat a thing but the buds and the tops."

Well, they told Jack he needn't mind about the cows any more; they 'uld feed 'em. So Will and Tom drove the stock out there and made Jack's cow eat all the buds off 'fore they turned their cows in. But their cows kept on gettin' poor and Jack's cow got so fat they couldn't make it out. They got madder and madder.

Will and Tom were standin' there lookin' at Jack's cow, and they were chewin' tobacco. Jack's cow belched and started chewin' her cud, and Will and Tom thought she was mockin' 'em. So they cut a tree on her and killed her for spite. They told Jack his cow had got in the way when they cut a tree and got killed. Jack went whistlin' on off up there and skinned her out. H'isted the hide up on his shoulder and lit out for the tan-yard.

Hit was a long way, but Jack he went steppin' right on. He stopped to rest when he wanted to, and everwhen he met anybody to talk to. On he went. And 'way along late in the evenin' he met up with a feller carryin' a crow on his arm.

"Howdy do, Jack. Where ye started with your cow hide?"

"Goin' to the tan-yard and sell it," Jack told him. "What you doin' with that pet crow?"

"Why this here is a talkin' crow, Jack. Now you can make a lot more money with a talkin' crow than you can tryin' to sell cow hides. How about swappin' me your hide for this talkin' crow? I won't ask no boot, bein' as it's you."

Jack swapped. Took the crow on his arm and started on back—talkin' to his crow. All hit said was "Squawk!"

He'd gone a right far piece and dark overtook him. So he had to find him a place to stay the night. He stopped at the next house he came to, and hollered Hello. Woman came to the door. Asked him what did he want.

"I want to stay the night."

"You'll have to go up in the loft. My man ain't home, and if he was to find ye here with me he 'uld kill ye sure. He's an awful jealous-hearted man. I'll have to lock ye in up there."

"All right," Jack told her. "I don't mind about that."

So he clume up the ladder to the loft and shut the lid to the scuttle-hole, and that woman latched it fast.

Jack he laid down and watched through the knotholes in the loft boards. Saw that woman fixin' a roasted shote and a big loaf of lightbread and some whisky. Directly a man came in and of course Jack he thought it was the man of the house. Then that woman brought out the roasted shote and the lightbread, and Jack saw 'em pull up to the table. And he could tell by the way that man rubbed his hands and started in eatin' that he must be a preacher. Well, they eat a little bit and the woman she started to pour out some drinks when

80

somebody rode up in the yard. She jumped up, says, "O Law! That's my old man!"

The old preacher headed for a barrel of tow was there by the door and scrouged down in it, and the woman piled tow up over his head. She grabbed up the roasted pig and the lightbread and whisky and went to hidin' 'em quick. Jack watched all that.

Her old man came on in the door. Smelled around, says, "What's that I smell, old woman?"

"Why I don't have no idea what you're talkin' about."

"Anybody been here?"

"Why no—except a poor little boy. Came here wantin' to stay the night and I let him in. But I knowed you'd not want him to stay down here and me all by myself, so I made him go up in the loft and I fastened him in."

"Well, let him down. No use to keep him locked up now."

So she unlatched the scuttle-hole, and Jack clume down holdin' his crow.

"What's your name, boy?"

"Jack."

"What-in-the-world ye doin' with that crow, Jack?"

"Hit's a fortune teller."

"Fortune teller? Humph!—Well come on here to the table. Maybe my old woman will bring us a bite of something to eat."

Jack and the old man they sat down, and the old woman brought out cold biscuits and buttermilk. Jack squeezed down on his crow's toe.

"Squawk!"

"You hush!"

"What did it say, Jack?"

"Not sure I ought to tell ye."

"Tell what it said, Jack, or I'll turn ye out of here."

"Well, hit said there was a roasted shote yonder in the trunk."

The old man went and looked. Brought it to the table and cut off some for Jack and him. Jack eat a bite or two, then he squeezed down on his crow again.

"Squawk!"

"You hush I told ye. You'll get us in trouble."

"What did it say then, Jack?"

"I think it said somethin' about a pone of lightbread under the mattress."

The old man went and reached around under the mattress

and found it. He and Jack ate right on. Then Jack got to thinkin' how good a little dram 'uld make him feel.

"Squaw-w-w-k!"

"Now I done told you to keep that blobber mouth shut."

"What did it say that time, Jack?"

"Hit might make a disturbance in the family."

"That don't differ. Tell what it said."

"I better ask it again to make sure.—Where did you say it was hid at?"

"Squaw-w-k!"

"Hit says it's under the piller yonder."

The old man reached and found the whisky. Poured Jack and him a drink a-piece. They sat there eatin' and drinkin'. Never offered the old woman a thing. She sat on there by the fireplace a-lookin' like she had swallered vinegar. Didn't say a word.

"Where'd you get that thing, Jack?"

"Oh hit took up with me when I came through a wilderness of a place out there."

"What'll ye take for it?"

"Oh you don't want my talkin' crow. You might not be able to make out what it says."

"You price it, Jack. I'll buy it. Just name any price you want to."

"Why I'd not sell it for a thousand dollars. Besides, hit's dangerous."

"Dangerous? What ye mean, Jack."

"You afraid of the Devil?"

"Don't know as I am. What's he got to do with it?"

"No, I'm afraid to tell ye."

"You tell me, Jack, or I'm liable to get mad and kill ye, and just take that thing anyhow."

"Well—this here crow can raise the Devil."

"Aw now! Surely not! Why I'd like to see that done! Go ahead. Let's see you try it."

"You better get the ax and stand there in the door with it. And if the Devil breaks to run you hit him in the head.—You and me we'll just put the preachers out of business."

The old man ran to fetch his ax. And Jack lit a splinter and got over behind that tow barrel. The old man got in the door with a good hold on his ax handle. Then Jack he raised that crow up over the barrel. Squeezed right hard——

"SQUAW-W-W-W-K!"

and Jack stuck his lighted splinter in the bung hole.

82

The tow flashed up, and that old preacher he shot right straight up with burnin' tow stickin' all over him and headed for the door. The man of the house was so flustered he couldn't get the ax raised up in time, and the old preacher ran right over the top of him and tore off down the road.

"Why hit shore is! Hit's the puore old Devil as shore's-the-world! Look at him run yonder in a light flame!"

That old man paid Jack twelve hundred dollars for his crow, and the next mornin' Jack went on in home.

Will and Tom asked Jack where he got all that money, and he told 'em, says, "Took my cow hide to the tan-yard. They cut it up into these here greenbacks."

So Will and Tom they ran right out and killed their cows, skinned 'em quick, and lit out for the tan-yard. When they got there they throwed down their hides, told the men they wanted 'em cut up into money. Said twenty-dollar bills would be all right. The men at the tan-yard thought they were crazy and ran Will and Tom out of there. They had to carry their stinkin' hides back with 'em. They were plumb give-out when they got in home, and they were both so mad at Jack they wanted to kill him right then.

Well, a day or two after that Jack's mother-in-law died and Jack had to get her fixed for the buryin'. Put her in a wagon and started drivin' to where he could buy her a good casket. Stopped at a house to get him a drink of water. There was a mill pond right there 'side the road, and Jack he propped his mother-in-law up on the wagon seat—on the side the pond was on. Went on to the house to get him his drink. The man of the house sent his little boy to get some fresh water.

"Who's that out in your wagon, son?"

"That's my mother-in-law."

"Don't she want a drink?"

"She might," says Jack.

So the man told his boy to take the water-bucket on out to see did that old lady in the wagon want a drink.

Jack told him, says, "She's right hard-of-hearin'. If she don't answer ye, you may have to punch her and ask her again."

So the boy ran out to the wagon. Asked Jack's mother-in-law did she want a drink. When she didn't answer, he hollered louder and asked her again. Then he reached up and punched her, and over the wagon wheel she went—headforemost right in the mill pond.

"Law look! He's done drownded my mother-in-law! I'm goin' to have him hung for that."

The boy came runnin' to the house scared to death, and his daddy begged Jack not to have him hung. Gave Jack a thousand dollars not to go to the law with it. So they laid the old lady in the wagon-bed, and Jack went on and bought her a fine casket.

Jack got back home and started countin' out his money. Will and Tom wanted to know where he got it. Jack said that was what they paid him for his mother-in-law. So Will and Tom they ran quick and knocked their mother-in-laws in the head, h'isted 'em in the wagon and pulled out. Carried 'em in to the undertaker and dumped 'em, says, "You can just let us have our money and we'll go on back. That'll be a thousand dollars a-piece."

And so Will and Tom got run off again. They had to get their mother-in-laws back in the wagon and get away fast 'fore the officers came. Had to make pine coffins and bury 'em themselves. And by then they were so mad at Jack they decided to kill him right then—and get *his* money.

So they set on him and pulled a feed sack down over his head, tied him hard and fast that-a-way, and headed for the river to drown him. Got to the river bank and took a notion to get good and drunk 'fore they throwed him in. Tied Jack against a tree and went to hunt some likker.

They'd not been gone long when here came an old man drivin' a hundred head of sheep. Jack heard all those sheep blate-in', heard the old man a-hollerin', "Shee-oo! Shee-oo!"

"Hello daddy!"

The old man fin'lly saw Jack, says, "Hello, son.—What-in-the-world are you a-doin' tied up that way?"

"I'm fixin' to go to heaven."

"Why you sound like you're too young to be goin' there. How old are ye?"

"Goin' on nineteen."

"Oh Law yes! Why'd a young feller like you want to go to heaven? You let me go instead."

"I don't know about that. I might get lost by the time I'm an old man, and land in the other place."

"I'll give ye all these sheep if you'll let me get in that poke and go in your place."

Jack fin'lly agreed and the old man untied him. Then Jack he rammed the sack down over that old man's head and tied him back good and tight against the tree.

"When them two angels come for ye," Jack told him, "they might talk a little rough, but you be sure not to say anything and you'll get to heaven all right."

And Jack he drove the sheep up the river a ways till he was out of sight.

Will and Tom came on back and grabbed up the old man. He never said a word, and they pitched him in the river and went on off. They looked back directly and there came Jack with ninety-nine head of sheep and a-ridin' the old buck.

"Why Jack, we thought we drownded ye. Where'n-the-world did you get all them sheep?"

"When you boys pitched me in I landed on this old buck and rode him out and the rest followed. There's several other big herds in there. I might 'a-got more but this was all I wanted."

"How about you pitchin' us in too, Jack? We'd like a few of them sheep ourselves."

"Got no time. I'll have to take my sheep on to pasture."

"Come on, Jack. We'll pay ye a hundred dollars to pitch us in the river."

"Well all right, but you'll have to get your own pokes."
So Will and Tom ran and brought the two feed sacks, and
Jack tied 'em up and shoved 'em in the river.
And right then I left and ain't heard from 'em since.

Jack and Old Strongman

Here, with several new touches, is Grimm's "Valiant Little Tailor"
who killed "seven at one blow." It comes from "Tom Hunt"[4] at
whose house we sat up and told tales from about dark one eve-
ning until daylight the next morning. In Tom Hunt's telling,
Strongman was a giant. The word "giant," in and around Beech
Creek, North Carolina, doesn't necessarily mean great size. Sometimes it means a male witch. In my telling of this tale, I have made
Strongman a big, "stout" (i.e. strong) man to make the run of the
tale a bit more plausible, especially the last event.

One time Jack was layin' under a big tree tryin' to sleep and
the flies kept botherin' him. He went to slappin' at 'em and
directly he looked and counted how many he'd killed. He got
up and went and gathered him some pokeberries. Squeezed
out the juice and then he wrote a sign on his fore-head—

KILLED FOURTEEN

Now there was a great stout feller came through that
country had killed seven men and he wore a big belt with

KILLED SEVEN

wrote around it. He was about the biggest and strongest man
that anybody had ever seen, and everybody got to talkin'
about him. And it wasn't long till he got acquainted with the
King's girl and he got struck on her right off. She liked him
pretty well, too. He said his name was Strongman Peters.
Well he ran across Jack one day, and when he saw that
sign on Jack's fore-head he didn't know what to make of it.
So he decided to take Jack for a buddy, get him to help him
work, and see was Jack really stout enough to out-do him

4 See *Grandfather Tales.*

86

that-a-way. And directly they went to work cuttin' firewood for the King.

Strongman he cut a big dead chestnut, trimmed it. Cut him another one, trimmed it. Picked up his two trees, one under each arm, and then he looked around where Jack was workin'. Jack hadn't cut ar' tree. He was twistin' him up a great long hickory wythe. Strongman went over there, set his logs down, says, "What you fixin' to do, Jack?"

"Why I'm just gettin' ready to take in my load of trees."

"But you ain't cut no trees yet."

"Oh I always fix my wythe first."

"Wythe? What for?"

"Why to tie the logs up. I always wythe my logs in a bundle 'fore I start totin' 'em in."

"How many do ye generally pack at one load, Jack?"

"Oh ten or twelve. Depends on how thick they are."

Strongman couldn't stand that—havin' Jack come in with more of a load than him. So he left his two logs layin' there and called Jack, says, "Let's let the wood go, Jack. We can haul it in with a team tomorrow. No use workin' ourselves to death."

"Come on. Let's take it back now."

"No, Jack. Let's wait."

So they went on back to where they were stayin'. Then Strongman thought he'd try Jack again. He got him a hogs-head-barrel and rigged up a big bail on it like a bucket. Brought that to Jack, says, "Jack, the King wants a little water fetched in this bucket. I'm fryin' us a calf for dinner or I'd go. Here's the bucket." And he set it down, went on back in the house.

Jack couldn't even lift the bucket off the ground. He went to the door, hollered, "Where's the mattick?"

"What you want with the mattick, Jack?"

"Why I wouldn't fool with takin' water anywhere in a little bitty old bucket like that. Hand me the mattick here. I'll just dig the well up and move it up there nearer the kitchen where they can get at it a lot handier."

"Just let it go, Jack. I'll fetch the water up directly.—Now you leave the mattick where it's at."

Strongman didn't know what to do. He'd got sort of scared of Jack by then. And besides that, Jack had been goin' over to see the King's girl and talkin' to her some. He saw the girl and Jack talkin' and laughin' about something, and sort of lookin' over to where he was, and it bothered him.

87

Strongman let Jack alone for a few days. And fin'lly Jack thought how he could banter Strongman to a contest. He waited that night till Strongman was snorin' right hard and then he went out with a big auger. Went to a good-sized white oak there a ways from the house, cut out a ring of bark and bored a big hole through. Cut the bark out right careful-like on the other side and then put all that bark back again just like it was.

Next mornin'——

"Strongman, let's you and me go up to that white oak in the pasture and see which one can knock the biggest hole in the trunk."

"With an ax?"

"Why no. Let's just hit in to it with our fists."

Strongman couldn't back down. So he went on with Jack. Drawed back and—kerslam!—he knocked a little dent in the bark and went to lickin' his knuckles. Jack whistled like he thought Strongman was pretty good. Then he drew his fist back a few inches and rammed through the tree clean up to his shoulder. Strongman saw the bark fly and saw Jack's fist pop out the far side and he was scareder than ever. Everything Jack told him to do after that, he done it.

But Strongman he kept on goin' down to the King's house Saturday nights, and the girl she liked him all right. He was a lot bigger than Jack, and—well, she sometimes liked him the best. Especially of a Saturday night. But she liked Jack, too. He was younger.

The King he liked Jack the best because he could tell Jack was sharper than old Strongman. So fin'lly he asked the girl which one she wanted to marry. She couldn't make up her mind.

So the King decided he'd fix a contest: see which one was the best hand to catch a lion. He said the one that brought back the lion's right forefoot could have the girl. He had one of his wild lions turned loose and it went tearin' off up a holler. Jack and Strongman took off after it. Jack told Strongman he 'uld let him have the first go at it and so Strongman went on ahead. Jack hid and waited. And it wasn't long till here came Strongman back down that holler a-goin' rippity-tuck! with the lion right in behind him. Well they tangled there close to where Jack was hid and Strongman he tried to get him a handhold on the lion and they started rollin' over and over.

Jack slipped around and waited till the lion was on top, then he jumped over there and hacked off his right paw, grabbed it and took off.

The King was right pleased and the girl she seemed to think a lot better of Jack. But Old Strongman came in directly all scratched up and his clothes nearly tore off, had the lion's other paw and said it was the only one the old lion had on him. Well the girl she got to suspectin' somethin' and she told the King she wasn't satisfied about the lion business. And so that got everything riled up again.

Then the King he told 'em, says, "All right. Now there's only one way to settle it: You'uns come on and eat supper now, and when we go to bed she can sleep between the both of ye and sometime durin' the night I'll come in, and the one she's facin' when I come to the door, that's the one she'll have to marry."

So just 'fore bedtime when Jack and old Strongman stepped

89

out, Jack went and pulled him a handful of mint and a big batch of ramps and wild onions. Then he called Strongman, says, "I saw her slip out in the kitchen after supper and eat her a big onion. We better eat some too. Then we'll not notice it so bad."

And Jack started eatin' that mint and handed old Strongman the onions. It was dark and when he heard Jack chewin' and chompin' he thought Jack was eatin' onions, so he crammed all them wild onions in his mouth and chawed 'em up.

So they crawled in the bed, one on one side and the other on the other. The girl she turned over to Strongman Peters.

"Phew!" she says and turned over to Jack.

She tried several times to turn toward Strongman but she just couldn't stand it, and when the old King came through the door a little after midnight she was facin' Jack.

So Jack got to marry her.

And the last time I was down there they were gettin' on fairly well.

THE FOOL IRISHMAN TALES

These are tales that were once told in England on "The Wise Men of Gotham." To "act like a pure Gotham fool" is an expression I have run across in the mountains of Virginia. One mountain woman had an explanation of why the town of Gotham got its reputation: King John sent a deputy to cut all their ears off because the Gothamites had cut trees across the road to bar the tax collector. When the deputy arrived the citizens put on several fool acts for his benefit. This so befuddled him that he decided to let them alone.

In Joseph Jacobs' *More English Fairy Tales* there are six "Wise Men of Gotham" tales. They are given there as contained in a *Shakesperian Jest Book*. Such tales have existed since the days of ancient Greece, where they were told on the Boeotians.

The Irish came to the United States later than the first settlers and consequently offered a good subject on which to hang these old "noodle" tales. These examples are from southwestern Virginia. I have no record of who my informants were for five of them.

90

Pat and the Mule Eggs

Pat never had seen any pumpkins. And one fall just after he had come to the U-nited States, he happened to go by a field full of pumpkins. The old farmer was shockin' his corn. Pat stopped and stood lookin' over the fence, and fin'lly he hollered at the old man, says, "Say, mister, what's all them little round yaller things?"

The farmer came over there, says, "Why, Pat, haven't you ever seen any mule eggs?"

"Mule eggs! Well faith-'n-be-jatters! Is them mule eggs?"

The old farmer reached down and picked up one, says, "Why yes, and they're ripenin' fast. Want to buy one?"

"Oh indeed yes, I'd like the best in the world to have me a little mule colt. How much are your mule eggs today?"

"Well this one here now, I reckon I can let you have it for twenty dollars—seein' it's you, Pat."

Pat paid him and took his mule egg and put off.

The old man hollered after him, says, "Put it on the south side of the barn, Pat, and at night you'll have to sit on it. Be careful and keep it warm. Some of 'em are just about ready to hatch now."

Pat went on hurryin' down the hill, and he was so tickled about hatchin' him out a colt he didn't watch his step and stumped his toe. The pumpkin jumped out of his arms and went rollin' down the hill. Pat took out after it, but it rolled and bounced and fin'lly it landed right in the middle of a bresh pile. It hit a rock in there and busted. Pat saw it bust and right then a rabbit ran out the other side of the pile of bresh. And Pat lit out after the rabbit, a-hollerin', "Cope,

91

colty! Cope colty! Here's your mammy! Here's your mammy!
Cope colty!"
Went back to that farmer, says, "Faith-'n-be-jatters! That
'un hatched 'fore I could get it home but I couldn't catch the
colt. Faith, it would have made a fine race horse. Can you
let me have another mule egg, one not quite so ripe?"

Pat and the Fire Engines

Two Irishmen came over here once. They never had seen
things the way they are here in the U-nited States. They just
had got off the boat, and they found 'em a room in a ho-tel
somewhere. Got their supper and went on to bed.

Then about midnight, a fire broke loose. Pat heard the
racket and jumped up, jerked the window open, poked his
head out to see what it was. One of them old-time fire engines,
the kind with a smoke stack, was tearin' down the street
headed right that way. But before Pat could turn around here
came another one, and they both went tearin' past: black
smoke boilin' and sparks shootin' up, and just then the fireman
opened the fire-door and all that red blaze lit up everything.

Pat ran to the bed and shook Mike, says,

"Mike! Mike! Get up quick and let's get away from here.
All Hell has done broke loose and two loads have just gone
by!"

Pat and the Rattlesnake

Pat and Mike came over to this country, and, you know, they
never had seen any snakes. They kept hearin' about snakes:
how dangerous they were, especially rattlesnakes, and what a
snake looked like 'n all. And they were awful scared of ever
runnin' across one.

Well they went 'way out in the country one day to see
somebody. Had to stop at a man's farm and ask the way.
The old farmer told 'em how they had to go: down a path
through a pasture-field, across an old rail fence, and up a
holler. So Pat thanked him and on they went. The old man
hollered after 'em, says, "You boys mind out goin' down
through there. We killed a big rattlesnake down that way a
couple of days ago."

Pat and Mike grabbed hold on one another and looked around over the ground, scared to death. But they didn't see anything, and directly Mike says, "Aw come on, Pat. We'll watch."

So they went on watchin' both sides of the path, and came to the rail fence. Mike he was in front, and he looked the fence over, didn't see anything, so he cloomb over. Then Mike turned around right quick to examine the other side of the fence.

Pat was climbin' over, and his big toe went through a knot-hole in one of the rails. Mike saw Pat's toe come through and he hollered, "Pat! Hold still! I see one!"

Pat was so scared he couldn't do a thing but freeze and hold fast. Mike picked up a big stick and slipped over slow-like, came down on Pat's big toe—BAM!

Pat hollered out, says, "Hit him again, Mike! He's done bit me!"

Pat and the City-billies

Most "Fool Irishman Tales" make fun of Pat. This one is the other way around.

One time two slick-lookin' city-billies were walkin' down the street, saw Pat comin' and they decided to have some fun out of him. They stopped Pat, says, "Pat, have you heard the news?"

"No, and what's that?" Pat asked 'em.

"Why, The Devil is dead."

Pat looked at them two city-billies a minute. Reached in his pocket, and handed 'em a quarter a-piece, went on.

The two fellers stood there lookin' at their quarters, then one of 'em hollered after Pat, says, "What's this for?"

Pat turned his head, says,

"In Ireland, where I come from, when the head of a family dies we always give something to the orphans."

The Irishman and the Fiddle

This tale is from R. M. Ward, verbatim. I have copied it from a field recording, taken down in shorthand years ago.

There was one Irishman[1] came over here by himself. He was lookin' all about the country learnin' everything he could. Fin'lly he come to somebody's house where they had a corn-shuckin' that day. And they'd done fixed to have a play[2] that night. Said that old Irishman happened to stop there and they called him in where all the people were sittin' about. And he didn't have a very good idea of all that. He was pretty excited bein' in such a big crowd.

Fin'lly the man who was goin' to make the music he got out the box that he had his fiddle in, took the fiddle out and started tunin' it. Pat slipped toward the door.

The man held his fiddle up and plunked the strings a little to see was it in tune, twisted the tunin'-pegs a time or two. Pat was tip-toein' along and reachin' for the doorknob. And about that time the fiddler raked the bow across the strings, and they all jumped up to get on the floor in their sets.

And they say that old Irishman shot out the door! Down the road he went: long hair a-flyin', coat-tail stickin' straight out. He ran about a mile, came to another house, and pitched right in the door.

The man of that house he ran and got hold of Pat, got him up off the floor, and said, "Hello here, whatever's the matter with ye?"

"Christ be-jabbers, I been tryin' to make legs save body!"

"What's wrong?" the man says.

"Well, I stopped at this next house back up there, and a large crowd of people was there. I don't know what they were all there for, but there was a lot of 'em—all settin' around. And there was a man there had something in a box. I don't know what kind of animal it was, but he h'isted it up and picked its ears and it squawked just a little. And then he took a stick and started beatin' that thing on the back, and —O, golly, what squawkin'! Everybody jumped up to run but I was the clostest to the door. My legs have saved my body. I don't know who else got killed."

[1] Usually pronounced "Arshman."
[2] *I.e.* a dance. "Dancing" is a sin, and we must use other words when we do any sort of country dancing.

94

The Seven Irishmen

Here's one told in the mountains of western North Carolina, as I heard it some fifteen years ago. It is also known, according to Dr. Stith Thompson, to the French, the Finns, the Germans, the Flemish, and the Zuni Indians.

One time there were seven Irishmen travelin' and night overtook 'em. They came to where the road ran alongside of a river. The moon was shinin' bright, and one of these Irishmen looked over in the water and saw the moon shinin' down in the water.

"Look!"

And they all stopped and came and looked.

"What-in-the-world is that now?"

"Hit's a yaller cheese."

"No," says Pat—he was the biggest 'un—"hit's a lump of gold, and faith-'n-b'-jatters we'll get it!"

"How'll we get it out from there?"

"Faith!" says Pat. "Now I'll tell ye. We'll all climb up in that tree there, see, and we'll all get out on that limb that hangs out just over where the lump of gold is at, see, and then I'll hang down on that limb, see, and then one of you fellers will climb down and take me by the heels, see, and then another'n will climb down over us, see, and take him by the heels, see, and then another'n will climb down and take *him* by *his* heels, see, and then we'll all get strung down like that, see, till the last man of all, see, can reach down and take hold on the gold, see, and he'll hand it up, see, and when it gets to me I'll take it down, see, and we'll break it and divide it amongst us all, see, and we'll all be rich forevermore! D'ye see now?"

They all thought that was just fine, and it wasn't long till the seventh man was climbing down to the bottom place. He caught on with one hand and was tryin' to reach for that lump of gold with the other, and Pat's string of men got to swingin' a little. Pat felt his hands about to slip, so he hollers out,

"You'uns there below! Hold fast a second while I spit on me hands!"

So Pat let go. And there they were strugglin' and stranglin' and beatin' the water with their hands. Pat he could

95

swim, so he got out quick and reached a pole to 'em and dragged 'em out.

"Oh faith, and now look at what you've done! And one of us poor fellers might have got drownded. Stand there now and let me count yet."

They stood there with the water dreenin' off 'em, and Pat he put his finger on his own chest, says, "Me and myself—" then he pointed at the others, says, "—and one, two, three, four, five, six! Oh, Oh! Now what'll we do? There's one poor feller's got drownded!"

Well, first one and then another would try to count, but none of 'em thought to count himself in, so they sat there all night lookin' in the water for the one that was drownded, and mournin' and carryin'-on over it till it was daylight.

Then a man came along and saw 'em sittin' there a-cryin' and boo-hoo-in', and asked what was the matter. So Pat told him how they'd tried to get the big lump of gold out the river, and how one of 'em was drownded for sure.

"How many of ye was there to start with?"

"Oh me!" says Pat. "There was seven 'fore that 'un got drownded. Poor feller!"

That man he made 'em stand up in a row and he counted 'em out loud: "One! Two! Three! Four! Five! Six!—" and then he slapped the next one on his back, says, "—and there's your drownded man—seven!"

But they wouldn't believe him. Said they'd already tried that countin' business themselves and they just knowed one of 'em was drownded. That man was about to go on, when a notion struck him. He pointed to a small-like mud hole[s] there in the road, about half dried-up, and he made all them Irishmen come and stand around it, says, "You fellers all get down on your knees and stick your noses into that, and then count the holes your noses make, and you'll see."

So they all got down and stuck their noses in. Pat sat back and counted seven holes. Then they all counted to make sure. And all at once they started laughin'.

"We're all of us here! None of us poor fellers got drownded!"

So they thanked the man and on they went.

[s] Or "a ripe cowpile," as it is usually told.

TALL TALES

The Norther and the Frogs

I have no record of where I learned this.

There was a man one time could prophesy about the weather the best of anybody I ever knew. He lived out in Oklahoma, and there's a wind out there they call The Norther. This man he could tell to the second when the weather was goin' to change. And one day late in April he was out lookin' at the clouds and sniffin' the air—and he took a notion.

Went down to a big frog pond there on his place. Sat down on a rock and started whistlin' right quiet-like till he'd whistled every frog out of the water and they were all sittin' there on the banks whistlin' back at him. Every now and then he'd wet his finger in his mouth and hold it up to test the wind. And finally he popped his hands all at once and hollered.

All the frogs jumped, and just as they hit the water that Norther struck. Froze the pond over solid.

The man went on home and next morning he came back with a scythe. The pond was covered with frogs stuck halfway down on top of the ice. So he mowed 'em. Raked up the frog legs. Packed 'em in a little ice and shipped 'em to Chicago. Made him quite a sum of money.

The Split Dog

I heard this somewhere in eastern Kentucky. It appeared in *Fisher's River* (North Carolina) *Scenes and Characters*, by "Skitt," published in New York, Harper & Brothers, 1859.

Had me a little dog once was the best rabbit dog you ever saw. Well, he was runnin' a rabbit one day, and some fool had left a scythe lyin' in the grass with the blade straight up. That poor little dog ran smack into it and it split him open from the tip of his nose right straight on down his tail.

97

Well I saw him fall apart and I ran and slapped him back together. I had jerked off my shirt, so I wrapped him up in that right quick and ran to the house. Set him in a box and poured turpentine all over the shirt. I kept him near the stove. Set him out in the sun part of the time. Oh, I could see him still breathin' a little, and I hoped I wouldn't lose him. And after about three weeks I could see him tryin' to wiggle now and then. Let him stay bandaged another three weeks—and then one morning I heard him bark. So I started unwrappin' him and in a few minutes out he jumped, spry as ever.

But—don't you know!—in my excitement, blame if I hadn't put him together wrong-way-to. He had two legs up and two legs down.

Anyhow, it turned out he was twice as good a rabbit dog after that. He'd run on two legs till he got tired, and then flip over and just keep right on.

Aa Lord! That little dog could run goin' and comin', and bark at both ends.

The Hickory Toothpick

This is from near Pine Mountain in eastern Kentucky. Percy Mac-Kaye wrote it up as told by Old Sol Shell. This tale, with its device of actually showing the toothpick, is a sure-fire after-dinner item.

One winter we sure had a big snow. I was livin' up a ways on Pine Mountain, south side, there where the Poor Fork of The Cumberland runs between The Pine and The Black. And one morning I tried to open the door, and I couldn't. I'd noticed the snow banked up on the windows, but when

I tried the door it looked like the snow had piled up plumb over the house.

I kept my stove goin'. Had me a fairly good pile of wood in the house—and enough rations for a day or two. But after about four days my wood was gone, and the meat, too. I tore out some shelves and kept my fire up. The snow didn't seem to thaw much, and after I'd burned up all my shelves and a couple of chairs I knew I had to get out of there and hunt me some firewood.

So I took the stovepipe down: knocked a few planks loose from around the flue, got my ax and crawled out. Well, the snow went up like a funnel, twenty or thirty feet, where my fire had kept it melted. So I hacked me some toeholds with the ax and finally made it out on top of all that snow. And like I said, it was a big snowfall: plumb over the tops of the tallest trees.

But 'way up on one cliff of Pine Mountain there was one tree—a hickory—the snow hadn't drifted over and buried. So I headed for it. The crust was hard enough to hold me and up I went. I could see directly where other folks' houses were snowed under. Putney, the settlement down at the foot of the mountain, looked like a little patch of doodlebug holes.

Got to that hickory tree finally—and it was full of coons. They'd gone from tree to tree, I reckon, and that hickory was ripe with 'em: frozen fast asleep. So I says, "Well, here's firewood, and meat too, to do me till a thaw sets in." I shook the coons out. A few rolled down the slope, but I picked up about a dozen: wythed a thin strip of bark off that hickory and tied 'em together by their tails.

Then I cut that tree. Went to trimmin' it. Piled up the limbs right careful, so's I'd have plenty of kindlin'. Oh, I saved every twig! But—don't you know!—when I hacked off that last limb, the log jumped and slid top foremost down the south side of the mountain. There went my stovewood!

I watched it slitherin' down, faster and faster. It was goin' so fast it shot across the bottom and up Black Mountain it flew. I thought it 'uld go right up in the air and over yon' side of The Black. But it slowed down just at the top of the ridge: stopped with its top teeterin'—and here it came back. Scooted across where the river was and headed up The Pine again. I cut me a few heel-holds, stepped down and thought I'd catch it with the ax when it got to me. But when I tried to nail it, it was about four inches too short. Stopped right at me, and down again. Hit through the bottom goin' so fast

99

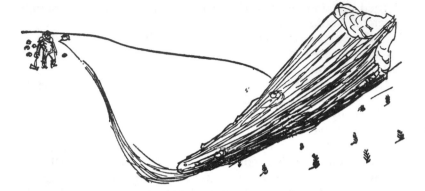

it was smokin'. Up Black Mountain, clean to the top, and back down this way again. Well I watched it see-sawin' a few times, and finally gathered up my coons and that pile of bresh and made it back to the house. Put the flue and stovepipe back and started my fire.

Well, I lived off coon-meat for about a week. Had to burn up all my chairs, and the table, to keep from freezin'. And I'd started burnin' the bedstead and was fryin' the last of my meat when I heard, drip! drip! drip! And there was a little daylight showin' at the top of the windows. So I shoved on the door, mashed the snow back, and got out. Snow was still about eight foot deep. Got my ax and headed for the nearest tree. Got me a good pile of wood in and fixed the fire till my little stove was red-hot.

Had to go fetch some meal and other rations. I was gettin' a little hungry. So I took off for the store at Putney.

I looked over the country and noticed a sort of trough there between the two mountains where that log had been slidin'. I went right down there. Couldn't see that hickory at all. But when I got to the bottom of that trough I looked, and there—still slidin' back and forth just a few inches— was my log. And—don't you know!—with all that see-sawin' that log had worn down to the size of a toothpick. I leaned over and picked it up. Stuck it in my pocket.

You may not believe me, but[1]—I've kept it to this day.— There. Look at it yourself.

Best toothpick I ever had.

---

[1] Having whittled down a twig of hickory—and maybe sandpapered it a bit—here you reach into your vest pocket and produce your hickory toothpick. An ordinary round toothpick, with one sharp end cut off to make it look more like a log, will do well enough, but isn't quite so convincing.

Old Hide and Taller

"Tales of the Tall Timbers" is a column that appears on the front page of *The Dickensonian,* published weekly in Clintwood, Dickenson County, Virginia. H. M. Sutherland, editor of the paper, has written this column about the doings up on The Devil's Apron for some years. A President of the United States has been among his subscribers. And so real does he make those folks up there that on my first visit to Mr. Sutherland I asked him, "Just how far is it from here to The Devil's Apron? I'd sort of like to go with you sometime." But Brandy Bill, and his oldest son, Bourbon, his twin boys, Rock and Rye, and the least young'un, Toddy, and Business Bill, Good 'Lige, Bad 'Lige, Little 'Bigie Birdsong, Aunt Marthy, Aunt Seraptheeny, Aunt Helfirey, and the other colorful citizens of that settlement live only in the imagination of Mr. Sutherland in the little basement office there in the County Seat, where *The Dickensonian* is edited, set up, printed, folded, and mailed, on every Thursday. I have been told that Mr. Sutherland composes each column direct on the linotype. Here is one of my favorites.

I was beginning to get a bit worried about Good 'Lige, since I hadn't seen him for some three weeks. It was with a feeling of relief when I knocked at his door last Sunday to hear his cheery voice call to me to enter.

He was sitting before the fire, reading his copy of the weekly newspaper, and he had a pot of "ginger stew" simmering in the coals on the hearth where a couple of hickory logs were blazing.

"Sit and help yourself," he urged hospitably, nodding toward some cups and saucers on a nearby table.

While we were talking, I glanced about the room at the magazine cover-pages with which he had papered the walls. Over the fireplace, resting on a pair of deer's antlers, lay a gun that caught and held my attention. It appeared to be a muzzle-loading, double-barreled weapon, with one barrel directly over the other. I arose and took the gun down to examine it more closely.

"That's old Hide-an'-Taller," explained Good 'Lige, "the best gun ever seen in the whole Apern country. I got her thut'y-forty years ago from one of the Eversoles when he was scoutin' in that French-Eversole war they had down in Kaintucky."

"Hide-and-Tallow?" I queried bewilderedly.

"Yeah, we used to have shootin' matches for beeves," said Good 'Lige, lighting the cigar I gave him. "Beeves wa'nt worth much then, an' the first choice was allus the hide and taller, because they was worth the most. I allus won with that rifle-gun there.

"She's a double-barr'l," he continued, taking the gun and caressing it. "Ye see the top barr'l is for a single ball an' the bottom barr'l is for shot. She shore has been a meat-gun. If it wa'nt so muddy out thar' I'd show ye how she shoots. I reckon she's got the longest range ever seen—around here anyhow."

Good 'Lige was silent a moment and a crinkle appeared at the corners of his eyes. I waited expectantly.

"I allus used a double charge of Frenchman's powder,[2] and greased my patchin', and the bullet sure did carry an onbelieveable distance. Of course the boys was exaggeratin' some, but they used to tell that I allus put salt in behind the bullets to keep the meat from sp'ilin' 'fore I could get to it and skin it out.

"She was the best b'ar gun that ever killed a b'ar in the Cumberlands. I never had to shoot but one time and the b'ar was mine, no matter how big it was, or how far away it was when I shot. I don't know how many b'ars I killed with her, but I used to sell b'ar meat to all the neighbors, and I killed so many I got plumb wore out with all the trouble I had skinnin' 'em. A b'ar is hard to skin, 'specially when he weighs about fo'-five hundred pounds.

"So one day I took old Hide-an'-Taller down and I loaded both barr'ls right careful. Put a good well-moulded ball in the top barr'l with two heapin' charges of powder. Then I loaded the shot barr'l: put in a double-charge of powder— wadded that in right good, wadded in a handful of carpet tacks on top of the powder, and then I took the blade out of an old Barlow knife, put it in the vise and twisted a little wing on it, and dropped hit down in there, wadded it in just enough so it would stay straight. Then I put off.

"I moseyed up toward the head of Wolf-Pen Creek, and fin'lly I heard somethin' thrashin' around, looked through the bresh and there was a big b'ar in there rakin' up a pile of chest-

[2] Du Pont, who made the first good powder.

102

nuts. I slipped through the paw-paw patch to where I could draw a better bead on him. Raised up this old gun here and hollered 'Hie!'

"That b'ar whirled around and I squeezed the top trigger, hit him right between the eyes—and just as he was about to fall I let loose with the other barr'l. That knife blade went twistin' through the air and skinned him out slick. And them tacks came right in behind the knife blade—tacked the hide to the nearest tree."

The Roguish Cow

This is given as it actually happened that day some years ago when I walked home with Gaines Kilgore, a gifted tale-teller. (See his "The King and Robert Hood's Horny Beast-es.") Later Gaines himself wrote out this tale about the roguish cow and elaborated it to the point where "World's War Two" was won with "all that lead she had in her,"—and her hide furnished elements for "the 'tomic bomb."

One day Gaines and I, on foot, were headed for his place up on "The Harricane" (a rural section just out of Wise, Virginia) and he started telling me about a cow that had been giving trouble in his neighborhood. At first it all sounded reasonable enough, but then Gaines remarked quite casually:

"She got into Elbert Mullins' feed house the other night and hit padlocked—locked when he went there in the morning; but his feed sacks were all slobbered up and cow tracks everywhere! He couldn't figure out who must have let that cow in and then gone and locked up after she left. And he knowed for sure he'd locked after he milked. So he and I watched the next night to see what-'n-all went on.

"Ten o'clock or so here came that roguish cow. She stood there and worried that padlock with the little keen points of her horns and blame if she didn't pick that lock! Flipped it out the hasp with her tongue, and in she went. We let her alone, and when she came out she nosed the door shut, picked up that padlock off the ground and mouthed it in place, and bit it locked again.

"Then Elbert let her have a load of buckshot and she left. She didn't seem to like that so well."

103

We were near the house now and Gaines went on in a most easy-going manner:

"She got in my oat stacks here about a week ago. I moved one of 'em, piled it in the barn loft, and put the rails up higher around that 'un.—See there?"

There stood a stack of oat bundles with rails rigged around it in a circle about eight feet high; and, sure enough, next to this stood an empty stack-pole with scraps of oat-straw on the ground around it.

"But two nights after I'd moved them oats, there was cow-sign up in the loft. I couldn't make it out: how-in-the-world she got up there now.

"So I got my flashlight and went out about eleven and hid right yonder in that blackberry thicket; had my shotgun. I didn't have long to wait. I heard her directly and when she got close enough I shined my light on her, and there she was —with a ladder on her horns. Ah, Lord, she had her a lad-der hid out in the bresh somewhere!"

Gaines paused, and at last he grinned a bit.

"That makes about eighteen times I've shot her myself. —Whoever owns that cow sure ought to sell her on the hoof. She bring a lot with all that lead she's got in her by now."

Only then did Gaines look straight at me. His eyes lit up and his grin widened, and we both broke into laughter.

The Snakebit Hoehandle

From many sources in the Southern Appalachians.

Copperhead made for me one day when I was hoein' my corn. Happened I saw him in time and I lit into him with the hoe. He thrashed around; bit the hoehandle a couple of times, but I fin'lly killed him. Hung him on the fence.

Went on back to work, and directly my hoehandle felt thicker'n common. I looked it over good and it was swellin'. The poison from that snakebite was workin' all through it. After I tried it a few more licks it popped the shank and the hoe-head fell off. So I threw that handle over by the fence: went and fixed me another'n. Got my corn hoed out about dark.

Week or two after that I was lookin' over my cornfield and I noticed a log in the fencerow. Examined it right close and blame if it wasn't that hoehandle! Hit was swelled up big enough for lumber. So I took it and had it sawed. Had enough boards to build me a new chicken house. Then I painted it and, don't you know!—the turpentine in the paint took out all that swellin', and the next mornin' my chicken house had shrunk to the size of a shoe box.—Good thing I hadn't put my chickens in it!

Big John Bolling and the Indians

This was written out by Boyd Bolling, of Flat Gap, Virginia, who lives "at the head of The Cumberland." Mr. Bolling used little punctuation. I have supplied just enough to make reading easier, and have paragraphed a bit. I have changed the spelling of only one word: " 'simmon," for which he had only one "m."

One of B. J. Bolling's tall tales of the Sixteen hundreds:
Back in the Early days of the settling of this country there was one John Ann Bolling settled in South Carolina near the

Sea Shore. He was a giant of those days: 7 feet tall, 340 lbs wt. He owned large farms.

One day he was working on a farm 1½ miles from home. All at once he heard a great noise, he looked and Behold here come five hundred indians on horse back down the mountains to kill him. He ran for a tall 'simmon tree about 4 hundred yards away, the indians yelling right after him. When he got there he jumped with all his might. It was 40 ft to the first limb. He missed it as he went up, but caught it as he came down.

Right up the tree he took, the indians yelling around and shooting arrows in him. He would jerk them out and stick a green 'simmon to the place so it would not bleed. They kept shooting him, he kept jerking them out.

At last they ran and piled rails around the Big tree and fired them. Still running around that tree with their war whoops and Dances. Still shooting them arrows in him. He kept pulling them out and sticking them green 'simmons to the place.

At last that big tree began to sway back and forth. Big John gave up to die. Finally he got hold of a big horn he had by his side. He put that horn to his mouth: gave three long blasts that meant great danger. In a few moments here came his wife and six sons on horses, with all sorts of guns.

They commenced shooting them down in piles. They started to run. Just then that big tree bent over to the ground. Big John leaped out, grabbed a gun and killed 30 of them before they could get to the mountains.

So they took Big John home, washed him and cleaned him up, and counted two hundred and thirty eight arrows had been shot in him, and—don't you think!—he never lost but about one spoonful of blood.

You See the mohawks never Bothered Big John any more.

2. Ballads, Songs and Hymns

[Folk songs] whose words are [often] incomplete or cor-
rupt, present a knotty problem to the collector who would
publish them for popular use. Only those who have tried can
realize the immense difficulty of the task. To be successful,
the editor must be in close sympathy with the [traditions] of
the folk poet. He must divest himself of all acquired literary
tricks, be alert to avoid anachronisms, [and all quaintness,
all "sham antiquity"], and contrive to speak in . . . simple
and direct language. The high estimation in which the best
Scottish traditional poetry is deservedly held, is due . . . to
the genius . . . of those who edited it . . . Scott [and] Burns.
. . . Who will do for our English [-American] ballads and
songs what Scott and Burns did for the Scottish?

Cecil Sharp in *English Folk Songs—Some Conclusions*
(Simpkin and Co., Ltd., Novello and Co., London, 1907).

The ballad, being founded on what is permanent and uni-
versal in the heart of man, will live forever.

quoted by Evelyn K. Wells in *The Ballad Tree.*

Our folk songs have always lived because of their intrinsic merits. They need no explaining. It is the same with all genuine art. Cecil Sharp has said, "It is a small demand that these things make: that of being known to be loved." And this is as true of the fine arts as of the folk arts.

I shall never forget the first time I heard a genuine English-American ballad. It was at Pine Mountain Settlement School in eastern Kentucky, when I was nearly twenty-one. The children were assembled, waiting for a program to begin. A child's voice raised the first line of "The Merry Golden Tree," and suddenly all of the children—without books, without any adult leader, without even a piano to accompany them—joined in, and the whole room was filled with their singing. The magic of the tune, of the sorrowful tale, of the "lone and lonesome" words, made my hair stand on end. When the ballad came to an end, two new voices each raised a separate song. There was a bit of a contest until a majority settled on one song and drowned out the other!

All the thirty years since that chance visit to Pine Mountain, this magic has held me fast in its spell.

When you sing these ballads and songs you are free to make them "make sense" *for you*—not too slow, not too fast. Articulate the words. Point up significant places in the sense: pause a bit before important words or points to be made. Observe the commas and periods, and do not pay too much attention to the *exact* length of measure or note. In songs of irregular rhythm it is helpful to give counts to each individual note rather than to try to count so many notes between the bars: quarter note "one," half note "one-two," dotted half "one-two-three," and so forth. Don't worry about the words falling in place with certain phrases or notes of the tune. Feel it out, and don't try to crowd anything. Tell the tale clearly. Think about the text, and, even as you use the tune make it more like talking than singing. For this reason (and following a precedent set by the 1940 Episcopal hymnal) we have omitted all time signatures. (See the general Introduction for further singing instruction.)

Concerning the style, or manner, in which these songs should be sung, the advice of Mr. Sharp is helpful: "Artistically, then, it will, I think, be found that the most effective treatment to accord the folk song is to sing it as straightforwardly as possible, and, while paying the closest attention to the clear enunciation of the words and the preservation of an even, pleasant tone, to forbear, as far as may be, from actively and deliberately attempting to improve it by the introduction of frequent changes of time, crescendos, diminuendos, and other devices of a like character.[1]"

Some of the songs that follow are for the lone singer singing for an audience. Some can be sung by a group. A few songs, a few variant tunes, are included because of their interest to musicians; and there are four songs especially for children.

A folk *ballad* tells a story, either in highly dramatic dialogue as in "The Devil's Questions," or as a plain narration as in "The Merry Golden Tree." A folk *song* is usually lyrical. It is more personal and emotional, and yet there are some folk songs that are also narrative. The distinction is not always clear. But a *folk* ballad or *folk* song is always traditional and of unknown authorship.

[1] From the Introduction to Cecil Sharp's *One Hundred English Folk Songs.* See Bibliography.

BALLADS

The Devil's Questions

It was at one of the folk festivals on White Top Mountain in southwestern Virginia that I first heard this ballad. One of the oldest songs in the language—No. 1 in Professor Francis James Child's great collection of 305 English and Scottish ballads—it is still sung here in America. The most ancient manuscript—"song ballot"—of this folk ballad "in a hand of about 1450," is in the Bodelian Library in England. The 1450 version begins:

> Inter diabolous et virgo.
> Wol ye here a wonder thynge
> betwyxt a mayd and the foule fende?
> Thys spake the fend to the mayd . . .

and from here the American version takes it up.

If you can't ans-wer my quest-ions nine —
Sing nine-ty nine and nine-ty!
Oh you're not God's you're one of mine.
And the crow flies ov-er the white oak tree!

2. Oh what is higher than the tree?
   Sing ninety nine and ninety!
   And what is deeper than the sea?
   And the crow flies over the white oak tree!

3. Oh Heaven is higher than a tree,
   Sing ninety nine and ninety!
   And Love is deeper than the sea.
   And the crow flies over the white oak tree!

4. Oh what is whiter than the milk?
   And what is softer than the silk?

5. Oh snow is whiter than the milk,
   And down is softer than the silk.

6. Oh what is louder than the horn?
   And what is sharper than the thorn?

7. Oh thunder's louder than the horn,
   And hunger's sharper than the thorn.

8. Oh what is heavier than the lead?
   And what is better than the bread?

9. Oh grief is heaver than the lead.
   God's blessing's better than the bread.

10. Now you have answered my questions nine.
    Oh you are God's, you're none of mine.

What was the *ninth* question? There are only eight given!

The Cambric Shirt

This tune came from Mrs. Fannie Norton of Norton, North Carolina. Some of these verses are from the Mother Goose versions, where the refrain runs

Parsley, sage, rosemary, and thyme!

Hilton Norton, Mrs. Norton's grandson, who first told me about this ballad, had written it out,

Rose de Marian Time!

This is another one of the ancient songs in our language—No. 2 in Professor Child's collection. It is also known in Virginia, (with a refrain "Lomma lomma linktum slomalee!") and in Vermont.

2. Tell her to make me a cambric shirt,
   Rose Marie and thyme!
   without any seam or needle work,
   and she shall be a true lover of mine.

3. Tell her to wash it in yonder well,
   Rose Marie and thyme!
   where water never ran nor rain never fell,
   and she shall be a true lover of mine.

4. Tell her to dry it on yonder thorn,
   Rose Marie and thyme!
   where leaf never was since Adam was born,
   and she shall be a true lover of mine.

5. I came back from yonder town,
   Rose Marie and thyme!
   she sent word to that young man,——
   If he would be a true lover of mine . . .

6. . . . tell him to clear me an acre of land,
   Rose Marie and thyme!
   between the sea and the salt sea sand,
   and he shall be a true lover of mine.

7. Tell him to plow it with a muley-cow's horn,
   Rose Marie and thyme!
   and sow it all over with one grain of corn,
   and he shall be a true lover of mine.

8. Tell him to reap it with an old stirrup leather,
   Rose Marie and thyme!
   and bind it all up in a tom-tit's feather,
   and he shall be a true lover of mine.

9. Tell him to shock it in the sea,
   Rose Marie and thyme!
   and bring it all home dry to me,
   and he shall be a true lover of mine.

10. Tell him to thresh it in an old shoe sole,
    Rose Marie and thyme!
    and crib it all in a little mouse hole,
    and he shall be a true lover of mine.

11. Tell him to gather it in a bottomless sack,
    Rose Marie and thyme!
    and bring it all home on a butterfly's back,
    and he shall be a true lover of mine.

12. Tell him when he's done this work,
    Rose Marie and thyme!
    come on to town and get his shirt,
    then he shall be a true lover of mine.

The Two Ravens

This extraordinarily good text came to me through Mrs. Willard Brooks, now of Washington, D. C. She could not remember where she learned it. Artus Moser collected it on Gashes Creek, Hickory Nut Gap, near Asheville, North Carolina, and Annabel Morris Buchanan has found it in Virginia. An "original" text appeared in a high school book in 1859, *A Compendium of English Literature* by Charles D. Cleveland. It was also recorded in the Southern Mountains by Mellenger Henry from a Mrs. Henry C. Gray now of Terre Haute, Indiana. The tune, "Ye Banks and Braes of Bonnie Doon," is used for Hymn No. 311 in *The Methodist Hymnal* (1939)—"Come, O Thou Traveller Unknown"—and is given there as a "Scottish traditional melody," from *The Hesperian Harp,* 1847. A somewhat similar text has been reported from Florida.

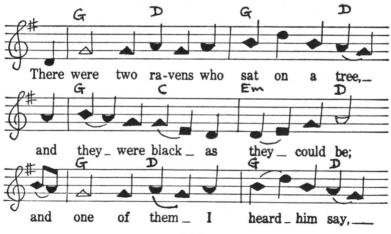

There were two ra-vens who sat on a tree,__
and they__ were black__ as they __ could be;
and one of them __ I heard__ him say,__

Oh where shall we go___ to dine___ to-day?

Shall___ we go down___ to the salt, salt sea,___

or shall we go dine___ by the green - wood tree?

Shall___ we go down___ to the salt,___ salt sea,___

or shall we go dine___ by the green - wood tree?

2. As I walked down on the white sea sand
   I saw a fair ship sailing near at hand.
   I waved my wings, I bent my beak,
   that ship she sank and I heard a shriek.
   There lie the sailors, one, two, and three,
   Oh shall we go dine by the wild salt sea?
   There lie the sailors, one, two, and three,
   Oh shall we go dine by the wild salt sea.

3. Come, I shall show you a far better sight—
   a lonesome glen, and a new-slain knight:
   his blood yet on the grass is hot,
   his sword half-drawn, his shafts unshot.
   And no one knows that he lies there
   but his hound, his hawk, and his lady fair.
   And no one knows that he lies there
   but his hound, his hawk, and his lady fair.

4. His hound is to the hunting gone,
   his hawk to fetch the wild fowl home,
   his lady's away to another mate.—
   Oh we shall make our feasting sweet!

115

Our dinner is sure, our feasting is free.
Oh come and we'll dine by the greenwood tree!
Our dinner is sure, our feasting is free.
Oh come and we'll dine by the greenwood tree!

5. Oh you shall tear at his naked white thighs,
   and I'll peck out his fair blue eyes.
   You can pull a lock of his fine yellow hair
   to thicken your nest where it grows bare.
   The golden down on his young chin
   will do to rest my young ones in.
   The golden down on his young chin
   will do to rest my young ones in.

6. Oh cold and bare will his bed be
   when grey winter storms sing in the tree.
   His head's on the turf, at his feet a stone.—
   He'll sleep nor hear young maidens mourn.
   Over his white bones the birds will fly,
   the wild deer run, the foxes cry.
   Over his white bones the birds will fly,
   the wild deer run, the foxes cry.

Lady Gay

This is a Southern Mountain version of the ballad called "The Wife of Usher's Well" in Professor Child's collection. The moral, as hinted in the last verse, is that excessive grief for the dead causes them unquiet. Lynn Gault of Brasstown, North Carolina, has made an exciting one-act "folk" play from this ballad. This ballad has been found in Alabama, Texas, Florida, Vermont, Mississippi, and Ohio.

Not too fast, but make it move right along.

There was a — la-dy, a — la - dy — gay,
and three fine sons — had — she;

116

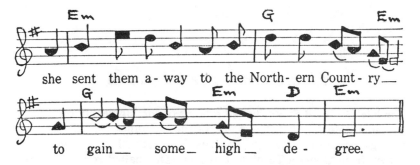

she sent them a-way to the North-ern Count-ry __
to gain __ some __ high __ de - gree.

2. They'd not been gone but a very short time,
   about a year and a day,
   when death, swift death, came a-hastening along
   and swept her sons away.

3. If there is a King in Heaven, she cried,
   a King that will grant my boon,
   he'll send to me my three young sons.
   Oh I pray that he send them soon.

4. It was just about Old Christmas Time
   when the nights were cold and clear,
   she looked and she saw her three young sons
   come walking home to her.

5. She spread a table with a clean white cloth,
   she set out cake and wine.
   Come eat, come drink, my three little sons,
   come eat and drink of mine.

6. We cannot eat your cake nor bread,
   we cannot drink your wine,
   for yonder stands our Saviour dear,
   and to him we must resign.

7. She made them a bed in their own back room,
   brought out her clean white sheets,
   and covered them over with a cloth of gold
   that they might soundly sleep.

8. Wake up, wake up! said the oldest one,
   the birds are singing for day.
   Our Saviour dear is a-calling loud,
   and away we must go—away!

9. Green grass, green grass grows over our heads,
   cold clay lies on our feet,
   and every tear you shed for us,
   it wets our winding sheet.

Home Came the Old Man

The late Dr. Reed Smith, ballad scholar of the University of South Carolina, told me that this is one of the old tunes for this ballad. College songsters some generations back set "I'm a Rambling Wreck from Georgia Tech" to this tune. This ballad is also known in Maine, Florida, and Ohio.

Oh home came the old man and home came he,
he saw a strange horse in the stall where his horse ought to be.
My dear wife, my dar-ling wife, my lov-ing wife, said he,
Whose horse is this with-in the stall where my horse ought to be?

2. You old fool, you blind fool, you dodderin' fool, said she;
   It's nothing but a milk-cow my mammy sent to me.
   A thousand miles I've travelled, a thousand miles or more,
   but—a saddle on a milk-cow I never did see before.

3. Oh home came the old man and home came he;
   he saw a strange coat on the rack where his coat ought to be.
   My dear wife, my darling wife, my loving wife, said he,
   whose coat is this upon the rack where my coat ought to be?

4. You old fool, you blind fool, you dodderin' fool, said she;
   it's nothing but a bed-quilt my mammy sent to me.
   A thousand miles I've travelled, a thousand miles or more,
   but—buttons on a bed-quilt I never did see before.

5. Oh home came the old man and home came he;
   he saw a strange hat on the hook where his hat ought to be.
   My dear wife, my darling wife, my loving wife, said he,
   whose hat is this upon the hook where my hat ought to be?

6. You old fool, you blind fool, you dodderin' fool, said she;
   it's nothing but a dinner pot my mammy sent to me.
   A thousand miles I've travelled, a thousand miles or more,
   but—a ribbon on a dinner pot I never did see before.

7. Oh home came the old man and home came he;
   he saw strange boots beneath the bed where his boots
   ought to be.
   My dear wife, my darling wife, my loving wife, said he,
   whose boots are these beneath the bed where my boots
   ought to be?

8. You old fool, you blind fool, you dodderin' fool, said she;
   it's nothing but some milk jugs my mammy sent to me.
   A thousand miles I've travelled, a thousand miles or more,
   but—spurs on a milk jug I never did see before.

9. Oh home came the old man and home came he;
   he saw a strange head on the pillow where his head ought
   to be.
   My dear wife, my darling wife, my loving wife, said he,
   whose head is this upon the pillow where my head ought
   to be?

10. You old fool, you blind fool, you dodderin' fool, said she;
    it's nothing but a cabbage-head my mammy sent to me.
    A thousand miles I've travelled, a thousand miles or more,
    but—a moustache on a cabbage-head I never did see
    before.

The Merry Golden Tree

The tune comes from Horton Barker, blind singer of Saint Clair's Creek, near Chilhowie, Virginia. The words are edited from many sources. This ballad is known throughout the Southern Mountains and in Maine, Michigan, and Mississippi.

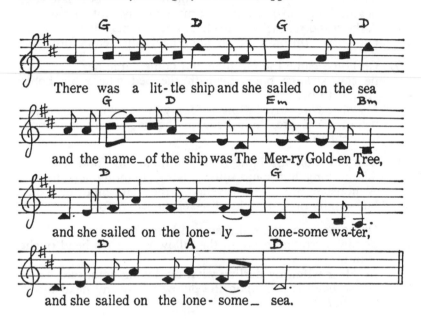

There was a lit-tle ship and she sailed on the sea and the name of the ship was The Mer-ry Gold-en Tree, and she sailed on the lone-ly ___ lone-some wa-ter, and she sailed on the lone-some ___ sea.

2. There was another ship and she sailed on the sea,
and the name of the ship was The Turkish Robbery:
and she sailed on the lonely lonesome water,
and she sailed on the lonesome sea.

3. There was a little sailor boy unto the captain said,
Oh captain, oh captain, what will you give to me
if I sink her in the lonely lonesome water,
if I sink her in the lonesome sea?

4. Two hundred golden dollars I will give unto thee,
and my youngest pretty daughter for your wedded wife
to be,
if you'll sink her in the lonely lonesome water,
if you'll sink her in the lonesome sea.

5. Oh it's down into the waves and away swam he;
   he swam until he came to The Turkish Robbery,
   where she sailed on the lonely lonesome water,
   where she sailed on the lonesome sea.

6. Then out of his pocket an auger he drew,
   and he bored nine holes for to let the water through,
   and he sunk her in the lonely lonesome water,
   and he sunk her in the lonesome sea.

7. He turned upon his breast and back swam he;
   he swam until he came to The Merry Golden Tree,
   where she sailed on the lonely lonesome water,
   where she sailed on the lonesome sea.

8. Oh captain, oh captain, won't you take me on board?
   Oh captain, oh captain, won't you be good as your word?
   For I've sunk her in the lonely lonesome water,
   for I've sunk her in the lonesome sea.

9. Oh I will not take you in, the captain he replied,
   for you shall never have my pretty daughter for your
      bride,
   and I'm sailing on the lonely lonesome water,
   and I'm sailing on the lonesome sea.

10. If it wasn't for the love I have for your men,
    I would do unto you as I've done unto them,
    I would sink you in the lonely lonesome water,
    I would sink you in the lonesome sea.

11. He turned upon his back and down sank he;
    Fare ye well! Fare ye well to The Merry Golden Tree!
    For I'm sinking in the lonely lonesome water,
    for I'm sinking in the lonesome sea.

Nickety Nackety

This tune is from Horton Barker, blind singer in Virginia. The text comes from many sources. This is known also as "The Wee Cooper of Fife," and "The Wife Wrapt in the Wether Skin."

I mar-ried my wife in the month of June —
Nick-e-ty, nack-e-ty, now, now, now!
I es-cor-ted her home by the light of the moon.
Nick-e-ty, nack-e-ty, nay down thack-e-ty!
Will-i-ty, wall-i-ty, rus-ti-co qual-i-ty!
Nick-e-ty, nack-e-ty, now, now, now!

2. One day when I came in from the plow,
    Nickety, nackety, now, now, now!
    says, Oh my good wife, is my dinner ready now?
    Nickety, nackety, nay down thackety!
    Willity, wallity, rustico quality!
    Nickety, nackety, now, now, now!

JRT

3. There's a little piece of cornbread on the shelf,
   Nickety, nackety, now, now, now!
   if you want any more you can bake it yourself.
   Nickety, nackety, nay down thackety!
   Willity, wallity, rustico quality!
   Nickety, nackety, now, now, now!

4. Oh I went out behind the barn,
   and I cut me a hickory as long as my arm.

5. Then I went out to my sheep pen,
   and I grabbed me up an old sheep skin.

6. I laid that skin all around her back,
   and with that stick I went Whickety-whack!

7. I'll tell my mother, I'll tell all my kin,
   how you hit me with a hickory limb.

8. You can tell your mother, you can tell all your kin,
   I was only tanning my old sheep skin.

9. Next day when I came in from the plow,
   says, Oh my good wife, is my dinner ready now?

10. She flew around and the board was spread,
    and Yes, my dear husband, was all she said.

Bold Robin Hood

That Robin Hood ballads should still be sung in modern America, four hundred years more or less after the many ballads on the outlaw were first sung, is one of the interesting facts about the Anglo-Saxon tradition. Some scholars believe that Robin Hood never really existed and is entirely "a creation of the ballad muse." This ballad came from Mrs. Cal Hicks of western North Carolina. Robin Hood ballads have been found in North Carolina, Virginia, Nebraska, Maine, Nova Scotia, Vermont, and Florida. Mrs. Hicks's version is rather curious, but it has many charming phrases. The text and tune are hers verbatim. See "The King and Robert Hood's Horny Beast-es."

Bold Rob - in Hood one morn - ing stood
with his back a - gainst a tree,
and he was a-ware of a fine young man,
as fine as fine could be.

2. Bold Robin put out to Nottingame Town
   as fast as he could ride,
   but who should he meet but a poor old woman
   as she came weeping by.

3. It's are you weeping for my gold, he said,
   or are you weeping for my store,
   or are you weeping for your three sons
   been taken from your body?

124

4. Oh I'm not weeping for your gold, she said,
   nor neither for your store,
   but I am weeping for my three sons
   that has to be hung today.

5. Bold Robin put out to Nottingame Town
   as fast as he could ride,
   but who should he meet but a poor old beggar
   as he came begging by.

6. Change clothing, change clothing, Bold Robin he said,
   pray change your clothing with me.
   Here's forty bright guineas I'll give you to boot
   if you change your clothing with me.

7. Bold Robin put on the bo' beggar's coat,
   was patched on every side.
   Good faith to my soul! Bold Robin he said,
   they'll say I just wear this for pride.

8. Bold Robin put out to Nottingame Town
   as fast as he could ride,
   but who should he see but the old town sheriff
   as he stood there close by.

9. Which way, which way, the old town sheriff said,
   which way, I pray to thee?
   I heard there's three men to be hung here today,
   and a hangman I want for to be.

10. Quick granted, quick granted, the old town sheriff said,
    quick granted, I say to thee,
    and you can have all of their gay, gay clothing
    and all of their bright monie.

11. It's I want none of their gay good clothing
    nor none of their bright monie,
    I want three blasts from my bugle horn,
    as happy as soldiers can be.

12. He wound his horn into his mouth
    and loud blasts he did blow.
    A hundred and ten of Bold Robin's men
    came marching all up in a row.
13. Whose men, whose men, the old town sheriff said,
    whose men, I pray to thee?
    They're brave men of mine, Bold Robin he said,
    come to borrow three sons from thee.
14. Oh take 'em, Oh take 'em, the old town sheriff said,
    Oh take 'em, I pray to thee!
    No lord nor knight nor no Christian dome
    can borrow three more from me.

Old Bangum and the Boar

This is from Jim Hayes, Jr. of southwestern Virginia, and is given
just as he sang it. "Little Jim" Hayes is the model for "Tom Hunt"
at whose house, one "Old Christmas Eve"—the night of the
Twelfth Day of Christmas which comes on the sixth of January
—we told tales from about dark till daylight the next morning.
    The notation is facsimile from John Powell's hand.

126

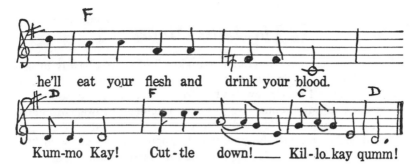

he'll eat your flesh and drink your blood.

Kum-mo Kay! Cut-tle down!___ Kil-lo kay qumm!

2. Old Bangum went to the wild boar's den,
   Dillum day! Dillum down!
   Old Bangum went to the wild boar's den,
   Dillum day! Dillum down!
   Old Bangum went to the wild boar's den,
   Dillum day! Dillum down!
   he saw the bones of a thousand men.
   Kummo Kay! Cuttle down! Killo kay gumm!

3. Old Bangum blew his bugle horn,
   Dillum day! Dillum down!
   Old Bangum blew his bugle horn,
   Dillum day! Dillum down!
   Old Bangum blew his bugle horn,
   Dillum day! Dillum down!
   caused the wild boar to come running home.
   Kummo Kay! Cuttle down! Killo kay gumm!

4. The wild boar came in such a dash,
   he cut his way through oak and ash.

5. Old Bangum drew his wooden knife,
   he swore he'd take the wild boar's life.

6. They fit four hours of the day,
   Old Bangum took the wild boar's life away.

The Little Mohee

This is "a chastened American re-making" of an old bawdy broadside ballad known in England as "The Indian Lass." It is one of the first songs I ever knew, and is widely known in the South, the Appalachian Mountains, New York, Michigan, Iowa, Montana, Texas, Alabama, Florida and Vermont. This text is almost an epic! The tune has recently become widely popular in its use with "On Top of Old Smoky." The rhythm of this version is unusual.

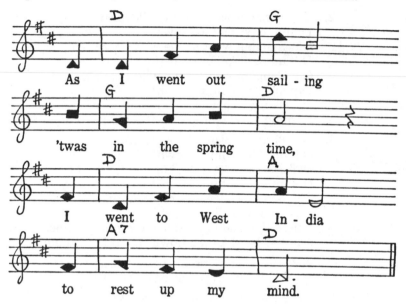

As I went out sail-ing 'twas in the spring time, I went to West In-dia to rest up my mind.

2. As I went out walking down by the sea shore,
   the wind it did whistle, the waters did roar.

3. As I sat amusing myself on the grass,
   O who did I see but a fair Indian lass.

4. She came and sat by me, took hold of my hand,
   said, You look like a stranger from a far distant land.

5. But if you will follow you're welcome to come
   and dwell in the cottage that I call my home.

6. Together we wandered, together did rove,
   till we came to a cottage in a cocoanut grove.

7. She asked me to marry and offered her hand,
   saying, My father's the chieftain of all of this land.

8. My father's a chieftain, a ruler is he,
   I'm his only daughter, my name is Mohee.

9. O no, my dear maiden, that never can be,
   for I have a true-lover in my own countree.

10. I will not forsake her, for I know she loves me,
    her heart is as true as any Mohee.

11. The sun was fast sinking far over the sea,
    as I wandered along with the Pretty Mohee.

12. I stayed in her country for a year and a day,
    and enjoyed the sweet love of the fair Indian maid.

13. It was early one morning, one morning in May,
    I broke her poor heart by the words I did say.

14. I'm a-going to leave you, so farewell my dear,
    my ship's sails are spreading and home I must steer.

15. The last time I saw her she stood on the sand,
    and as my ship passed her she waved me her hand.

16. Saying: When you get over to the girl that you love,
    remember the Mohee in the cocoanut grove.

17. And when I had landed on my own native shore,
    both friends and relations gathered 'round me once more.

18. I looked all around me, not one did I see
    that could really compare with the Little Mohee.

19. And the girl I had trusted proved untrue to me,
    so I said I'll turn my course back over the sea.

20. I'll turn my ships backwards on the dark stormy sea
    I'll go and spend my days with the Little Mohee.

The Rich Old Lady

This came originally from Irving Gross, a Virginia singer, through Winston Wilkinson of Charlottesville. I first heard it as sung by Horton Barker at one of the White Top Folk Festivals in southwestern Virginia. John Powell included it in his Five Virginian Folk Songs with piano accompaniment.

A rich old lady in ou-er town, in ou-er town did dwell, ____ she loved her hus-band dear-ly but a-no-ther man twice as well. ____ Sing Too de um! Sing Too de um! Whack! Fa lal a day! ____

2. She was listenin' in at the door one day
   when she heard the old man say
   if you snuffed a few old marrow bones
   it 'uld take your sight away.
   Sing Too de um! Sing Too de um!
   Whack! Fa lal a day!

130

3. So she went down to the butcher shop
   to see what she could find,
   intent upon buying a thing or two
   to make her old man blind.
   Sing Too de um! Sing Too de um!
   Whack! Fa lal a day!

4. She bought twelve dozen old marrow bones,
   she made him snuff them all:
   says he, Old Lady, I now am blind,
   I cannot see at all.

5. And I would like to drown myself
   if I could only see—
   Just take my hand, dear husband,
   and come along with me.

6. She bundled him up in his old gray coat,
   she led him to the brim.
   Says he, I cannot drown myself
   unless—you push me in.

7. The old lady went up on the bank a ways
   to get a running-go,
   the old man stepped a little to the side
   and she went off below.

8. She bubbled and gurgled and bawled out
   as loud as she could squall.
   Says he, Old Lady, I'm *so* blind
   I can't see you at all.

9. The old man being kind-hearted
   and knowing she could not swim,
   he went and cut him a very long pole
   and—pushed her further in.

Verse 2 is my own invention. It points up the tale much
better. The idea came from a tale dealing with this identical
situation.

Locks and Bolts

This is from Mrs. Rebecca Jones who lived near Raleigh, North Carolina. The extra line in verse 3 is unusual. And the text contains some striking phrases: *e.g.* "my true-love she *sought my voice.*" The words are substantially Mrs. Jones's. The closing verses are from various sources. A version of this ballad is given in Sandburg's "American Songbag."

1. I dreamed of my true love last night
all in my arms was ly - ing,
but when I woke it was not so,
I was forced to lie with - out her.

2. Her pret-ty yel-low hair like straw of gold

(To music B, C, D, as for verse 1.)

      all tangled on my pillow—
      Before I eat or drink or sleep
      I'm intending to be with her.

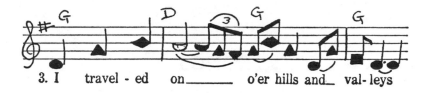

3. I travel - ed on＿＿＿ o'er hills and＿ val- leys

(*To music A, B, C, D as for verse 1.*)

> I travelled to her uncle's house,
> and there I expected to find her.
> Her uncle said, She is not here—
> which filled my heart with sorrow.

(*From here on use the tune as for verse 1.*)

4. But my true-love she sought my voice,
   came running to the window,
   says, Oh my love, I would be with you
   but locks and bolts do hinder!

5. I stood a moment all in amaze,
   considering my surrender.
   My passion flew, my sword I drew,
   I burst the door asunder.

6. I took my sword in my right hand,
   my true-love in the other,
   said, If any man loves you any better than I,
   one man must slay another.

7. Her uncle and another man
   straight after me did follow.
   I slew them both, I left them there,
   in their own heart's blood to wallow.

8. We'll join right hands and swear our love
   to bind us both forever.
   Till fatal death doth spend our breath
   we'll live our days together.

SONGS

The Darby Ram

This, the biggest lie ever told or sung, was (I have often heard)
George Washington's favorite song. Some years ago I met an old
man in Virginia who told me that his great-uncle used to tell how
Mr. Washington had taken him on his knee many a time and sung
him "The Darby Ram,"—including all the "naughty verses."
These naughty verses are not clever enough to merit including
here. I have known this song from many sources. The most recent
was from Mrs. Martha Field Blair of Lynchburg, Virginia. This
song is also known in Texas, Michigan, Mississippi and Ohio.

Recitative. Like talking. Keep it moving right along.

And there I saw the big-gest ram that ev-er was fed on hay!

2. And if you think this is not so,
   for maybe you'll think I lie—
   Oh you go down to Darby Town
   and you'll see the same as I—
   and you'll see the same as I.
   Oh you go down to Darby Town
   and you'll see the same as I.

3. This ram he had four feet, sir,
   on four feet he did stand,
   and every track he made, sir,
   it covered an acre of land—
   it covered an acre of land.
   And every track he made sir,
   it covered an acre of land.

4. The wool on this ram's back, sir,
   it grew up to the sky;
   the eagles built their nests up there—
   I heard the young ones cry.

5. The wool on this ram's belly, sir,
   it grew down in the ground;
   the Devil cut it off, sir,
   to make himself a gown.

6. And one of this ram's teeth, sir,
   was hollow as a horn,
   and when they took its measure, sir,
   it held a bushel of corn.

7. The man that butchered this ram, sir,
   stood up to his knees in blood;
   the boy that held the basin, sir,
   got washed away in the flood.

135

8. The blood it ran for forty miles—
   I'm sure it was not more.
   It turned the water wheels so fast
   it made the mill-stones roar.

Mrs. Blair's first verse ran:

There was a ram in Darby,
as I have heard it said;
he was the biggest ram, sir,
that ever wore a head.

Instead of the tag ending "sir," "boys" is sometimes used.

The Deaf Woman's Courtship

Tune from Miss Margaret Purcell of Albemarle County, Virginia.
I first heard it from John Powell, and Miss Purcell sang it for
some children once at Konnarock, Virginia, while sitting on the
top step in front of a school. I have edited the text from Mary
Cecily Baker's *Old Rhymes for All Times,* and from the singing
of Horton Barker. The tune is a good one. It comes, not from a
Kentucky mountain cove where, as some imagine, the natives go
barefoot and speak "pure Elizabethan English," but from a
descendant of two branches of Virginia's finest first families: the
Randolphs and the Harrisons. The air was known in the reign of
King George II, and was used in a ballad opera in 1729.

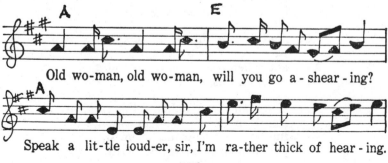

Old wo-man, old wo-man, will you go a - shear - ing?

Speak a lit-tle loud-er, sir, I'm ra-ther thick of hear - ing.

Old wo-man, old wo-man, are you good at weav-ing?

Pray speak a lit-tle loud-er, sir, my hear-ing is de-ceiv-ing.

2. Old woman! Old woman! Will you go a'walking?
   Speak a little louder, sir, or what's the use of talking?
   OLD WOMAN! OLD WOMAN! Are you fond of
      spinning?
   Pray speak a little louder, sir. I only see you grinning.

3. Old woman, old woman, will you do—*my knitting?*
   My hearing's getting better now. Come nearer where I'm
      sitting.
   Old woman, old woman, shall I kiss you dearly?
   Oh! Lord-have-mercy-on-my-soul, sir! Now I hear you
      clearly!

———◆———

Four stiff-standers,
four down-hangers,
two lookers, two crookers,
one dirty switch-about lags along behind.

A cow.

Six set, and the seventh sprung.
From the dead the living come.

Quail's nest in a horse's skull. Six eggs in the nest. The mother bird flew away.

Lolly Too Dum

This tune is from Horton Barker, with one phrase as sung at Pine Mountain, Kentucky. The text comes from many sources—oral and printed. The song has also been reported from Texas, Alabama, and Mississippi.

As I went out one morn-ing to take the morn-ing air —
Lol-ly too dum, too dum! Too lol-ly day!
—as I went out one morn-ing to take the morn-ing air,
I heard a wid-ow wo-man talk-ing to her daugh-ter fair.
Lol-ly too dum, too dum! Lol-ly too dum day!

2. Whistle, daughter, whistle, and you shall have a cow—
Lolly too dum, too dum! Too lolly day!
Whistle, daughter, whistle, and you shall have a cow.
I cannot whistle, mother, because I don't know how.
Lolly too dum, too dum! Lolly too dum day!

3. Whistle, daughter, whistle, and you shall have a pig—
Lolly too dum, too dum! Too lolly day!
Whistle, daughter, whistle, and you shall have a pig.
I cannot whistle, mother, because I am too big.
Lolly too dum, too dum! Lolly too dum day!

4. Whistle, daughter, whistle, and you shall have a sheep—
   Whistle, daughter, whistle, and you shall have a sheep.
   I cannot whistle, mother, and I'm just about to weep.

5. Whistle, daughter, whistle, and you shall have a man—
   Whistle, daughter, whistle, and you shall have a man.
   (*Whistle:* Whee whee whee-ee! Whee whee-whee-whee-ee
   whee-ee!)

Here is another set of words for this same tune:

1. As I went out one morning to take the morning air—
   Lolly too dum, too dum, too lolly day!
   As I went out one morning to take the morning air
   I heard a widow-woman talking to her daughter fair.
   Lolly too dum, too dum! Lolly too dum day!

2. You better go wash them dishes and hush that clattering
       tongue—
   I know you want to marry, and that you are too young.

3. Oh pity my condition just like you would your own—
   For seventeen long years I've been sleeping all alone.

4. Yes, I'm seventeen and over, and that you will allow—
   I must and I will get married for I'm in the notion now.

5. You might be in the notion but where'd you get you a
       man?
   Oh never you mind, dear mother, I could get old Dandy
       Sam.

6. Suppose Sam was to slight you, like you did him before?
   Oh never fear, dear mother, I could get a dozen more.

7. Such as doctors and lawyers and men of high degree—
   Some wants to marry and some would marry me.

8. Then there's peddlers and tinkers and boys that follow
       the plow—
   Lordy mercy, mammy! The fit comes on me now.[1]

9. Now my daughter's married and well-for-to-do.
   Gather 'round, young fellers! I'm on the market too!

[1] There is a seventeenth century country dance with the title "The Fit
Comes on Me Now."

The Bashful Courtship

Once, a young man had to walk many miles to court his girl. And often, there being no bed for "company," he and the young lady had no choice but to sit by the fire and "talk"—that is, court—all night. This song is sung "down the Watauga toward Tennessee," not far from Beech Mountain, North Carolina. I first heard it at Pine Mountain, Kentucky, as "Aunt Sal's Song."

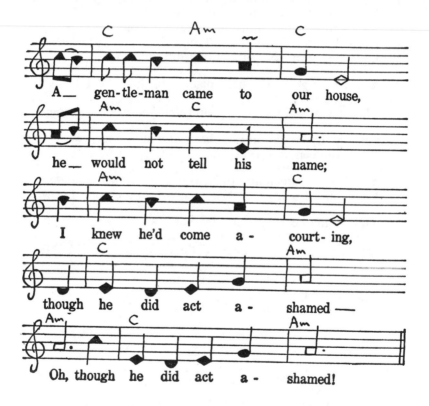

A— gen-tle-man came to our house,
he— would not tell his name;
I knew he'd come a - court- ing,
though he did act a - shamed —
Oh, though he did act a - shamed!

2. He drew his chair up to my side,
   his manners pleased me well;
   I thought the spirit moved him
   some handsome tale to tell:
   Oh some handsome tale to tell!

140

3. But there he sat the livelong night
   and never a word did say;
   he only sat and sighed and groaned
   while I did wish for day:
   Oh while I did wish for day!

4. The chickens they began to crow,
   the daylight did appear—
   How do you do? Good morning, sir!
   I'm glad to see you here:
   Oh I'm glad to see you here!

5. I was weary of the livelong night,
   I was weary of my life!
   If this is what you call courting, boys,
   you'll never get a wife:
   Oh you'll never get a wife!

6. Now when he goes in company,
   the girls all laugh for sport,
   saying, Yonder goes that ding-dang fool
   who don't know how to court:
   Oh who don't know how to court!

Here is a very curious riddle. We have tried to learn a better constructed, better rhymed version. Perhaps some of our readers know the "right" way this one should be given, and will send it in to us.

He was neither No-e[1] nor No-e's son,
but was with No-e in the Ark.
His robe was neither silk nor wool.
His beard and hair they both were flesh.
Never married, he had many wives.
And a short sermon once he preached
that made a man go out and weep.

[1] Noah.

A rooster. (Luke 22: verses 61 and 62.)

141

Clinch Mountain

The Oxford Book of Light Verse devotes two-and-a-half full pages to this rowdy old song. It is also called "Rye Whiskey, Rye Whiskey" or "The Drunken Hiccups." The tune is an ancient one, and its uses are many and varied: with "Sweet England" in *English Folk Songs for Schools* by S. Baring Gould and Cecil Sharp, with "The Children's Song of The Nativity" in *The Oxford Book of Carols* to a text by Frances Chesterton, and it is also known as a hymn tune under the name "Stowey," but I have not as yet located it in any hymnal. This version is known in Texas, and is included in the Lomax books and in Carl Sandburg's *American Songbag.*

Way up on Clinch Moun-tain I wan-der a-lone,
as drunk as the Dev-il and a long ways from home.
Oh, (hic-cup!) O— Lord-y! How sleep-y I be!
Oh— (hic-cup!) O Lord-y! How good I do feel!

2. I'll eat when I'm hungry, I'll drink when I'm dry,
   and if hard times don't kill me I'll live till I die.
   Oh, (hiccup!) O Lordy! How sleepy I be!
   Oh, (hiccup!) O Lordy! How good I do feel!

3. Jack-a-diamonds! Jack-a-diamonds! I know you of old.
You rob my poor pockets of silver and gold.
Oh, (hiccup!) O Lordy! How sleepy I be!
Oh, (hiccup!) O Lordy! How good I do feel!

4. If the river was whiskey and I was a duck,
I'd dive to the bottom and drink my way up.

5. Oh Lulu! Oh Lulu! Oh Lulu my dear!
I'd give this whole world if my Lulu was here.

6. Her parents don't like me; they say I'm too poor.
They say I'm not worthy to enter their door.

7. My foot's in the stirrup, the bridle in my hand.
Fare-well my sweet Lulu, I'm leaving this land.

8. I'll tune up my fiddle and rosin my bow,
and make myself welcome wherever I go.

9. Rye Whiskey, rye whiskey, rye whiskey, I cry.
If I don't get rye whiskey I shorely will die.

10. Oh it's beefsteak when I'm hungry, and likker when
I'm dry,
and greenbacks when I'm hard-up, and Heaven when
I die.

11. Oh if I drink whiskey, my money's my own,
and them that don't like me can leave me alone.

12. Way up on Clinch Mountain I wander alone,
as drunk as the Devil and a long way from home.

The Miller's Will

This song is from Dr. E. E. Ericson, formerly Associate Professor of English at the University of North Carolina, who learned it as a boy in Nebraska. It has been found also in Florida, Michigan, Ohio, and Vermont.

There was an old mil-ler so I've heard told;
he had three sons that were al - most grown.
He was a - bout to make his will,
and all that he had was a lit-tle grist mill.
Hi! Fol! Did- dle all day!

2. So he called to his oldest son,
   Son, Oh son, I'm almost gone,
   And if to you this will I make,
   Oh tell me the toll that you mean to take.
   Hi! Fol! Diddle all day!

3. Father, you know my name is Heck;
   out of a bushel I'll take a peck.
   For if my fortune I would make,
   now that is the toll I intend to take.
   Hi! Fol! Diddle all day!

4. Son, Oh son, I'm afraid you're a fool,
   you have not learned to follow my rule.
   To you this mill I will not give,
   for by such a toll no man can live.
   Hi! Fol! Diddle all day!

5. Then he called to his second son.
   Son, Oh son, I'm almost gone,
   and if to you this will I make,
   Oh tell me the toll that you mean to take.
   Hi! Fol! Diddle all day!

6. Father, you know my name is Ralph;
   out of a bushel I'll take a half.
   For if my fortune I would make,
   now that is the toll I intend to take.
   Hi! Fol! Diddle all day!

7. Son, Oh son, I'm afraid you're a fool,
   you have not perfect learned my rule.
   To you this mill I will not give,
   for by such a toll no man can live.
   Hi! Fol! Diddle all day!

8. Then he called to his youngest son.
   Son, Oh son, I'm almost gone,
   and if to you this will I make,
   Oh tell me the toll that you mean to take.
   Hi! Fol! Diddle all day!

9. Father, you know my name is Paul;
   out of a bushel I'll take it all:
   take all the grain and swear to the sack,
   and beat the old farmer if he dares to come back.
   Hi! Fol! Diddle all day!

10. Glory be to God! the old man says,
    I've got one son that's learned my ways!
    Hallelujah! the old woman cried,
    and the old man he straightened out his legs and he died.
    Hi! Fol! Diddle all day!

The Gambling Suitor

This song came from Miss Ella Shiflett, who lived on a mountain in Greene County, Virginia. It has been found also in Michigan, Arkansas, and Tennessee.

Sir, I see you ___ com - ing a - gain;
pray tell me what it's for.
When I left you in ___ Bar - bour - ville, ___
I told you to come no more,
I told you to come no ___ more.

2. Miss, I have a very fine house,
   newly built with pine;
   and you may have it at your command
   if you will be my bride.
   if you will be my bride.

3. Sir, I know it's a very fine house,
   also a very fine yard,
   but who will stay at home with me
   when you're out playing cards?
   when you're out playing cards?

146

4. I never played a card in all my life,
   I never thought it right;
   if you'll consent to be my bride,
   I'll stay away n'ary night.

5. Miss, I have a very fine farm,
   it's sixty acres wide,
   and you shall have it at your command
   if you will be my bride.

6. Sir, I know it's a very fine farm,
   full of very fine fruit;
   as you come in I'll drive you out—
   for you know a hog must root.

7. Miss, I have a very fine horse,
   he paces like the tide;
   and you may have him at your command
   whenever you wish to ride.

8. Sir, I know he's a very fine horse,
   also a very fine barn,
   but his master drinks and gambles so,
   I'm afraid his horse will learn.

9. Madam, he is a very fine horse,
   he pulls my buggy well.
   I'll drink my fill, and throw my cards,
   and you may go to—Baltimore.

Sourwood Mountain

This is a country dance tune—a "jig song." There are many verses
—comic couplets—that wander from one jig tune to another, but
this particular one has established a sequence all its own. It is
usually associated with the Southern Mountains. *The Archive of
American Folk Song* at the Library of Congress lists eleven variants from eastern Kentucky, eight from southwestern Virginia,
four from western North Carolina, one from Tennessee, and one
each from Mississippi, Ohio, Wisconsin, and Washington, D. C.

Chick-ens crow-in' on Sour-wood Moun-tain.
Hey my rink-tum, a did-dle lol-ly day!
Get your hat and we'll go a-court-in'.
Hey my rink-tum, a did-dle lol-ly day!

2. I got a gal in the head of the holler.
   Hey my rinktum, a diddle lolly day!
   She won't come, and I won't call her.
   Hey my rinktum, a diddle lolly day!

3. Big dog bark and a little one bite you.
   Hey my rinktum, a diddle lolly day!
   Big girl court, and a little one spite you.
   Hey my rinktum, a diddle lolly day!

148

4. My true love is a blue-eyed daisy.
   She won't work and I'm too lazy.
   (or—If I don't get her I'll go crazy.)

5. She sits up with Old Si Hall.
   Me and Jeff can't go there at all.

   *(Or, usually, "Me and——" naming someone
   in the immediate crowd of listeners.)*

6. Some of these days before very long
   I'll get that gal and home I'll run.

7. Old man, old man, I want your daughter.
   to bake me bread and carry me water.

8. Old man, old man, now can I get your daughter?
   O yes, young man, take her if you want her.

9. Bundle up her old clothes, take her up behind you.
   Take her on home, and whup her till she'll mind you.

10. Chickens crowin' on Sourwood Mountain.
    So many pretty girls I can't count 'em.

Variant refrains:

> Hey! Ho! Diddle um a day!—or, Diddle all day!
> Hey diddy ump, diddy iddy ump day!
> Hey, day, de lingle dum day!

Paddy O'Doyle

Strictly speaking, this is not a folk song. It came from John Hunt who lived in Marion, Virginia. "Sailor Dad" once shipped out of Liverpool. He knew many good chanteys, and was a great favorite at The White Top Folk Festival. He was an expert gardener. The second verse comes from another old Irish song, for Dad Hunt had forgotten his own second verse.

Oh Pad-dy O' Doyle lived in Kil-lar-ney,
court-ed a girl named Bid-dy O' Toole;
his tongue was tipped with I-rish blar-ney,
at mak-in' love he was no fool.
Whack to my loo-ral, lau-rel, lay-rel!
Whack to my loo-ral, lau-rel, lay!
Whack to my loo-ral, lau-rel, lay-rel!
Whack to my loo-ral, lau-rel, lay!

150

Verse 2

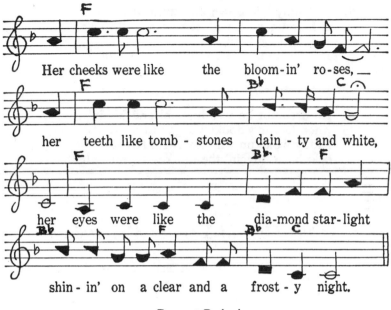

Her cheeks were like the bloom-in' ro-ses, —

her teeth like tomb - stones dain - ty and white,

her eyes were like the dia-mond star-light

shin - in' on a clear and a frost - y night.

Repeat Refrain

(Tune as for verse 1.)

3. 'Twas late at night in one November
   Paddy went out to meet his love;
   what night it was I don't remember
   but the moon shone brightly from above.
   Whack to my looral, laurel, layrel!
   Whack to my looral, laurel, lay!
   Whack to my looral, laurel, layrel!
   Whack to my looral, laurel, lay!

(Tune as for verse 2.)

4. That day the boy had got some likker
   which made his spirits bright and gay.
   Said, What's the use of me a-walkin' any further
   when I know she'll meet me on the way?
   Whack to my looral, laurel, layrel!
   Whack to my looral, laurel, lay!
   Whack to my looral, laurel, layrel!
   Whack to my looral, laurel, lay!

151

(Tune as for verse 1.)

   5. So Paddy laid down and went to sleep
       in Doran's barn with the cows and sheep,
       and there he slept and there he lay
       and dreampt of Biddy till the break of day.

(Tune as for verse 2.)

   6. He dreampt he was huggin' and kissin' Biddy,
       when Doran's donkey began to bray.
       Paddy woke up with an awful fright—
       he'd been huggin' the donkey all that night.

At the Foot of Yonder Mountain

This is from the singing of Horton Barker. It is given in John Powell's *Five Virginian Folk Songs* as recorded by Annabel Morris Buchanan from Miss Lillie Williams of Marion, Virginia.

    Mr. Powell says of this song: "Among American songs of this group may be mentioned: 'The Wagoner's Lad,' 'On Top of Old Smoky,' and 'Pretty Saro.' Lucy Broadwood and Anne Gilchrist have written articles which set forth the hypothesis with such logic and insight as to bring conviction that this song is derived from an ancient mystical hymn to the Virgin. They identify its locality with that of Saint Michael's Mount, strangely predominant in Cornish lore since pre-Saxon, even pre-Christian, times."

    Related English songs are: "Sweet England," "Come All You Little Streamers," and "Linden Lea." There are related tunes from Scotland and Ireland. (See also, "Clinch Mountain.")

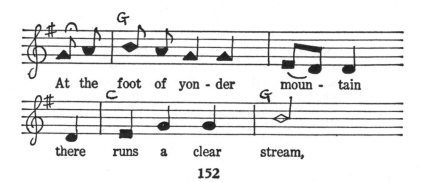

at the foot of yon - der moun - tain
there lives a fair queen.
She's hand - some, she's pro - per,
and her ways — are com - plete;
I ——— ask no bet - ter pas - time
than to be — with my sweet.

2. But why she won't have me I well understand:
   she wants some freeholder and I have no land.
   I cannot maintain her on silver and gold,
   and all the other fine things that my love's house should
   hold.

3. Oh I wish I were a penman and could write a fine hand!
   I would write my love a letter from this distant land.
   I'd send it by the waters just for to let her know
   that I think of Pretty Mary wherever I go.

4. Oh I wish I were a bird and had wings and could fly,
   it's to my love's dwelling this night I'd draw nigh.
   I'd sit in her window all night long and cry
   that for love of Pretty Mary I gladly would die.

Devilish Mary

I learned this from Horton Barker. It is in the Lomax collections, and is also known in Florida.

When I was a young man grow-in' up,

thought I'd nev-er mar-ry;

saw so man-y pret-ty lit-tle girls,

but none of them would have me.

Rah, rah, rink-tum, a hood-le-um a rink-tum!

Rah, rah, rink-tum a ra-zy!

Rah, rah, rink-tum, a hood-le-um a rink-tum!

Her name was Dev-il-ish Ma-ry!

2. One little girl I came across
   lived in London's Dairy,
   her hair was red as a golden thread,
   and her name was Devilish Mary.

Rah, rah, rinktum, a hoodleum a rinktum!
Rah, rah, rinktum a razy!
Rah, rah, rinktum, a hoodleum a rinktum!
Her name was Devilish Mary!

3. Hadn't been courtin' but a week or two,
    we both got in a hurry;
    both agreed right on the spot,
    and married the very next Thursday.
    Rah, rah, rinktum, a hoodleum a rinktum!
    Rah, rah, rinktum a razy!
    Rah, rah, rinktum, a hoodleum a rinktum!
    Her name was Devilish Mary!

4. Hadn't been married but a week or two,
    she acted like the devil;
    every time I'd open my mouth
    she'd crack my head with the shovel.

5. She wropped the broom all around my neck,
    striped my back with switches;
    jumped on the floor and popped her fist
    and swore she'd wear the britches.

6. One night when I was late gettin' in,
    a-makin' an awful blunder,
    she picked up a big old vinegar jug—
    I thought I 'uz struck by thunder!

7. Hadn't been married but about two months,
    she decided we'd better be parted;
    picked up her little bundle of duds,
    and down the road she started.

8. If ever I get married again
    it'll be for love nor riches,
    it'll be a little gal sixteen foot high
    that can't get in my britches.

155

The Riddle Song

In *The Oxford Book of Light Verse* there is an ancient version
of this song, but no source or date is given.

I have a young suster fer beyondyn the se;
many be the drowryis that sche sente me.
Sche sente me the cherye withoutyn ony ston,
and so sche dede the dowe withoutyn ony bon. . . . &c.
How schulde ony cherye be withoute ston? . . . &c.
Quan the cherye was a flour than hadde it non ston. . . . &c.

There is also a rollicking version:

I have four brothers over the sea—
Perry, merry, dixie, dominee!
They each sent a present home to me.
Perry, merry, dixie, dominee!
Petrum, patrum, paradise-a-tempore!
Perry, merry, dixie, dominee!

Wherever I have sung old songs for groups of adults or children
this one has been one of the most immediately beloved. The version that follows, simple and short as it is, has had much thought
and care put into it to get both tune and text just right. The tune
is that sung by Horton Barker, with one phrase changed by John
Powell. The text is from several sources. And the third line I
learned from Susie Reed. The song is known also in Maine,
Michigan, and Ohio.

I brought my love a cher-ry that has no stone,
I brought my love a chick-en that has no_ bone,
I told my love a sto-ry that has no end.
I brought my love a ba-by and no cry-en.

2. How can there be a cherry that has no stone?
   How can there be a chicken that has no bone?
   How can there be a story that has no end?
   How can there be a baby and no cryen?

3. A cherry when it's blooming it has no stone;
   a chicken in the egg it has no bone;
   the story of our love shall have no end;
   a baby when it's sleeping there's no cryen.

Johnny's Gone to Hilo

This is a sea chantey sung by "Sailor Dad," John Hunt, who lived in Marion, Virginia. Also, see "Paddy O'Doyle."

If I should die and be bur-ied at sea,
a mer-maid's sweet - heart I would be.
John-ny's gone to Hi-lo! Hee - lo!_ Hi - lo!
My John-ny's gone, _ what shall I do!
John-ny's gone to Hi - lo!

HYMNS

The Garden Hymn

This appears in *The Southern Harmony,* 1st edition, 1835.

The Lord in-to his Gar - den comes,

the flow - ers yield a rich per - fume,

the lil - ies grow and thrive,

the lil - ies grow and thrive.

Re - fresh-ing showers of grace di - vine

from Je - sus flow to eve - ry vine,

and make the faint re - vive,

and make the faint re - vive.

2. Oh that this dry and barren ground
   in springs of water may abound,
   a fruitful soil become, a fruitful soil become,
   the desert blossom as the rose,
   and Jesus conquer all his foes,
   and make his people one, and make his people one.

———◆———

Here are two riddles from Boyd Bolling of Flat Gap, Virginia.
We print them exactly as he sent them to us.

"a old time riddle
out of Blood and Bones came i as all other creatures do
yet neither Blood nor Bones remain in me
it was all by my mother's side where I was bravely bred
and when i Became of Perfect age they cut off my head
they gave me such Strong drink to drink
and such a Strength it had
it made diference Between rich and Poor
and makes trulovyers mad.

Here is one more

one thing another i sent to my Brother
all full of holes and no holes nother

unridle those
don't look on the other side."

And on the other side of the paper Mr. Bolling wrote:
"an old time goose quill Pen
Honey Comb"
It may be that some of our readers know other versions of the goose quill
riddle and will send them in.

Wondrous Love

This appears in many of the old shape-note hymnals. The tune is given here as sung by the Reverend Joseph R. Morris, Huntsville, Alabama, grandfather of Annabel Morris Buchanan, and was given me by Mrs. Buchanan, who learned it in her childhood. The rhythmic structure of this song is akin to "Captain Kidd" and "Samuel Hall," and as such goes back to the sixteenth century.

What wond'-rous love is this, O my soul! O my soul!
What wond'-rous love is this, O my soul!
What wond'-rous love is this that caused the Lord of bliss
to send such per-fect peace to my soul, to my soul
to send such per-fect peace to my soul!

2. Ye wing-ed seraphs fly, bear the news, bear the news!
   Ye wing-ed seraphs fly, bear the news!
   Ye wing-ed seraphs fly like comets through the sky,
   With loud and joyful cry bear the news, bear the news!
   With loud and joyful cry bear the news!

3. To God and to the Lamb I will sing, I will sing.
   To God and to the Lamb I will sing.
   To God and to the Lamb, Jehovah great I AM,
   and Christ the Son of Man, I will sing, I will sing.
   And Christ the Son of Man I will sing.

4. When we're from sorrow free we'll sing on, we'll sing on.
   When we're from sorrow free we'll sing on.
   When we're from sorrow free, we'll rise and joyful be,
   and through eternity we'll sing on, we'll sing on.
   And through eternity we'll sing on.

———◆———

There was a man who had no eyes,
and out he went, and looked at the skies.
He saw a tree that had good apples grown;
he took no apples off, he left no apples on.

The answer is in the use of the plural. He was a one-eyed man, and the tree had only two apples on it, "and one apple's not *apples!*"

I went to the fields and I got it.
I brought it home in my hand because I couldn't find it.
The more I looked for it, the more I felt it.
And when I found it, I threw it away.

A briar. "No, it's not a thorn. A thorn's too big."

161

The Wayfaring Stranger

This hymn is sung, passed on by word-of-mouth, throughout the Southern Mountains. It became widely known when Burl Ives sang it on his radio program some years ago. I have worked for about twelve years to compile the best text possible. The tune is from the collection of Annabel Morris Buchanan who wrote it down for me as given here. In Virginia I once heard it used with the carol "We are the true-born sons of Levi." The tune is known in Ireland.

I am a poor way - far- ing strang- er
Wand'-ring through this world of woe,
but there's no sor - row, toil, nor dan - ger
in that bright land to which I go:

I'm go-ing there to see my fa-ther,
I'm go-ing there no more _ to roam,
I'm just a - go - ing _ o - ver Jor - dan,
I'm on - ly go - ing o - ver home.

2. I know dark clouds will gather 'round me,
I know my way is rough and steep,
but golden fields lie out before me,
where all the saints their vigils keep:
I'm going there to see my mother,
she said she'd meet me when I come,
I'm just a-going over Jordan,
I'm only going over home.

3. I'll soon be free from every trial,
my body rest beneath the sod,
I'll drop the cross of self-denial
and stand before the throne of God:
I'm going there to see my Saviour,
to sing his praise forevermore,
I'm just a-going over Jordan,
I'm only going over home.

Here are two interesting variants of this tune.

As sung by Horton Barker of Saint Clair's Creek, Virginia:

In Cecil Sharp's *American-English Folk-Songs, 1st Series,* with an excellent piano accompaniment, there is a "love song" which uses the first part of this tune: "The Dear Companion." Following are the words as I know them:

1. Oh once I had a dear companion,
   indeed I thought his love my own
   until a black-haired girl betrayed me,
   and now he cares no more for me.

2. Just go and leave me if you want to,
   it will never bother me.—
   Oh in your heart you love another,
   and in my grave I'd rather be!

3. Last night you lay sweetly sleeping,
   dreaming in some sweet repose,
   while I, a poor girl broken broken-hearted,
   listen to the wind that blows.

4. Oh when I see your babe a-laughing
   it makes me think of your sweet face,
   but when I see your babe a-crying
   it makes me think of my disgrace.

Jesus Walked in Galilee

This tune is from Sam Russell who lived in Marion, Virginia. His first verse was "Jesus born in Bethlea and in the manger lay" which would lead one to think it might be a Christmas carol. There is a four-part vocal arrangement of this (by Annabel Morris Buchanan) in *Twelve Folk Hymns* edited by John Powell.

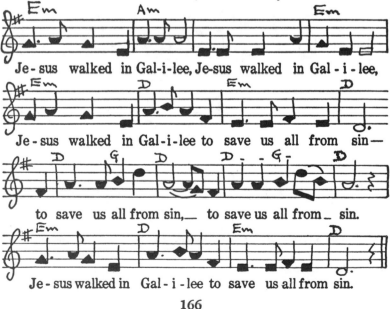

Je-sus walked in Gal-i-lee, Je-sus walked in Gal-i-lee,

Je-sus walked in Gal-i-lee to save us all from sin—

to save us all from sin,— to save us all from— sin.

Je-sus walked in Gal-i-lee to save us all from sin.

2. Judas he betrayed him,
   Judas he betrayed him,
   Judas he betrayed him,
   and nailed him to the tree—
   and nailed him to the tree—
   and nailed him to the tree.
   Judas he betrayed him,
   and nailed him to the tree.

3. Joseph begged his body,
   Joseph begged his body,
   Joseph begged his body,
   and laid it in the tomb—
   and laid it in the tomb—
   and laid it in the tomb.
   Joseph begged his body,
   and laid it in the tomb.

4. One morning early,
   just at the break of day—

5. —down came an angel
   and rolled the stone away.

6. Mary came a-weeping,
   her loving Lord to see.

7. What's the matter, Mary?
   They've stolen my Lord away.

8. Jesus has arisen,
   arisen from the dead.

9. Go and tell his brethren,
   he's gone to Galilee.

10. The tomb it could not hold him,
    he's burst the bonds of death.

The resemblance of this tune to "For He's a Jolly Good Fellow" or "The Bear Went Over the Mountain," may not be apparent at first, but I have actually heard this hymn sung thus:

(Quietly. Not too fast.)

See also "Molly Brooks" for more notes of interest concerning this tune.

Oh Lord, How Long?

This strange and beautiful spiritual was given me by Annabel Morris Buchanan who recorded it from a singer in Grainger County, near Bean Station, Tennessee. The tune is in the rare Lydian mode—keynote *fa*.

This time — an-o-ther year we may — be

dead and gone, — bur-ied in some lone-some — grave - yard. — O — Lord, how long?

Rise, · fa-thers, and trim your lamps. — O — Lord, how long?

King — Je - sus is rid - ing a - round your

camps. — O — Lord, how long?

Over Yonders Ocean

This is from Mrs. Rebecca Jones who lived near Raleigh, North Carolina.

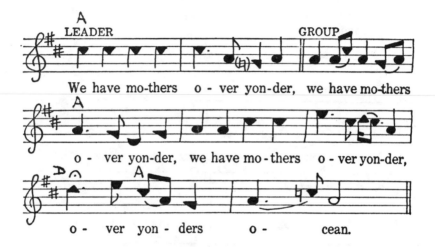

We have mo-thers   o - ver yon-der,   we have mo-thers

o - ver yon-der,   we have mo - thers   o - ver yon-der,

o - ver yon - ders   o -   cean.

   2. Bye and bye we'll go and see them,
     Bye and bye we'll go and see them,
     Bye and bye we'll go and see them,
     Over yonders ocean.

   3. Won't that be a happy meeting,
     Won't that be a happy meeting,
     Won't that be a happy meeting,
     Over yonders ocean.

The song continues in this same three-verse pattern substituting "fathers," "sisters," and "brothers."

SONGS TO SING YOUR CHILDREN

Fiddle-i-Fee

This is from "the Jack Tale man," R. M. Ward, who lived on Laurel Creek near Beech Mountain, North Carolina. His selection of animals has more charm, I think, than any other version I've ever heard. Usually the words are, "I bought me a cat, the cat pleased me . . ." But one day after I sang it this way with some children at an orphanage one little boy told me I had sung it "all wrong." I have been singing it *his* way ever since.

1. I had a lit-tle cat, the cat loved me,
   I fed my cat un-der yon - der tree.
   Cat went fid - dle - i - fee!

2. I had a little chicken, the chicken loved me,
   I fed my chicken under yonder tree.

   Chick-en went Chee - mi - chack! Chee - mi - chack!
   Cat went fiddle-i-fee! (*as at first*)

3. I had a little duck, the duck loved me,
I fed my duck under yonder tree.

Duck went Quack - quack! Quack - quack!

Chicken went Cheemi-chack! Cheemi-chack!
Cat went Fiddle-i-fee!

4. I had a little goose, the goose loved me,
I fed my goose under yonder tree.

Goose went Snoo - sy! Snoo - sy!

Duck went Quack-quack! Quack-quack!
Chicken went Cheemi-chack! Cheemi-chack!
Cat went Fiddle-i-fee!

5. I had a little guinea, the guinea loved me,
I fed my guinea under yonder tree.

Guin-ea went Pot - rack! Pot - rack!

Goose went Snoosy! Snoosy!
Duck went Quack-quack! Quack-quack!
Chicken went Cheemi-chack! Cheemi-chack!
Cat went Fiddle-i-fee!

6. I had a little pony, the pony loved me,
I fed my pony under yonder tree.

Po - ny went Trot - a - trot! Trot - a - trot!

Guinea went Pot-rack! Pot-rack!

Goose went Snoosy! Snoosy!
Duck went Quack-quack! Quack-quack!
Chicken went Cheemi-chack! Cheemi-chack!
Cat went Fiddle-i-fee!

7. I had a little mule, the mule loved me,
   I fed my mule under yonder tree.

Mule went   Hee - hawn!   Hee - hawn!

Pony went Trot-a-trot! Trot-a-trot!
Guinea went Pot-rack! Pot-rack!
Goose went Snoosy! Snoosy!
Duck went Quack-quack! Quack-quack!
Chicken went Cheemi-chack! Cheemi-chack!
Cat went Fiddle-i-fee!

8. I had a little rabbit, the rabbit loved me,
   I fed my rabbit under yonder tree.

Rab- bit went   Lit- tle jump!   Lit-tle jump!

Mule went Hee-hawn! Hee-hawn!
Pony went Trot-a-trot! Trot-a-trot!
Guinea went Pot-rack! Pot-rack!
Goose went Snoosy! Snoosy!
Duck went Quack-quack! Quack-quack!
Chicken went Cheemi-chack! Cheemi-chack!
Cat went Fiddle-i-fee!

9. I had a little deer, the deer loved me,
   I fed my deer under yonder tree.

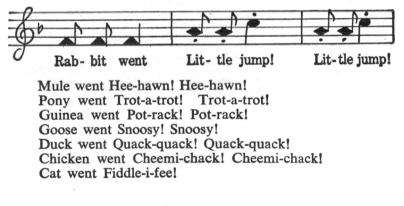

Deer went.   Big   jump!   Big   jump!

Rabbit went Little jump! Little jump!

173

Mule went Hee-hawn! Hee-hawn!
Pony went Trot-a-trot! Trot-a-trot!
Guinea went Pot-rack! Pot-rack!
Goose went Snoosy! Snoosy!
Duck went Quack-quack! Quack-quack!
Chicken went Cheemi-chack! Cheemi-chack!
Cat went Fiddle-i-fee!

I had a little turkey, the turkey loved me,
I fed my turkey under yonder tree.
Turkey went — GOBBLE-GOBBLE-GOBBLE-GOBBLE-
GOBBLE-GOBBLE!

At this last, of course, the singer jumps at the nearest child.

The Swapping Song

This is from Greene County, Virginia.

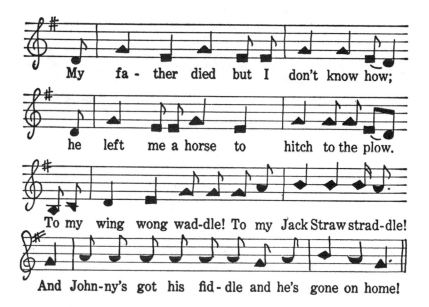

My fa - ther died but I don't know how;

he left me a horse to hitch to the plow.

To my wing wong wad-dle! To my Jack Straw strad-dle!

And John-ny's got his fid - dle and he's gone on home!

2. I swapped my horse and got me a cow,
   and in that trade I just learned how.
   To my wing wong waddle! To my Jack Straw straddle!
   And Johnny's got his fiddle and he's gone on home!

3. I swapped my cow and got me a calf,
   and in that trade I lost just half.
   To my wing wong waddle! To my Jack Straw straddle!
   And Johnny's got his fiddle and he's gone on home!

4. I swapped my calf and got me a pig,
   the poor little thing hit never growed big.

5. I swapped my pig and got me a hen
   to lay me an egg every now and then.

6. I swapped my hen and got me a cat,
   the pretty little thing by the chimney sat.

7. I swapped my cat and got me a mouse,
   his tail caught a-fire and he burned down the house.

8. I swapped my mouse and got me a mole,
   the dad-burned thing went straight down its hole.
   To my wing wong waddle! To my Jack Straw straddle!
   And Johnny's got his fiddle and he's gone on home!

The Old Gray Goose Is Dead

This is one of the most widely known and best loved of all our songs. Usually it is only the first two verses that are known. My putting-together of the song as given here is the result of some thirty years of selection and rejection. There are many different "Aunts"—Nancy, Rosie, Rhody, Tabby, Abbie, Mandy, Dinah, and Patsy. I have sung this song before audiences in Los Angeles, Denver, Chicago, and in Flint, Michigan; and "Aunt Rhody" was the favorite. I like it best because the "O" sound *sings* better.

I first learned the song from Mrs. Neida Humphrey Pratt, of Huntsville, Alabama, when she was an active student of the opera. I cannot remember the source of the third verse. The fourth verse came from a concert singer in New York City, John Langstaff. It would be fine to learn of other possible verses. (See "Amateur Collector's Guide.")

The melody is also known in hymnals as "Greenville," (No. 187 in the Methodist Hymnal) or "Rousseau's Dream," and in this use it has a second part. It appeared in an opera written by Jean Jacques Rousseau in 1750, and it is said that Rousseau dreamed he went to Heaven and heard angels singing this melody as they stood around the throne of God.

2. The one that she's been a-savin',
   the one that she's been a-savin',
   the one that she's been a-savin',
   to make a feather bed.

3. She died in the mill pond,
   she died in the mill pond,
   she died in the mill pond,
   standin' on her head.

4. She left nine little goslins,
   she left nine little goslins,
   she left nine little goslins,
   to scratch for their own bread.

5. So run and tell Aunt Rhody,
   run and tell Aunt Rhody,
   run and tell Aunt Rhody,
   the old gray goose is dead.

A full version of the tune is given here as set down by John Powell, who found it in an old shape note hymn book. Its unusual rhythm is due to the words to which it was set.

Cock Robin

This came from a singer near Chapel Hill, North Carolina, whose name I failed to record. I remember singing it over and over as I walked back some three miles from his home out in the country. The kinship of all folk music was once made clear to me out in Arizona when I was visiting an Indian reservation. There were present a white man and his family, a Hopi couple, a Navajo couple, and myself. We had been trying to get the Indians to sing Indian songs and, as a part of the warming-up process, I hummed this tune. "Sing that again," one of the Indians said. I hummed it again. "Did you ever know anything like that?" I finally asked. Another Indian spoke up, "Sure! That's a Shoshone night chant. I've heard it many times."

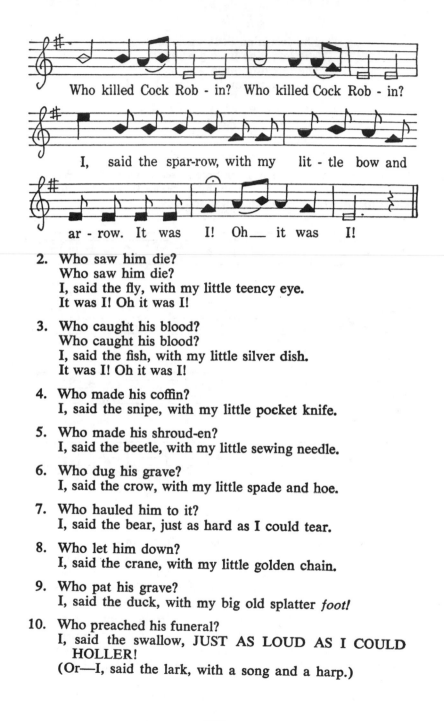

Who killed Cock Rob - in? Who killed Cock Rob - in?

I, said the spar-row, with my lit - tle bow and

ar - row. It was I! Oh— it was I!

2. Who saw him die?
   Who saw him die?
   I, said the fly, with my little teency eye.
   It was I! Oh it was I!

3. Who caught his blood?
   Who caught his blood?
   I, said the fish, with my little silver dish.
   It was I! Oh it was I!

4. Who made his coffin?
   I, said the snipe, with my little pocket knife.

5. Who made his shroud-en?
   I, said the beetle, with my little sewing needle.

6. Who dug his grave?
   I, said the crow, with my little spade and hoe.

7. Who hauled him to it?
   I, said the bear, just as hard as I could tear.

8. Who let him down?
   I, said the crane, with my little golden chain.

9. Who pat his grave?
   I, said the duck, with my big old splatter *foot!*

10. Who preached his funeral?
    I, said the swallow, JUST AS LOUD AS I COULD HOLLER!
    (Or—I, said the lark, with a song and a harp.)

SONGS AS SUNG BY ORA CANTER

The following five songs are given exactly as sung by Miss Ora Canter who lives near Mountain City, Tennessee. They were recorded on tape by Marjorie Loomis of Forest Hills, New York. Miss Ora has no electricity in her house, as yet, and so we made the recordings in the offices of the nearby Rural Electrification Administration. Miss Ora is nearly blind. She lives alone in a small house which she keeps spotlessly clean and neat. She is one of the sweetest, most cheerful people I have ever known, and was very particular about my getting the words set down "right." Her repertory of traditional English folk songs, hymns, and ballads seems well-nigh endless.

Johnny Jarmanie

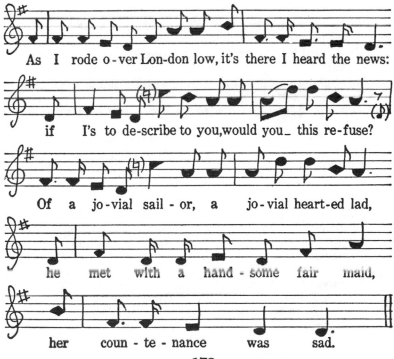

As I rode o-ver Lon-don low, it's there I heard the news:

if I's to de-scribe to you, would you_ this re-fuse?

Of a jo-vial sail-or, a jo-vial heart-ed lad,

he met with a hand-some fair maid,

her coun-te-nance was sad.

2. Oh my pretty fair maiden, what makes you so cast down?
   She answered him with modesty and neither smiled nor
     frowned,
   Now my true love's forsaken me and from me he is gone,
   he's left me not a token whenever he'll return.

3. Oh my pretty fair maiden, perhaps I've seen him at sea.
   If I's to right describe to you would you answer me?
   And if his shapes and features do to you explain,
   would you consent to marry me if he never comes again?

4. He's handsome in his features, though courage he doth
     lack,
   he's handsome in his features whene'er he turned his
     back.
   Belonging to The Rainbow, and mate to Captain Glow,
   his name is Johnny Jarmanie. Is this the man you know?

5. Then she jumped for joy, saying, That's the very man!
   Come tell me more about him, and do no longer stand.
   Cheer up, cheer up, my pretty fair maid, the truth you
     soon shall know:
   your loving Johnny Jarmanie's been dead five months ago.

6. Then she wrung her lily-white hands and tears fell down
     her cheeks,
   she turned herself straightway around, into her chamber's
     gone,
   sad sighing and lamenting, still wishing she could die.

7. This young man he wheeled his horse, and back on board
     he went.
   Little did this fair maid think what was his intent.
   He dressed himself in scarlet red and back to her he came
   with jovial resolution to comfort her again.

8. Open your door, dear Polly, some comfort you shall hear.
   Open your door, dear Polly, leave sorrow all behind.
   'Twas just to oblige him she opened it immediately,
   saying, Who can this young sailor be but my loving
     Jarmanie?

9. Johnny, Oh Johnny, how could you serve me so?
   Johnny I do love you and this you do know.
   'Twas just to try your constitute, to see whether you'd be
     true or no.
   There's n'ary a turtle dove that's ever exceeded you.

180

10. Polly, you are my jewel, my joy and heart's delight.
    I never will prove cruel but love you day and night.
    You're brighter than the morning sun, and sweeter than
        the rose,
    you're like some blooming flower—your color comes and
        goes.

11. Here's adieu to this country since Polly's won my heart.
    Perhaps we'll have a wedding before we do depart.
    Adieu to The Rainbow and a mate to Captain Glow,
    adieu to The Rainbow, adieu forevermore.

The Wagoner's Lad

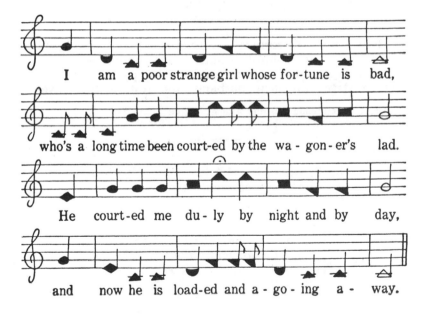

I am a poor strange girl whose for-tune is bad,
who's a long time been court-ed by the wa-gon-er's lad.
He court-ed me du-ly by night and by day,
and now he is load-ed and a-go-ing a-way.

2. Your horses are hungry, go feed them some hay,
    and set you down by me as long as you stay.
    My horses ain't hungry, they won't eat your hay.
    So fare you well Nancy, I've no time to stay.

3. Your wagon's to grease, your bill is to pay.
   Set you down by me as long as you stay.
   My wagon is greased, my whip's in my hand,
   so fare you well Nancy, I've no time to stand.

4. He mounted his horse, away he did go,
   he left this girl weeping as you very well know,
   but when he returned she crowned him with joy
   and kissed the sweet lips of the wagoner's boy.

5. So early next morning as he did arise,
   he crossed the deep waters with tears in his eyes,
   to think he must leave her and see her no more.
   He left this girl weeping on New River's shore.

6. Some say that I'm wicked, some say that I'm vile,
   some say that I'm guilty of many bad crimes.
   I'll prove them all liars by the powers above,
   for I'm guilty of nothing but innocent love.

7. Your father doth[1] hate me because I am poor,
   and thinks me scarce worthy to enter his door,
   but I hope he will rue it—it all is in vain—
   for love is a killing and a tormenting pain.

8. How hard is the fortune of all womankind!
   They're always controlled and always confined—
   controlled by their parents until they're made wives,
   then slaves for their husbands the rest of their lives.

[1] Miss Canter pronounced this with a long O: "dōth."

———◆———

Older than Adam, if Adam were still alive.
Just four weeks old, and never shall be five.

The moon.

The man that made it didn't want it.
The man that bought it didn't need it.
The man that used it didn't know it.

A coffin.

Riddle to my riddle to my rocket!
What a poor man throws away,
A rich man puts in his pocket.

"There's no polite way to answer that 'un, son: it's just plain snot."

182

The Little Family

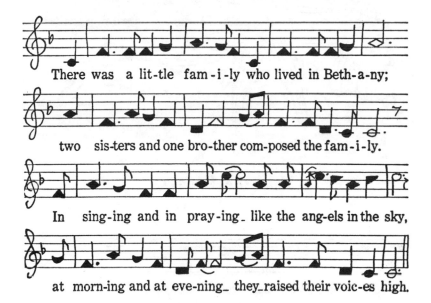

There was a lit-tle fam-i-ly who lived in Beth-a-ny;

two sis-ters and one bro-ther com-posed the fam-i-ly.

In sing-ing and in pray-ing_ like the ang-els in the sky,

at morn-ing and at eve-ning_ they_raised their voic-es high.

2. They lived in peace and pleasure, a many a long year,
   till Lazarus was afflicted beyond this vale of tears.
   Poor Martha and her sister, they wept aloud and cried,
   but still he grew no better, but lingered on and died.

3. When Jesus was a-coming Martha met him on the way,
   and told him how her brother had just died and passed
     away.
   When Jesus was a-coming Mary ran and met him too—
   down at his feet a-weeping rehearsed this tale of woe.

4. He blessed them and he cheered them and told them not
     to weep,
   for Lazarus in full vigor shall be risen from his sleep.—
   Now, if we do love Jesus and do his holy will,
   like Martha and like Mary, we'll always please him well.

(Repeat last half of the tune . . .)

From Death he will redeem us and take us to the skies,
and bid us live forever where pleasure never dies.

Will the Weaver

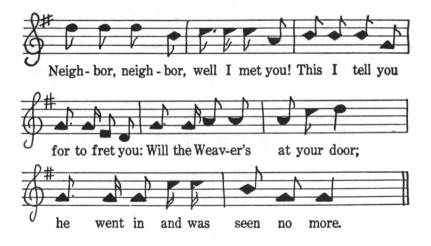

Neigh-bor, neigh-bor, well I met you! This I tell you for to fret you: Will the Weav-er's at your door; he went in and was seen no more.

2. He ran home all in a wonder,
   kicked the door and it groaned like thunder.
   Who's that? Who's that? the weaver cried.
   'Tis my husband and you must hide!

3. Up the chimbley he did venture,
   for her husband she let enter;
   searched the house, the room all 'round,
   not a man to be found.

4. Up the chimbley he was gazing,
   there he saw in all amazing—
   there he saw the wretched soul
   perched upon the lubber pole.

5. Oh, my lad, I'm glad I found you,
   I'll neither kill, hang, nor drown you,
   this he thought, nothing spoke:
   I'll stuff you well with smoke.

6. Just to please his own desire,
   built himself a rousing fire;
   his wife called out of her free good will,
   Husband, there's a man you'll kill!

7. He kindled on some other fuel,
   his wife cried out. My dearest Jewel,[a]
   husband dear, to be your wife,
   take him down and spare his life.

8. He catched him by the heels and down he jerked him,
   with his fists so well he worked him;
   every lick thus he spoke,
   Come no more to stop my smoke.

9. Who's as black as Will the Weaver,
   he's as black as a chimbley sweeper,
   all his face, hands, and clothes—
   two black eyes and a bloody nose.

10. He ran home, his wife she met him,
    up with a club and down she let him,
    turned his black all into red—
    Hush, the Will the Weaver's dead.

[a] Miss Canter seemed to sing "duel."

The Old Woman All Skin and Bones

There was an old wo-man all skin and bones and
this old wo-man she lived all a-lone and
Oh - h! — and Oh - h!

2. This old woman she thought one day
   she'd go hear the parson preach and pray: and Oh-h,
   and Oh-h!

3. When she got to the meeting-house stile
   she thought she'd sit down and rest a while: and Oh-h,
   and Oh-h!

4. When she got to the meeting-house door
   she thought she'd sit down and rest some more: and Oh-h,
   and Oh-h!

5. And when she got to the church within
   she thought she'd sit down and rest ag'in: and Oh-h,
   and Oh-h!

6. She looketh up, and looketh down,
   she spied a ghost (corpse) upon the ground: and Oh-h,
   and Oh-h!

7. From the top of its head and down to its chin
   the worms crawled out and the worms crawled in: and
   Oh-h, and Oh-h!

8. The old woman to the parson said,
   Shall I look so when I am dead?—and Oh-h, and Oh-h!

9. The parson to the old woman said,
   Yes, you shall look so when you are dead: and Oh-h,
   and Oh-h!

10. The old woman to the parson said . . . *Eeeeeeee!*

3. Games and Country Dances

Traditional social and ritual dances exist over the whole world. English folk dances used for social recreation are called country dances, and the American Square Dance is one of these—a country dance that developed from traditional sources to suit the various environments and needs this side of the Atlantic. English country dances were developed from native sources in the courts of Henry VIII, Elizabeth I, and the Jameses. An English publisher named John Playford brought out a book called *The English Dancing Master,* which ran through seventeen editions from 1650 to 1728.

This form of social dance spread from England to the continent, and migrated to America with the colonists. In France the same kind of dance was known as the "contre-danse," and in Germany as the "kontra tanz"—both names being based on the English words "country dance."

A History of Dancing, published in England in 1710 reported: "Country dancing is a growth of this nation, though now transplanted to all the courts of Europe, where it has become in the most august assemblies the favorite diversion. This dancing is a moderate and healthful exercise, a pleasant and innocent diversion if modestly used and performed at convenient times and by suitable company."

In America much of our country dance tradition has kept the dignified gaiety which gives this kind of social dancing its value and keeps it perennially popular. The best of it is phrased to the music for each dance, and needs no "calling," once the dancers know the dance. Examples of good country dancing abound in New England: "Lady Walpole's Reel," "The Sicilian Circle," and "The Lady of the Lake." In the South, "The Virginia Reel" (Sir Roger de Coverly), is the best-known, "Molly Brooks," given here, is very much like a court dance. American formations, "sets," include: longways (mostly New England), four-couple squares (New England, Ohio, Midwest, Texas, the Far West), big rings (New England, the South) and in Virginia there is one tradition of a big hollow square of several couples at the "head and foot" and on the "sides" of a set.

187

Ritual dances, English Morris dances, and sword dances, traditionally done by teams of men, are performed only on specific seasonal occasions. These dances did not come over with our early settlers, but the tunes for both Morris and sword dances did cross the Atlantic, and found their way into early hymn books!

Children's singing games, known in similar forms in all parts of England and America, are ritualistic in origin. We are told that many of them spring from the pre-Christian rites of our pagan ancestors. Playparty games (folk games) are a step up from children's singing games for ages about twelve and up. Often with certain rural groups or at church parties, they are good for all ages.

These singing figure-dances developed in many American communities where *dancing to fiddle music* was considered "sinful." But "playing games" to a singing accompaniment was allowed, even though the same dance figures were done as when a fiddler might be present!

Granny London Tells About Old Times

R. CHASE: Then what kind of fun did you used to have, after the work was caught up?

GRANNY: Ha! We had it all right! Aa Lord! This generation that's comin' up now, they've not had no chance to learn how to play—and *really* have a good time. Get in a car. Go tearin' around. It's pityful! But when I was a girl, people lived a lot further apart than they do these times, but it seems like they could get together even more than they do anymore.[1] We had quiltin's, and cornshuckin's, and even corn-hoein' parties.

---

[1] *i.e.* "now-a-days."

Everybody 'uld come and work together till it was all done, and then they'd play games.

It was: "Come to my corn-shuckin' next Saturday. We're goin' to have a big play."[2] Well, they'd all come, and after the corn was shucked, and supper was done. Oh, yes, they'd always fix a big supper for everybody! "Now let's play."

Then one young man would start out and get his sweetheart, and everybody'd start singin' and they'd all drop in one by one and get partners and march around until they'd all be in the game. Let me see now can I remember how it went—

Lon-don Bridge is washed a-way! Dance on my la-dies all! Lon-don Bridge is washed a-way! To my high gain de day!

2. Mend it up with sticks and clay!
    Dance on, my ladies all!
    Mend it up with sticks and clay!
    To my high gained de-day!

The other verses were:

3. Sticks and clay will wash away!
4. Mend it up with sword and steel!
5. Sword and steel will bend and break!
6. Break a lock and steal a girl!

GRANNY: Then when the last ones were in, they'd get in two lines, and be facin' one another.—We're goin' to talk sugar-talk now:

Ground hog married the baboon's sister;
smacked his mouth, and how did he kiss her?
Kissed so hard he raised a blister!
First couple out on the floor! . . .

Oh Law! There was a lot more to it. I can't remember it all now.

[2] "We had to call it that. The preachers would get after you if they thought you were goin' to dance!"

189

CHASE: When you got tired of playin', what would you do?

GRANNY: Why, pull our chairs up in a circle, or just sit on the floor, around the big fireplace, and make somebody sing, or get to askin' riddles. But I liked it best when some of the old folks would start tellin' tales.

TOM HUNT: You remember any of the old tales?

GRANNY: Yes. I can tell 'em.

GIRL: She was tellin' us one just last night.

HUNT: Would you tell us one now?

GRANNY: Well, I don't care to.[3] Which one do you reckon this feller would like, Tom?

HUNT: Do you know "Jack and the talkin' crow"?

GRANNY: I used to know it.

TURNER: Did you ever hear that 'un about Jack and his bull?

GRANNY: Screwed off the bull's horns to get his bread and milk. Law, yes. I know that one good. —Did you ever hear about the time Jack had with Old King Marock? Hit's got one mean [4] place in it.

HUNT: Tell that. That's the one!

GRANNY: Hit's an awful long 'un.

TURNER: That's the very kind we like.

GRANNY: You know, I've often thought of it: a body ought to keep them old tales alive some way or other.

HUNT: That's exactly what we aim to try to do, Granny. Dick and Jeems here, they're settin' the old tales down to go in a book.

GRANNY: A book? Law, that's fine! You take folks today, now: they don't have no way of knowin' the old tales. But 'way back when I was a child, my mother had to card and spin wool for our clothes. We had a big gang of sheep, and they'd run into burrs. Get just full of 'em. And when we'd shear the wool off we'd have to pick all that out: burrs, and twigs, and trash. My mother'd get a wool-fleece out, of a night, put it on the floor, and everybody—all us children too—had to help pick that big fleece. And she 'uld tell us tales to keep us awake. She'd get in the middle of one of them old tales, and we'd just pick for life! —Now, you really want to hear all that about Jack and King Marock?

. . . And Granny London told the old "mean" tale, laughing heartily when the bawdy part came along.

[3] *i.e.* "I don't object."
[4] Granny's word for "bawdy."

190

We're Marchin' 'Round the Levee

Children's singing games are the simplest of English folk dances. This one seems to indicate a ritual processional " 'round and 'round the village." Today, the village of Helston in Cornwall celebrates such spring rites when a long processional "parade" of dancers "go in and out the windows"—doors rather—of the town to bring in the May and good luck.

The game given here has several "new" verses learned recently from children in Marion, Virginia, and in Buncombe County, North Carolina.

"Levee" here has no connection with flood control! It must mean a morning party or reception. (*See* Webster.) Such levees were held during the War Between The States to celebrate victories . . . "For we have gained the day."

This can be played with the average classroom, first grade through fourth—about thirty children. It takes a minimum of twelve. Start with a ring holding hands and let one child stand in the center.

The ring circles left with a brisk but easy-going walking step.

1. We're marchin' 'round the levee,
   we're marchin' round the levee,
   we're marchin' round the levee,
   for we have gained the day.

The ring stops. They raise their joined hands. The child in the center goes in and out under the arches.

2. Go in and out the window,
   go in and out the window,
   go in and out the window
   for we have gained the day.

191

The child in the center goes around pulling down the joined hands of those in the ring.

    3. Go fasten down the shutters . . .
        for we have gained the day.

The ring squats, their hands still joined, and the child in the center goes jumping in and out the ring over their joined hands.

    4. Go jumping over the doorsills . . .
        for we have gained the day.

The ring stands up. The child in the center makes washing motions in front of the faces of several in the ring.

    5. Go wash your tiny windows . . .
        for we have gained the day.

The ring walks toward the center, and walks backward, twice.

    6. Go up and down the ladder . . .
        for we have gained the day.

The center player goes and stands in front of the "lover."

    7. Go forth and face your lover . . .
        for we have gained the day.

The one in the center kneels.

    8. I kneel because I love you . . .
        for we have gained the day.

The kneeling child measures off its love on one finger and forearm, more and more until both arms are held out wide on the last line. Often a child will measure less and less "just for meanness," but always end with arms stretched out wide. (Once I saw children literally measure the lover, as for a fitting. A handkerchief, or an imaginary tape measure, was used.)

    9. I measure my love to show you . . .
        for we have gained the day.

The center player stands up and stays put. The ring circles left.

    10. Good-by, I hate to leave you . . .
         for we have gained the day.

The ring circles back, to the right.

> 11. I'm coming back to see you . . .
> for we have gained the day.

. . . and so brings the lovers together again.

The one inside takes the lover into the center, and now you start all over again with two inside the ring. These two choose lovers from the ring, and on the third round there are four in the middle—and so on. Every child, thus, will eventually have a "lover." (If there is an odd number, the teacher, if present, can take the child who is left over.)

When the ring can no longer join hands because most players are in the center, they move left and right in a horseshoe or in scattered groups holding hands where possible.

The last round may be varied, and the game brought to a good ending, by swinging each other in couples (hands joined straight across—R in L and L in R—and turning clockwise) with a skipping step, singing . . .

> We're swinging 'round the levee,
> we're swinging 'round the levee,
> we're swinging 'round the levee
> for we have gained the day.

Skip to My Lou

This folk game is an old favorite and has been tried even in Hollywood! These three versions each have their uses according to the social situation. Version I is easy but can become monotonous. Version II is not difficult but can get wild if the "shooting" of the odd one toward the center is done too vigorously. Version III is a simple "square" dance, and currently the most popular.

1. Lou, Lou, skip to my Lou,
   Lou, Lou, skip to my Lou,
   Lou, Lou, skip to my Lou,
   Skip to my Lou, my darlin'!

2. Lost my partner, what'll I do?
   Lost my partner, what'll I do?
   Lost my partner, what'll I do?
   Skip to my Lou, my darlin'!

3. Get me another one, pretty as you,
   Get me another one, pretty as you,
   Get me another one, pretty as you,
   Skip to my Lou, my darlin'!

4. Pretty as a redbird, prettier too!

5. Can't get a redbird, a bluebird'll do.

6. Can't get a biscuit, cornbread'll do.

7. Little red wagon, painted blue.

8. Flies in the buttermilk—Shoo, fly! Shoo!

9. Ants in the sugar bowl, two by two.

10. Kittens in the haystack—Mew-mew-mew!

11. Mule's in the cellar, kickin' up through.

Refrain verses:

A. Lou, Lou, skip to my Lou . . .
B. Lou-Lou, Lou-Lou, skip to my Lou . . .
C. Skip, skip, skip to my Lou . . .
D. Gone again! What'll I do? . . .

There are many other verses, and there is no set order for those given here. Every community has its own tradition of verses for this game. And often new verses are made up on the spur of the moment.

Look at that greenhorn, don't know what to do! . . .
Look at that girl with a number ten shoe! . . .

Usually the rhymes are all "loo," "too," "do," etc. Only near Luray, Virginia, have I ever heard a different pattern:

I got a gal eats turnips raw,
brushes her teeth with a handful of straw,
combs her head with a crosscut saw!—
Skip to my Lou, my darlin'!

194

The success of this game depends particularly on a hearty participation in the singing. Anyone can, and should, raise any verse he can think of, or make up. Sing one or two of the refrain verses over and over, if necessary, but be sure to *keep the music going.*

FIGURES FOR THE THREE VERSIONS

Version I

Formation: A ring of couples. Girl on the boy's right. Only *couples* holding hands. (Not a closed ring.) One extra boy in the center.

Action: The extra boy skips around counterclockwise inside the set. He takes ("steals") any girl from the ring, takes her left hand in his right (or crosses hands, R in R and L in L, as for promenading), and skips on around until they both come to the empty place in the ring which they fill—standing quickly out of the way of the "stealer" (or couple) coming behind them! For—the partner of the stolen girl starts skipping out as soon as she is taken away from him. And he steals himself another, returning to *that* empty place after one circuit—and so on. Don't be a "greenhorn" and stand too long in the ring after your partner is stolen. When you lose your partner, you can, if you wish, steal the very next girl in the ring. Keep singing, and "keep it up till half-past-two," if you wish.

Version II

Formation: Same as Version I, but an extra boy and an extra *girl* may both be in the center. It is best not to skip in this dance, even though you are singing "Skip, skip——." A lively walk, with a good *lift* (*i.e.* almost a skip but without letting the supporting foot actually leave the floor) will work best—a quick strut.

Action: Each extra dancer in the center goes anywhere in the ring and makes a three-handed circle with any couple. This three-hands-around moves to the left, clockwise, about once-and-a-half around until the boy whose partner is being stolen is facing the center of the big ring. Then an arch is made by the stealing boy and the stolen girl under which the other boy is shot into the center of the set. In popping the dancer under this arch, the one to be popped should hold back slightly so that the other two can really "shoot" him through like an ox row. The girl in the center steals the same way; she and the boy shoot the other *girl* through into the middle.

The leader of this dance may, as the game progresses, start another pair stealing by taking the girl with whom he happens to be standing into the center and both of them start stealing.

Then after several rounds with these four active, the leader may keep increasing the number of stealers until the game breaks up.

Version III

This is a handy device in starting a group of inexperienced dancers. There is almost no need for "instruction," since the verses carry their own directions. My first knowledge of this use of "Skip to My Lou" came from Dr. Glenn Gildersleeve of Madison College in Virginia.

Formation: A closed single-ring of couples, all holding hands. At least one extra man in the center. You can have several if enough extra men are present. In joining hands in the ring the men should *take* the women's hands: men's palms up, women's palms down. Woman is always on the man's right. To get the ring in good shape keep joined hands at about waist level (*i.e.* not limply hanging, not stiffened either), and as the ring moves keep a *slight* pull away from the center of the ring. Maintain a springy connection, always, in the hands and arms. "Show your muscles," as a boy said once—but don't pull too hard. This makes for the greatest enjoyment of the whole group moving and changing direction *together,* and keeps the dancers evenly spaced. Use a lively quiet walking step throughout. Younger dancers may skip for verse 6— "Swing your partner . . . ," but trying to skip elsewhere makes things too boisterous and even impossible!

Action: The "Caller" should be sure to sing out on the last two beats of the last line, every time—*i.e.* on the word "darlin'!"

When there are extra women present, promenade "the wrong way": in a clockwise direction so that the men are on the outside. Then call, "Gents turn back!" at the end of verse 7, and, "Grab, girls! Grab!" at the end of verse 8.

You can get couples on the floor by singing:

"March around two by two . . ."

Then get the ring all set, and start in!

(*Caller: "Circle left!"*)

    1. Circle left, skip to my Lou,
      circle left, skip to my Lou,
      circle left, skip to my Lou!
      Skip to my Lou, my darlin'!

(*"Circle right!"*)

    2. Circle right, skip to my Lou . . .
      Skip to my Lou, my darlin'!

196

("All to the center!")

Now all will move toward the center with seven shorter steps—a light and lilting sort of strut. Be sure to keep moving forward until you hear the words "—back again!"

3. All to the center, all the way in,
   all to the center and—back again!
   Back again, skip to my Lou!
   Skip to my Lou, my darlin'!

("Ladies in!")

4. Ladies to the center, all the way in,
   ladies to the center and—back again!
   Back again, skip to my Lou!
   Skip to my Lou, my darlin'!

("Gents in!")

5. Gents to the center, all the way in,
   gents to the center and—back again!
   Back again, skip to my Lou!
   Skip to my Lou, my darlin'!

Alternative verse 5:

Gents to the center with a rebel yell,
gents to the center and *(Yell!)*.
Back again, skip to my Lou!
Skip to my Lou, my darlin'!

("Swing your partner!")

To get the best fun swinging, try this:

1. Join hands straight across (R in L & L in R), and ; . .
2. keeping a little to the side of your partner, each of you facing (clockwise) in opposite directions, and . . .
3. pulling apart, through the shoulders, balance your weight against your partner's, and . . .
4. keeping this balance, with arms springy (not limp—not stiff) and elbows bent about 90° ("Show your muscles!") . . . then
5. just *go!*—with a lively lilting walking step.

(Younger couples may, if they wish, swing with a skipping step.)

6. Swing your partner 'round and 'round . . .
   Skip to my Lou, my darlin'!

("Promenade!")

197

In promenading, near hands may be joined (woman's L in man's R), or hands joined across (R in R & L in L); or, the man may put his R arm around his partner's waist holding her L hand in his L or with her L hand holding on to the man's R shoulder. (The women are on the outside.)

7. March around two by two . . .
   Skip to my Lou, my darlin'!

("Ladies turn back!")

The men, releasing their partners, keep on circling around counterclockwise inside the set, and here the extra men get in with the other men. The women, turning out to their right, go back the other way, clockwise, around the outside of the set.

8. Lost my partner! What'll I do? . . .
   Skip to my Lou, my darlin'!

("Grab, boys! Grab!")

Every man takes, quick, the *nearest* woman, and gets set in promenade position. In a large set, the women whom the men have not, as yet, spotted, should move into the center of the set so the men can find them. There will be a lot of dashing about through the center of the set until the men—all but one! (or however many extra men there are)—have found new partners.

9. Get me another one, pretty one too! . . .
   Skip to my Lou, my darlin'!

(Promenade!")

Skipping step is all right if the set is *all* younger dancers. Otherwise, sing "March around two by two . . . ," and walk instead.

10. Skip, skip, skip to my Lou! . . .
    Skip to my Lou, my darlin'!

Slow up at the end of this verse, and get ready to start over. Stop and catch your breath, until your caller says, again— *"Circle left!"*

For groups about 13 years old and younger, the "—to the center" verses (3, 4, and 5) can be omitted.

This dance can also be done to any good square dance music (recorded or live) by using just the Calls given above. It is fun to call, *"Grab, boys! Grab!"* in the *middle* of verse 4 (or in verse 5, when the extras are women), particularly when there is a bashful boy (or girl) in the center who failed to grab a partner on the round before.

The Tennessee Wagon Wheel

This is a combination of square dance figures, based on a version done at Berea College, Kentucky.

Any good square dance tune will do for this dance. (See "Skip to My Lou.") *Note*: Nearly all country dance tunes have two parts, and each part has 16 beats. In this dance the "Calls" should be given in time to start each successive figure on the first beat of each part of the tune. Most of the movements take the full 16 beats without any change of direction. A few are divided into 2 movements of 8 beats each (8 + 8). Each figure as numbered below requires one phrase of the music: the full 16 beats.

Formation: a single-ring for any number of couples. Country dance walking step throughout.

I.

CALLS:	FIGURES:
Circle left!	1. Do it. (16)
Circle right!	2. Do that. (16)
Swing your partner!	3. Swing each other clockwise. Hands joined straight. (See "Skip to My Lou.") Keep swinging the full phrase (16 beats).
Promenade!	4. (See "Skip to My Lou.") Use the full phrase. (16) Keep evenly spaced and out from the center so you can make a neat ring again for the next figure.
All to the center!	5. (See "Skip to My Lou.") Sometimes we give a yell as we reach the center, on the 7th beat. (8) Move the ring back to places. (8)
Back again! Ladies to the center!	6. The women move in, not too fast. (8) The men be ready to move in as soon as the women start back.

199

Ladies back, *and gents* *to the center . . .* *with a* *Right Hand Wheel!*	The men go in, while the women back up to their places. (8) Men stay in the center for the next figure.
	7. The men circle left, on the inside, making a right hand "chain gang" —*i.e.* a Right Hand Wheel, moving clockwise. Take the right shoulder of the man ahead of you with your right hand. (16)
Back the other *way with a* *Left Hand Wheel!*	8. Each man turns in, a half-turn clockwise, and takes the left shoulder of the man now ahead of him, and the Wheel circles counterclockwise. (16) Keep hold of this Wheel for the next figure.
Pick up your *partners!*	9. Ladies lay their left hands in their partners right hands, and go with the Wheel as it continues to move. (16)
Swing your *partner!*	10. Keep your feet under you! Don't swing too fast! (16)
Promenade!	11. As before. This figure and the next do not require any fixed number of beats.
	12. The Tunnel. (Keep on promenading.)

Raise the tunnel! Leading couple through, and everybody follow!

Each couple (man holding his partner's L hand and his R) raises an arch, and all keep moving as the couples start coming through the Tunnel. One couple—the leader of this dance and his partner—ducks back and starts through the Tunnel. Just swap hands with your partner (her R hand now in your L). All follow these leaders. On reaching the other end of the tunnel, swap hands again (woman's L in man's R), and carry your arch over the heads of the couples coming through. All follow. Leading couple now promenade. All follow. Leading couple should hold back a bit, *i.e.* not promenade too fast, but watch the last couples coming through the tunnel, and close the promenade ring just as the last couple comes through. This completes the first half of The Tennessee Wagon Wheel.

II.

The second part is the same as before for figures 1, 2, 3, 4, and 5. On 6, the men go to the center and the women move in as the men move back. On 7, the women, staying in the middle, make a Right Hand Wheel. 8. Left Hand Wheel, and the women *"Pick up your partners!"* Then, 9, women continue with the Wheel, taking the men with them (man's L hand in woman's R). 10. *"Swing your partner!"* 11. *"Promenade!"*

This dance may end with either of two figures: 12. The Basket: *"All to the center!"* (8) *"Ladies stay in, and the gents come back!"* (8)—*"Gents circle left! Ladies to the right!"* (16) *"Back the other way!"* (16)—*"Gents duck under and wheel the basket!"* The women, keeping their ring, raise arches, while the men, keeping their ring (and making sure that each man has his partner on his right) duck under. This forms the Basket. Keep all joined hands at waist level, and "wheel the basket" to the left. This has to be done with pivot step: double time—only the right foot now taking the beat of the music. Let the left foot stop short of the instep of the right foot. Propel the basket with the left foot, dropping down on the right. Thus: RIGHT, left, RIGHT, left, RIGHT, left, RIGHT—instead of RIGHT, LEFT, RIGHT, LEFT.

Finally every dancer in the Basket will fall into this rhythm and the whole set begin to move quite fast. Continue wheeling the Basket a reasonable length of time for the full enjoyment of this swift movement. Then, *"Swing your partners!*—and *Promenade off the floor!"*

Or this final figure may be done. (It does not require the pivot step.) 12. *"Circle right!*—*Wind up the first man!"* The leading man lets go of the hand of the woman on his left, and, while the rest of the ring continues to circle right, he, holding his partner's hand and the rest of the ring still holding fast, moves toward the center of the room where he stands still. Then his partner stops. The next couple stops. And so forth. Each couple stops in its turn, until the last couple has come to a halt. Each dancer must watch his turn to stop moving, and must stop without letting his arms get too stretched out. There should be at least a two-foot space between the coils of the spiral. The figure ends in the shape of a watch spring. Now the first man works his way straight out from the center toward where the last couple are standing, a path being made for him by arches raised, and passing under the arch made by the last couple, the first man moves clockwise around the outside of the set, drawing all the other dancers with him. All will soon be circling left. Then, *"Wind up the last lady!"* All keep circling left, while the woman on the first man's left lets go his hand and moves to the center. All, keeping hands still joined, now wind up around this dancer. All stop in turn as before, and the last lady "threads the needle" out, as did the first man, passing under an arch made by the first couple. She now leads the dancers around the outside in a counterclockwise direction until all are again in a single circle moving right. *"Swing your partners, and promenade off the floor!"*

Molly Brooks

The figures for this dance came through Miss Annie Ball and Mrs. John Hunter, of Richmond, Virginia. There is some indication, through the family traditions that preserved this country dance, that it may have been known to George Washington and Thomas Jefferson. The tune came from Uncle Jim Chisholm of Albemarle County, Virginia. At certain country dance parties I have had many Virginians, especially the older ones, ask me, "Can you show us how to do 'Molly Brooks'?" It has been a very popular number wherever I have led it. Actually, this version is a restoration, as well as it could be figured from the information received. It may have been a four-couple square. At any rate, as given here "it works." It may be that some of our readers can give us better instructions for the "old way" these figures were run. See "Amateur Collector's Guide."

Formation: a ring of 8 couples. (Can be done with 10 couples. With 12 couples it might be better to form two 6-couple sets.)

Step: a quiet brisk walk throughout—almost a strut. It is a quiet dance, but lively—even in the "Honors" done to the B part of the tune.

Before starting the dance the leader numbers the couples by Ones and Twos.

Figures: Each figure is timed exactly to its phrase of the tune. Part A is 16 beats and its movements are divided into 8 + 8 or 4 × 4. The number of beats required for every figure is given in parentheses. Parts B and C have 8 beats each.

MUSIC: FIGURES:

A. (16) All join hands in the big single-ring and move forward 3 steps (4), bringing feet together on the 4th beat, and back (4), and do that again (4 + 4). Keep a good lilting lift throughout. There is no stopping on the 3rd step; keep taking one step after another—R L R L: R L R L: R L R L: R L R L—balancing your body on each 4th beat enough to change direction forward or back.

B. (8)   Honor partners (4). Honor corners (4).—Your corner is the woman on your left.—The Honor is a slight bow on the part of the man. The woman curtsies. It is best not to exaggerate these Honors. Just "recognize" each other with a grin.

C. (8)   All the Number One couples, with near hands joined, move out and face the next couple (No. 2 couples) on their right. (8).

A.   Any four-handed country dance figure that can be phrased to fit this part of the tune may be done here. (16 beats: 8 + 8 or 4 × 4.)—See below.

B.   "Oh the ladies cross over and bow!" The two women change places, passing right shoulder to right shoulder (4). The two men change places, passing left shoulders (4). This is a swift movement ending with a quiet Honor to the person with whom one changes places. It is not necessary to take any specific number of steps to do this. "Zip" across, get poised, and then "honor," on the third beat.

C.   Join hands in a ring of four, and circle left; and as the No. 1 couples come around, they release the couple with whom they have just done the figure and move quickly on to face the next No. 2 couple (8).

A.B.C.   Repeat these figures with each couple in turn all
          around the ring, until the No. 1 couples are about to
          reach their home places again; then . . . (*on* C.)

C.   . . . the No. 1 couples finish their last circling-left
          by taking their places again in the big ring (8). This
          time, in the "circle four," the No. 1 man keeps hold
          of the No. 2 woman's hand while his partner (the
          No. 1 woman) releases the No. 2 man's hand. This
          helps each dancer to regain his place in the big ring.

NOTE: This dance now *ends on part* A of the tune.

A. (Last time)   The ring moves forward to the center (4)
          and back (4), and do that again (4 + 4). Retard the
          last two notes of the tune, and all honor partners.

Repeat the whole dance with the No. 2 couples leading out
with the same four-handed figure, or with a different one.

FOUR-HANDED FIGURES

Hands Across (or "Right Hand Star and Left Hand Back").

A. The two men join right hands, the two women join right
   hands, and this "Star" wheels clockwise (8); change to
   left hands across and wheel back counterclockwise
   to places (8). Change hands on beats 7-8. Release hands,
   on 7-8, when coming back to places.

Arches Over (or "Duck and Dive").

A. The leading couple (inside the set) raises an arch and
   goes over the standing couple (facing the center) who
   move forward to go under (4), all turning in toward
   partners and changing hands to go back. Leading couples,
   now on the outside, go back under an arch made by the
   other couples, and all return to places (4). And do that
   again (4 + 4). The arch goes over four times, twice for
   each couple. The arch goes *over* from the *inside*. Each
   change takes 4 beats, but it is best to move under, or over,
   in *two* swift steps, changing hands and getting poised to
   return on beats 3 and 4. Another way of getting ready to
   go back, over or under, is for each couple to keep hold
   of hands— woman's L in man's R—and the man, as they
   cross, move backward helping the woman into place on
   his right each time as they face the other couple.

Other four-handed figures, well-known in the recent revival
of "square dancing" throughout England and America, that
will work well in this country dance are: "Right and Left
Through," "Two Ladies Chain," "Lady 'Round the Lady and

the Gent also! Lady 'Round the Gent and the Gent don't go!"
"Figure Eight"—or make up your own figure! (But be sure
it times out a full 16 beats: $8 + 8$ or 4×4.)

This is a quiet dance. However its movements are all quite
lively, even in the "Honors." But skipping would be entirely
out of place anywhere in this country dance.

The tune for "Molly Brooks" is an interesting and beautiful variant of "The Bear Went Over the Mountain." See also
"Jesus Preached in Galilee," where this dance tune is used
for a hymn (!).

There is a French folk song with practically the same tune:

> *Malbrough s'en va-t-en guerre,*
> *Mironton, ton, ton, mirotaine!*
> *Malbrough s'en va-t-en guerre.*
> *Ne sait quand reviendra.*
> *Ne sait quand reviendra!*
> *Ne sait quand reviendra!*
> *Malbrough s'en va-t-en guerre.*
> *Ne sait quand reviendra.*

There are various theories about the age and origin of this
melody. One record says the song, as given above, was com-
posed "after the battle of Malplaquet in 1710, on an air going
back to the Middle Ages." Another report: "This tune was
once known throughout the world, from Paris to Constanti-
nople," and that it existed "for six hundred years among the
Arabs." And I have heard that it was the marching song for
one of the Crusades.

Malbrough, The Duke of Marlborough, in American folk
tradition became "Molly Brooks"! In Virginia I have heard
these verses sung to the tune:

> Molly Brooks has gone to the war,
> and I fear she'll never return.
> Molly Brooks come out of my orchard,
> and leave my apples alone.
> Molly Brooks come out of the water,
> till you learn how to swim.

And there is a playparty game, same tune, with these verses:

> Oh my mother and father were Irish,
> and I am Irish too.
> Oh we bought a peck of potatoes,
> and they were Irish too.
> Oh we kept a pig in the parlor,
> for it was Irish too.

4. Fiddle Tunes

The notations for these country dance tunes are printed in facsimile from John Powell's hand. All but the last have been used in orchestral works by Mr. Powell.

I Love Somebody, Yes I Do!

(DO SCALE)

Another title is "My Love Is But a Lassie Yet." This is from John Powell's own memory. A Scottish version of the air was set for orchestra by Beethoven. Mr. Powell used it in his Overture, *In Old Virginia*. It is the tune for a country dance, "The Cumberland Square Eight," currently popular in England and America.

Give the Fiddler a Dram

(SOL SCALE)

This was taken down from C. B. Wohlford, a banjo player who lived in Marion, Virginia. John Powell's *Symphony in A* starts with this tune.

Old Salt River

(RE SCALE)

This came from Hezikiah Pigge of Pittsylvania County, Virginia. It is used in the first movement of *Symphony in A.*

Natchez on the Hill

This was set down from Mrs. John Hunter of Richmond, Virginia, who was one of the first in that state to write down these
old tunes "for posterity." Mr. Powell used this one in an orchestral suite named *Natchez on the Hill*. Kindred tunes are "Turkey
in the Straw" and "Old Zip Coon." Another variant is the English
Morris dance tune "Old Mother Oxford."

5. Odds and Ends

Here are miscellaneous traditions which are hard to classify. "A Field Trip" gathers some of them into one piece. "How to Plant Crops" is given from print. "Old Brindle" is what our mountain people call "a crazy speech." "Love Verses" have no tunes, and therefore cannot be placed with "Songs." "Deaths on Three-Mile Creek" is strictly speaking not folklore, but is given here on account of its pioneer flavor and color and its human interest. Four "Jokes" are included for good measure.

The Bedtime Prayer

This is based on a version appearing in *English Folk Songs for Schools* by Cecil Sharp and Baring-Gould, with a tune in the *mi* scale. We print this without any music, hoping that some of our readers can send in a good American tune for these verses. (See "Amateur Collector's Guide.") In Vermont this song is known as "The White Paternoster," as reported by Helen Hartness Flanders and Marguerite Olney.

1. Matthew, Mark, and Luke, and John
    bless the bed that I lie on.
    Four corners to my bed,
    four angels there be spread.
    One to watch and one to pray,
    two to guard my soul alway.

2. God is the branch and I the flower.
    Pray God send me a bless-ed hour.
    Now I lay me down to sleep
    I give the Lord my soul to keep,
    and in the morning when I wake
    the Lord's path I shall surely take.

209

A Field Trip

The red bud is out. Patches of its reddish purple show warmly through bareness of woodland as we drive. A thin yellow spring mist tints the tops of early-leafing trees. Dogwood will not bloom for several weeks yet, but the white mass of a Sarvice Bush stands out here and there as we go deeper into the forest.

Today, Tom Hunt and Jeems Turner and I hope to set down at least one good tale from Old Robin Weaver. We had not said much since we entered the thick woods, for we had all three been looking for signs of spring. Then Jeems spoke up.

TURNER: My wife set an old hen on Easter Sunday. She says the little diddles will be all colors if you do that.—I reckon they'll hatch that way all right; our chickens are a mixed bunch.

HUNT: Did she plant her pepper on Good Friday?

TURNER: Yes, and beans too. We always plant our beans on a Good Friday, before sun-up. You know it's said you ought to plant pepper when you're mad about something. Makes 'em stronger. Callie believes that, and I tried to get her mad when she was fixin' to put in her pepper seed; but it didn't work. She got to laughin' at me instead.—I don't like my pepper too hot anyhow.

CHASE: When do you plant corn?

HUNT: We always plant our corn when oak leaves are as big as squirrels' ears, or when whip-poor-wills commenced to holler. There's the Signs, too. Plant corn when the moon's in The Crab (that's the sign of The Breast) and the grains will fill over the end of the cob. Plant it in the sign of The Twins and you'll have two ears to every stalk. The sign of The Thighs— What's the other name for that?—The Archer, that's hit, if I recollect right—that'll make big ears. Plant potatoes in the sign of The Feet you'll get nothing but little pindly toe-'taters.

TURNER: Light of the moon for crops above the ground. Dark of the moon for root crops.

HUNT: Nothin' to it, some say; but we've always done it, planted by the signs, and it generally does seem to make a difference.——By the way now, all this red bud bein' out reminds me of somethin' I remember my father tellin'. Judas Tree, that's another name for red bud. It's said hit used to grow big as a maple or an oak. But that was the tree Judas hanged himself on, and it's been stunted ever since. Looks like clotted blood on the limbs, too, all them little red blooms.

We turned off the main road when we sighted our landmark —a mailbox made of an old square oil tin. We had some doubts about the rocky brushy trail into which we had turned, until we saw automobile tracks ahead. We wound on through laurel bushes, bumped over a small creek, and finally twisted our way up into the green wide yard of Robin Weaver's house.

It was a neat frame dwelling painted white and green— everything about it fresh and well-kept for all its remoteness. Two Irish junipers stood, like sentinels, on either side of the door. Robin Weaver's father, Old Robin, will, we hope, be here and not be "feelin' puny" today.

Mrs. Weaver comes to the door. She is a slender woman with a quick smile. She wears glasses and has on a neat cotton-print dress.

"Well, Tom Hunt! What in the world are you doin' away back here on the ridge? Glad to see you. Come in! Come in!"

We enter a neatly furnished parlor complete with rug, easy chair, sofa, bookshelves, bright curtains, house plants. Everything indicates care and good taste. Turner and I are made known to the woman of the house; and while I glance around wonderingly at the order and beauty of this place, "away back on the ridge," I hear Tom stating our mission and asking about Old Rob's health.

"Oh he's feeling just fine today. He's in the next room yonder. We could fix a fire in here but if you don't mind we can all sit and talk with father in there where there's a good fire already lit."

We go into the other room, and there on the edge of a bed sits a merry-looking old man. Grey beard and grey hair well-trimmed, a pleasant ruddy face and eyes that have a quick look of mischief. He does not rise as we are introduced. His handclasp is a little shaky but his voice is a hearty one.

"Pleased to meet ye! Pleased to meet ye! What in the nation are you fellers after 'way out here in the woods? Eh?"

"They came to see you, father."

"Me? Well look at me all you want, boys. I ain't much to look at now, but when I was a young feller I had sweethearts up every creek and holler from here to Clinch River."

This was followed by a bouncing burst of laughter that squeaked the bed springs.

"Why I thought you'd come to look at them dolls—like so many do. It's a sight in the world what my girl here started when she commenced makin' them things. You'd never guess what she makes 'em out of, either."

211

"Dolls?"

"Dolls, poppets, play-pretties! She sends 'em all over the country. Even sent one to that girl in England. And we got a letter from her. Go get it, honey. I know these boys would like to see that."

Protesting a little, Mrs. Weaver went to the mantlepiece and took down a small envelope. It bore a London cancellation and inside was this simple note:

The lady-in-waiting to her royal highness
The Princess Elizabeth
is commanded to thank Mrs. Robin Weaver, Jr.,
for the beautiful gift of dolls made from maize husks.
Buckingham Palace
June 7, 1940

We clamored then to see "them dolls." Mrs. Weaver brought out a large carton and set it on the floor beside her chair. She took out a tiny figure of Bo-Beep, the little shepherdess complete with dainty red slippers, petticoat, apron with a big bow in the back, puffed sleeves, bonnet, and crook—all beautifully colored and made entirely of cornshucks. She stood Bo-Peep on a small table by the hearth and set a cornshuck sheep beside it. Next came Little Jack Horner sitting with a pie in his lap and a purple plum held proudly on his thumb. Then Tom, Tom, the Piper's Son with the pig under his arm and his legs stretched in flight. Robin Hood appeared gripping his long-bow and clad in a bright green jerkin, a jaunty red feather in his cap. There were three musicians with fiddle, banjo, and guitar; and a four-couple set of country dancers to go with them. Then she set out a drove of little horses with manes and tails made of cornsilk. Each horse had his own color, was neatly saddled and bridled, and in each saddle sat a fiercely cornsilk-bewhiskered rider wearing blue overalls and a black hat.

"These are a special order."

"How do you market them?" I asked.

"The Episcopal Church has a Handcraft Guild in this county. We sell a lot of things folks make in here: woven coverlets and quilts, and things the men whittle—dogs and rabbits and squirrels and bears."

"The church had a show of all that stuff over in Coalwood some years back," Tom said. "One feller had made a sign out of a piece of white poplar. Carved it out where the letters went and filled 'em in with black walnut. The sign said

212

It's a lot better to be whittlin' something
than just to be a-whittlin' whittlin's.

"Hunph! That's right too now!" shouted Old Rob.

"One of the men happened to say that to Miss Martin one
day—that's the lady who helps with the Guild—and it's been
one of our mottos ever since."

"Those horses are sure pretty," said Tom. "They look like
they are about to run off."

She gave us leave to pick up the figures and look at them
more closely. For all the commonness of the materials no de-
tail is left out, and every piece has a spirited liveliness about it.
Bo-Peep's petticoat has a lace-like fringe. The pig under The
Piper's Son's arm is squealing loudly. The little horses toss
their heads proudly and really do seem to be wanting to gal-
lop away.

"I make the Christmas scene too. Lots of people want them.
I have to make Joseph and Mary and the Child in the manger,
three wise men and a camel, three shepherds—two old ones
and a young one—three sheep, and a horse and a cow. The
church sure keeps me busy on all that. I have to get started
in August."

"Did you ever hear about that Episcopalian feller here years
ago?" boomed forth Old Rob. "That was when they had the
first mission worker in here. Wasn't many had joined the
church back then. This feller, he was one; and he came up
here surveyin' or somethin'. Anyhow, he got lost back on
Splashdam somewhere, and fin'lly got to a house. Had to ask
how to find his way back to the public road. Well, there wasn't
nobody home but the old woman. She told him how to find
his way out again, and he got to talkin' to her, happened to
ask her, says, 'Do you know, ma'm, if there's any Episco-
palians in this part of the country?'

"She told him, says, 'Well I don't know rightly about that
now, but my old man's a powerful hunter and out there behind the barn he keeps a lot of skins nailed up. You can just
go out there and look if you've a mind to.' "

Again that hearty laughter which this time nearly bounced
the old man off the edge of the bed. We had nearly forgotten
what we'd come for, with our sudden interest in dolls.

TURNER: You remember how they used to sit around the fire
of a winter night and tell old tales, back when you were a boy?
We thought you might recollect a tale for us.—I reckon you
know a tale or two like that, don't ye?

213

ROB: Humpf! I've done forgot more than most men ever knowed. Sure, I can recollect such as that: get too cold to work, gather at somebody's house, tell tales, make music. We had no books much, no novels, no kind of shows in here in them days. But when a crowd would gather like that they'd be likely to sit up all night a-tellin' big lies, or them great long old grandfather tales about Jack and Will and Tom. The biggest 'uns was about when somebody-or-other went out huntin' with his old hog-rifle. Old man Bollingbroke'd tell it like it really happened to him: Honey River and that fritter tree, bendin' his rifle to shoot around a hill, roasted pigs runnin' around with knives and forks stuck in their backs a-squealin' "Who'll eat me? Who'll eat me?" You never heard the like!

CHASE: Have you always lived here in Crockett County?

ROB: Made one trip—out West. Thought I'd make it a big 'un while I was at it. Went clean to Californy and viewed the Pacific Ocean. Comin' back I took me a look at that place out there—What do they call it?—the Grand Canyon. Right smart of a gully.

CHASE: Your people, 'way back, they all from this part of the mountains?

ROB: Some of my people came down here from the Valley of Virginia. Germans. Yes, we're Germans. This nation was settled by all nationalities, not just the Scotch-Irish. Germans are good people now, but their rulers ain't. They're the wittiest people in the world, and the prettiest people in the world —and I take after 'em!

And Old Robin told us "grandfather tales" until long after dark had fallen.

How to Plant Crops

Fertility rites, and their connection with worship of the Great Earth-Mother, Ishtar, brought down the wrath of Yahweh and Moses, on the Children of Israel. And after three thousand years or more one would think that such practices had been completely obliterated. But Vance Randolph has recently written an article [1] on relics of these customs as known to exist in twentieth century America. Mr. Randolph reports one old man as saying, with a grin, "Yes, I've heard of such doings. It's

[1] "Nakedness in Ozark Folk Belief," *Journal of American Folklore*, Vol. 66, No. 262, October-December, 1953.

supposed to make the corn grow tall." Other excerpts from the articles: "—that certain crops grew better if the persons who sowed the seed were naked. . . . Four grown girls and one boy did the planting. They all stripped off naked. The boy started in the middle of the patch with them four big girls a-prancin' around him. . . . The boy throwed all the seed, and the girls kept a-hollerin' 'Pxxxer deep! Pxxxer deer!' . . . There ain't no sense to it, but them folks always raised the best turnips on the creek. . . . Soon as they got their bread planted, [he] would take his wife out to the patch at midnight. —Take off every stitch of clothes and run around the crop three times. And then he would throw her right down in the dirt and have at it. . . . Wash off in the creek and go on back home."

This procedure was said to protect the corn against damage from frost, drought, crows, and cutworms.

And here are excerpts from an account [2] of this rite in prehistoric times and amongst primitive peoples: "When sex was understood to cause birth, a new magic had to be added. . . . Mating was needed as a spell, a ritual to bring increase to people and . . . crops. . . . At the beginning of history, gods and goddesses must marry, and around these marriages grew such custom as the orgies of Saturnalia. To make the fields produce, use human methods. For centuries, the Egyptians reiterated the marriage of Isis and Osiris. . . . In India, the gods still have lawful wives, and in some simple villages there the priest and priestess act as divinities, offering their intercourse for blessing of the crops. . . . In some parts of Java a farmer and his wife would mate in the fields by night."

[2] *The Wisdom Tree*, Emma Hawkridge. Boston: Houghton Mifflin Co., 1945. *See also, The Golden Bough* (Abridged), Sir James George Frazer. New York: The Macmillan Co., 1944. Chapter XI, p. 135 ff.

Old Brindle

This is one of the "crazy speeches" and exists in many forms. It is the essence of the Doctor's speech in nearly all Mummers' Plays, and is like the verse in "Oh Suzanna!": "It rained all night the day I left, the weather it was dry," etc. See also "The Skoonkin Huntin' " in *Grandfather Tales,* and "Sir Gammer Vans" in Joseph Jacobs' *More English Fairy Tales.* This version shows traces of "wild bull rides" described by Mark Twain, George Washington Harris ("Sut Lovingood's Yarns," (1867) and "Scroggins" who had it as "Deacon Smith's Bull, or Mike Fink in a Tight Place." (1851)[8] Mark Twain used the tale in *Joan of Arc.* When recited, or read, it should be rattled off with no pauses and with complete deadpan. I learned about Old Brindle near Luray, Virginia.

I pulled off my old red huntin' shirt and was a-bathin' my back in moonshine when Old Brindle passed me by. He pawed and scraped like he was goin' to dig my grave. I told him, "Old Brindle, as you go back by here I'll go for ye." As he went back so I went for him. Took him by the tail and we whipped 'way out yonder on dry land in Mike Harmon's Bottom and I wropped his tail around a white oak stump. I said, "Old Brindle, you got to stand or pull this stump out by the roots of your tail." I looked him in the eye and I knowed he was goin' to stand. But here come the dogs and I knowed what they'd do: join up with Old Brindle and dog-gone near kill me or quite. So I said, "Old Brindle, let's be partners. I'll jump on your back and we'll leave here." So I hopped on his back and away we went flippity-flop, and there we met a great big tall

[8] D. M. McKeithan, *Southern Folklore Quarterly,* Vol. XVII, No. 4, December 1953.

rawboned bandyshanked man about the size of a boy, had on a chestnut colored blue overcoat wove dimity fashion, brand new hat without rim, brim, nor band with a buckle, new rifle over his shoulder without lock, stock, nor barrel with a loop. Hit was Old Lawson's hoss-doctor, three meals a day and supper till midnight. So we threw the old sow at a little hungry boy had brought a custard pie for a levee and throwed it back through a brick wall nine foot thick, and had to jump over. Broke his right ankle just above the knee, and the old cat had nine turkey gobblers while a high wind blew "Yankee Doodle" in the frying-pan. So we went on down to Johnny Whimpler's mill, told him to grind me nine yards of steel fine as sawdust and the best cornmeal. Said he wouldn't and I thought he couldn't, so I kicked him through the barrel, broke his devilish neck and that ended all the dispute. Got down to Jeems Wilson's Salt Works beterminate to fight bears and wildcats right on down to rattlesnakes and the little toenails off big bears, up the right-hand holler off the left side of Goosebristle Creek hot enough to melt pure pine lumps. So the next thing I knowed Old Brindle humped himself and throwed me up in the high forks of a huckleberry tree where there was a hornet nest and a peck-and-a-half of stingin' worms. Some stung me, some stung the dogs, and some stung Old Brindle. So I hugged Old Brindle's neck and he hugged mine. So Old Brindle and the dogs and me, we limped on back to the house, and there the old woman stood wide open with the door in the bed. I said, "Old Brindle, what's the reward?" Old Brindle he stopped and thought, looked at me, says,

> Little boy, come home with me,
> and I'll treat you to
> a pint of pigeon's milk
> strained through a side of sole leather,
> churned in an old sow's horn,
> and stirred with a green cat's feather.

Love Verses

These rhymes which were collected in southwestern Virginia by Emory Hamilton of Wise, Virginia, are often written in autograph books and in love letters. There is a large collection of this sort of verse: *Yours Till Niagara Falls*[4], collected by Lillian Morrison.

217

Ducks in the millpond,
geese in the pasture;
if you want to marry,
you'll have to talk faster.

I love you little, I love you lots.
My love for you would fill all the pots,
buckets, pitchers, kettles, and cans,
the big wash-tub, and both dishpans.

(—or: piggins, keelers, kettles, and cans,
a four-foot tub, and ten dishpans.—

A *piggin* is a small old-time bucket with one stave sticking up with a hole in it for a handle. A *keeler* is a wooden
skimmer. "While greasy Joan doth keel the pot.")

Green grows the willow,
it has a yellow bark;
if you want to marry,
now's the time to spark.

If all this world were a sheet of paper,
and the sea an ink of blue,
and the trees on the hills were eagle quills,
it couldn't write all my love to you.

(There is an English rhyme, and country dance tune, that
runs thus:

If all the world were paper,
and all the seas were ink,
and all the trees were bread and cheese,
what would we have to drink?
If all the bottles leak-ed,
and none but had a crack,
and Spanish apes ate all the grapes,
what would we do for sack?[5])

The old sow whistles,
and the little pigs dance;
all the girls are marrying
but I can't get a chance.

[4] Published by Thomas Y. Crowell Co., New York, 1950.
[5] "Sack"—*Wyne seck, vin sec,* dry wine.

Kiss me now,
kiss me cunning,
kiss me quick,
mama's coming.

The road is long that has no crook;
I hope someday you'll be my cook.

You are the honey,
I am the comb;
I wish we were married
and in our own home.

Limestone water and cedar wood;[6]
a kiss from you is twice as good.

If a woman's eyes are gray,
listen to what she's got to say.
If a woman's eyes are black,
give her room and clear the track.
If a woman's eyes are brown,
never let your own fall down.
If a woman's eyes are green,
whip her with a switch that's keen.
If a woman's eyes are blue,
take her, she's the one that's true.

[6] Clear cool water, pure and with no taste of sulphur as in some wells in southwest Virginia; and kept in a cedar bucket.

Deaths on Three-Mile Creek: 1841 to 1915

These items were given us by Mrs. Sloop of Crossnore, North Carolina. Obituaries are, of course, not strictly folklore, but they are so full of pioneer color and human interest that I include them here. They were written down by Uncle Jake Carpenter of Three-Mile Creek, Avery County, in the mountains of western North Carolina. I copied them from an old typewritten copy of Uncle Jake's notes, and added only enough letters to make his curious spellings more quickly readable. Uncle Jake's records were read to "Aunt Naomi" once, and her comments were added. Here then is a *Spoon River Anthology* of Three-Mile Creek.

Wm Davis   age 100.8   dide oc 5   1841
    wars old soldier in rev w[a]re   and got his
      thie brok in last fite at Kinge['s] monte
      he wars farmer   and made brandy
      and never had Drunker[d] in famly

Franky Davis his wife   age 87   dide Sep 10   1842
    she had nirve fite wolves all nite at shogar camp[7]
      to save her caff   throde fier chonks
      the camp wars half mile from home
      noe she must have nirv to fite wolf all nite

[7] "shogar camp"—sugar camp, *i.e.*, where maple sap was boiled down to sugar.

Charley Kiney   age 72   dide may 10   1852
wars farmer live in mt on bluey rige at kiney gap
he had 4 wim[min] cors ["of course"] marid to one
                    res[t] live on farme
all went to felde   work to mak gra[i]n
    all wen to crib for ther br[ea]d
    all went smok ho[u]s for there mete
he cilde⁸ bote 75 to 80 hoges eve[ry] yere
and wimen never had worde[s] bout him
              haven so many wimin
    [if] he wod be [living] this times
              wod be hare pulde
    thar wars 42 children blong to him
    th[ey] all wento preching togethern
noth[ing] sed   des aver bod[y] go long smooth
              help one nother
              never had any foes
    got along smooth with avery bodi
              I nod him

JACOB CARPENTER

Joseph Carpenter   ag 18   did aug 18   1862
    he fot for his contery   los his lif.

Sooney Ollis   ag 84   did march 15   1871
    grates Deer honter   & turkies
bee tree[s] by honder[d]s   and ratel snak by 100
        cild deer by thousan
              I no him well

Pegey Wise   age 75   dide oc 15   1864
    she was granny womin⁹ for contery

Aunt Naomi explained that Peggy Wise was Nute Wise's
mother. She said: "I remember when there was a big dam
above Linville Falls. Was for a forge to make iron. They had
a big forge hammer so heavy that very few men could lift it.
Such men as Tom and Nute could, but common men
couldn't."

⁸ The letter "C" for the sound "K" was also used by D. Boone who "cild
a bar—"
⁹ "Granny-woman"—midwife.

Henery Barer   ag 78   dide march 15   1871
     wars fine honter   cil bare by 100

Aunt Naomi: "He often went out before breakfast and killed deer."

Margit Carpenter   age 87   dide Jun 5   1875
    wars good womin for pore [to help the poor—?]
    She did not have no bed to slep on when she marid
        she slep on deer skin til marid
        but that lo[o]k lik hard times
   when she had to li on derskins when she was mared

Wm Carpenter   ag 70   dide nov 15   1881
         wars fine honter
   cil bare and wolves by 100 der by 100

Aunt Naomi: "He was an awful sorry [worthless] man."

Kim Kone   ag 73   dide oc 15   1888
        wars black smith
   he had 6 girles that cod work in shop
      tha[y] wars 6 feet hy

David Frank   age 72   dide Dec 22   1891
        wars fine man
    mad[e] some brandy wars good

Samel Hoskin   ag 70   dide may 5   1896
     wars farmer   and grate lier

Aunt Naomi: "Pretty braggy old fellow. Not much at him."[10]

Los Frank   ag 72   July 8   1899
      wars fine man
    he sed wot he thot

Aunt Naomi: "Cuss you all to pieces, if he liked you."

Homer Hines   age 28
shot himself cos of bad wimen and whisky
trete his wife me[a]n as dozn[11]

[10] i.e., "Nothing much to him."
[11] "mean as the devil"? Or does this mean to treat one person mean enough to do for a dozen people at once?

Homer Withman   age 18   Dec 26   1914
    shote his self bout gal gon back on him

The age of this boy, and the date of his suicide, imply in so few words some tragedy that might make a wonderful story to tell.

For all the overwrought romanticizing that has grown up around the name of Jesse James, and for all the songs and the movies built on the famous gang, this is all that Uncle Jake put in his record:

Frank James   age 74   dide in Alabam Feb. 20   1915
    he wars grate bank rober him Jesy James and Bob Forde
    Bob Forde shot Jescy James for [re]warde of Thirty
                        Thosen Dolars
            in his ho[u]s wars fixing pick[t]er
            when shote him   for money
                he wars one of gang

Jokes

"Fat or Lean" was told to me in Wise County, Virginia.

One time there was an old man crippled up with rheumatism. Hadn't walked a step for twelve years. Most of the time he just sat on the front porch in a big chair full of quilts. They had to carry him in to put him to bed every night. He said he didn't reckon he ever would be able to walk again. Doctor said so too.

Well he was sittin' there one day all bent down in that chair and a young feller stopped and got to talkin' to the old man about a certain house in that section, house nobody had lived in for several years. The boy told how folks was sayin' it was han'ted—wouldn't nobody stay in it even one night.

"Ain't nothin' to it," says the old man. "Why, I'd stay all night, if I could get down there."

"Will you go there and stay with me?" that boy asked him. "I'll tote ye on my back."

The old man told him, sure he'd go if the boy 'uld get him there. So they made it up to go that very night.

Well, it happened there was two rogues had come into that

223

settlement that same day, and they'd laid 'em a plan to steal a sheep that night and cook it in that same old house. One of 'em said he'd steal the sheep and told the other one to steal some meal and salt, and said he'd meet him at that house. So that one he stole some meal and salt; went on down to the old house about dark and gathered enough wood to roast the sheep. Then he cloomb up in the loft and laid down. About half the boards were broke out and he got fixed up there where he could watch for the other rogue to come in the door.

That young feller come along carryin' the old man on his back. Went on in that house, and when the rogue up in the loft seen 'em he thought it was his buddy totin' the sheep, stuck his head down out the loft, says, "Is he fat?"

That boy throwed the old man on the floor, hollered, "Fat or lean, you can have him!"

Lit out down the road as hard as he could tear.

Slowed down a little when he got to the settle-ments, and there was that old crippled man sittin' on the front porch rockin', says, "What-in-the-nation took *you* so long to get away from there?"

Ah Lord, that old man never was bothered with rheumatism any more!

"Granny and the Matches" was told to me in Wise County, Virginia.

One time an old woman was just about to light her pipe. She was pokin' in the ashes for a hot coal. And right then one of her boys came in. He'd just come from the store and had bought some matches. They were the first matches ever sold in here: about four inches long with a big gob of stuff on the end. They called 'em Long Toms. Cost twelve for a penny.

"Here, granny! Let me light your pipe for ye."

So he struck one of his matches up under the fireplace. Held it down, and it smoked and fumed and dripped brimstone and finally flared and lit. He held it for Granny to light her pipe. The old lady opened her eyes sort of wide and puffed till her pipe was goin'. She thanked him. Didn't say nothin' much.

"Granny, I'm goin' to give you some of these. Here."

—And he handed her several.

Well, they ate supper directly and finally they were all sittin' around the fireplace again. Granny got out her pipe, cut some tobacco off her twist, crumbled it in her hand and got her pipe filled. Looked down at the ashes like she 'uld rather light up with a coal-of-fire. Then she stuck the little reed stem in her mouth, and made up her mind: reached in her apron pocket and pulled out one of them Long Toms.

She held it up and looked at it. There were several kids standin' around. Granny told 'em says, "Stand back out the way now, you young'uns. Granny's goin' to scratch the Hell Fire out of this here splinter."

I first heard "Did You Break My Pitcher?" from my grandmother, Mrs. Homer Nathaniel Chase of Buckfield, Maine. She says she learned it from a book of rhymes by Holman Day of Auburn, Maine, and that it was called "Aunt Shaw's Jug."

The old man wanted to go to the cellar after cider. His wife couldn't find a clean jug, so she let him have her best pitcher.

"You be careful now. Don't you dare let anything happen to my pitcher."

Some bottles had been left there at the head of the cellar stairs, and the old man happened to kick one. It rolled over and he stepped right on top of it.

Well he started down the stairs twistin' and turnin' and rollin' every which-a-way so's to keep that pitcher from gettin' broken. Hit the cellar floor with his elbows skinned and his back and his hips bruised and his head just about bashed in.

The old woman came runnin', poked her head around the door jam and hollered at him, says, "Did you break my pitcher?"

The old man looked up from where he sat, says, "No! But now—by—God—I—will!"

225

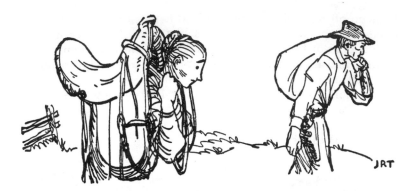

"That's Once" is from H. M. Sutherland of Clintwood, Dickenson County, Virginia.

There was a woman, one time, couldn't nobody get along with. Good worker, good cook and housekeeper and all, but she was so vigrous[12] nobody 'uld marry her.

One man, though, he decided he'd try it. So he went for her. She took him, and they got their license and went on to a preacher, and finally they started back.

Now this feller he'd gone to fetch her on a horse that was so old and worn-out he wasn't any good to anybody any more. They'd bought some rations and a little house plunder of one sort or another. Had all that tied on behind the saddle. The man got on and pulled his woman up behind him, and they put off.

The old horse stumbled directly—threw 'em. The woman she never said much. The man got the horse back on his feet, raised his head up by the bridle, says,

"That's once!"

Got back on, and on they went. The old pack-horse gave way again after a mile or so and they both landed on the ground— hard. The woman got up, brushed the dirt off her, and she didn't complain too much. That feller pulled on the reins, got the horse up again, says,

"That's twice!"

[12] vigrous: (vi-grus) severe, sharp-tongued. "Br'er B'ar say he's the strongest . . . Br'er Wolf say he's the most vigrous." Does this word have any connection with *virago*?

Well, the next time the old horse tripped and just sprawled. Turned that woman sort of upside down, but still she didn't make too much of a fuss over it. Then the man he jerked on the bridle till the horse scrambled up on his feet, looked right at him, says,

"Confound ye, that's three times!"

Pulled out his pistol and—BAM—shot the old no-'count horse right between the eyes. Time the horse fell that woman was so surprised she just stood there gapin'. But then she caught her breath and she started in——

"What did ye do that for? You must be crazy! Now we got to pack all that stuff ourselves! What did ye go and shoot him for that way? We could 'a-walked and let him tote all this stuff! And I'll tell ye right now I'm not goin' to pack one thing on *my* back! I'll say! Shoot him, will ye? It's mighty little sense you got."

On she went—her tongue rattlin' like a clatterbone. And the man he just stood there, and let her shake her finger in his face. Then when she'd give out of breath, he just looked at her straight, says—

"That's once."

—He put the rations and stuff in a poke he'd brought along, and—Ah, Lord!—he made her pack the saddle. She got to the house with the saddle on her back and the reins around her neck!

227

6. Amateur Collector's Guide

Every song, ballad, hymn, carol, tale, singing game, dance tune, set of dance figures, or even bit of dramatic dialogue that comes from unwritten, unpublished, word-of-mouth sources may contribute immeasurably to the future culture of our nation. It is conceivable that some readers of this book may have preserved in their own family, songs, tales, games or other traditions that have hitherto never been recorded, or important variants of those that are known. We urge our readers to share these traditions with others. It is hoped that this book may reawaken memories of half-forgotten songs or tales, and make more and more people aware of the importance of preserving these "old ways."

This section may help the amateur in finding English folk songs and tales in America. Many young people nowadays are keenly interested in our folklore. They sing folk songs; they do country dances, and some of them are going out amongst "the folk" to try to learn these traditions at first hand.

It should be easy, in these days of tape recorders, for young enthusiasts to do important work in locating true and culturally valuable folk traditions in many hitherto unexplored parts of the nation and these general principles of collecting apply to any other language-group or non-English tradition in the United States.

Remember that a good place to start is in your own region of your own state, your own town, city, or settlement—even in your own family. That strange old song even you yourself have "always known," because you heard your mother, grandfather, or great-aunt, sing it, may be the one "rare ballad" that folklorists thought was "lost" several generations ago!

If you visit any rural family (or even an urban family), or any individual, for the purpose of writing down, or mechanically recording, any sort of folk tradition, it is good to come to the point the moment you enter the house. After that don't try to rush things. Some people may respond at once. With others, it make take several visits before they feel enough

228

at home with you to open up. In any case, let a conversation flow naturally. This is often necessary because an informant may not immediately be able to sing for you, or share with you one of the old tales. He may need a period of warming up. At its best, this singing or tale-telling is always a *sharing with you,* not a "performance," and you must *never* applaud. Your own approach must be based on genuine feeling and appreciation and you must go equipped with some knowledge of the field. We "folk" are quick to sense any attitude of mere curiosity, or any feeling that an "outsider" is merely being amused by something "quaint."

It is best, usually, not to use the word "folk." We call these things the *old* songs, the *old* music, the *old* tales. Nor do we know the word "ballad." A "song-ballot" (or "ballett") means the *written-down text* of some old song—more often on sheets of paper pinned or sewed (or glued) together into a long ballot-like strip and kept in a box or tied in a roll and kept in a trunk or drawer. "Do you have any song-ballots?" is a good question to ask. Usually, among mountain families, there are only two kinds of music: sacred songs, and "love songs." The latter term can mean any song and every song that is *not* sacred. Often a "love song" will prove to be a genuine English ballad. Nor do we concern ourselves with the authentically traditional nature of what we sing. Frequently the collector has to listen to a lot of fairly recent songs: "Omie Wise," "Johnson's Old Gray Mule," "Floyd Collins," "The Preacher and the Bear," etc., before the real old songs will come out. If you are going to look for genuine traditions of "ancient Anglo-Saxon" origin you will need patience, and you will need to know what to keep asking for. This list is for lore in the English language. Collecting French-American, Spanish-American, or other such traditions is not in the scope of this guide.

When you do find any genuine item you probably will feel an extraordinary sense of excitement, a real tingling—even though the words may sound curiously incomplete or may seem difficult to grasp.

The genuine *ballad* is only one type of folk song. Your "ballad" is not a true *folk* ballad unless it is closely kin to one of the 305—no more, no less!—in Professor Child's great collection. Only about one third of the 305 have, so far, been recorded in America. The first volume of Mr. Sharp's *Appalachian* collection is all folk ballads. The second volume is all folk songs. Your nearest college or state library is likely to have these books.

This list of "finders" starts with the commonest traditions and goes on to important items less easy to discover. The list is based on one made by Fletcher Collins, Jr., of Staunton, Virginia, and his suggestions are:

Welcome any song which the singer offers in response to any of these finders. You may thus hear a fine song which is not on the partial list.

The catch-lines as given will not always be identical with the version known to the singer. Assure him that his version is the *right* one, for him and you. There is no *correct* or *standard* version of any traditional song. The freedom of such songs to change, evolve, develop, is the essence of their being.

The words of a traditional song are only half the task of recording, and only a third of the folk game (play part game). Be sure to record the music, and the dance-pattern (the dance figures) of the play party or singing game.

City people, if of a community settled by the English or Scotch, are as likely prospects as are country people.

Listed below are typical titles and typical lines for you to suggest to your informant, when you are helping him refresh his memory. Any one of these titles and lines may call forth a song or a tale that is associated with the title or line on your "finders" list that you suggest. But you may find that one title may bring to mind another that has no connection with the title you first suggest THREE LITTLE BABES, for example, might remind the person from whom you are "collecting" of THE GREEN WOOD SIDE, which is also known in some parts of the country as THE CRUEL MOTHER. The typical *titles* of songs and tales are printed here in capital letters; the typical *lines* are in quotation marks. Only contributions that have been handed down by *word-of-mouth* will be of interest.

All information received will be acknowledged gratefully. Furthermore, whatever is sent in will be passed on to The National Archive of Folklore in The Library of Congress. Certain items may be sent to *The Journal of American Folklore* for publication if the sender so consents.

Information may be sent to Richard Chase, % Dover Publications, Inc., 180 Varick Street, New York, N. Y. 10014.

I. Folk Traditions frequently encountered

Ballads

BARBARA ALLEN. "It was in the merry month of May . . ."
PRETTY POLLY. LADY MARGARET. FAIR ELLINOR. FAIR
ELLENDER.
LORD LOVELL. LORD THOMAS. LORD BATEMAN. LORD BAKE-
MAN. LORD RANDAL. LORD BANNER. LORD DONALD. LORD
ARNOLD.
". . . part of your father's gold, and part of your mother's
fee . . ."
"Wake up, wake up, you seven sleepers."
THE TWO SISTERS. "Bow down!" "The boughs they bend to
me!" "The oldest pushed the youngest in."
"Where have you been all the day, Randal, my son?" JOHN
RANDOLPH. JIMMY RANDALL.
"I am sick-hearted and I want to lie down."
THE HOUSE CARPENTER. "I once could have married a King's
daughter." "Will you forsake your house and land?"
LITTLE MATTY GROVE. ". . . he went to town, the holy word
to hear." "The little foot page was standing by . . ."
GEORGE COLLINS. ". . . rode home one cold winter night."
THE GYPSY DAVIE. THE BLACK JACK DAVIE. "Oh what care I
for my house and land?" ". . . sleep in a cold open field . . ."
OLD BANGUM AND THE BOAR. "Dillum down!" "Kullo key!
Cut him down! Killo quay qum!" "Kubbo kye! Cuddle down!"
"Two brothers at the school . . ." ". . . try a wrestle fall."
". . . and bind it 'round my bleeding wound . . ."
"What will you leave to your father?"—mother, brother, etc.
"Come in, come in my old true love."
SWEET WILLIAM. ". . . he rose on a merry May morn."
"Six kings' daughters I've drownd-ed here, and the seventh
you shall be."
"There were two crows sat on a tree."
"Mother, O mother, come rede my riddle!"
"In New York City where I did dwell . . ." "In Jersey
City . . ." ". . . a butcher boy I loved so well . . ."
BEAULAMBKIN. "Beware of the Lamkin, he's a-walking
about."

231

"Hangman! Hangman! Hold your rope!" "O father have you brought my gold?" ". . . but I have come to see you hanging on the gallows tree."

"Jack he went a-sailing . . ." ". . . the wars of Germany."

LOWLANDS LOW. "She loved her driver boy . . ."

"What is higher than a tree?" "I brought my love a cherry that has no stone." "Perry merry dixie, Dominee!"

THE BOY IN THE ROAD, AND THE KNIGHT. "Oh where are you going, boy? . . . I'm a-going to my school. Oh I wish you were on the sea. . . . Yes, and a good boat under me."

SWEET JANE. "—for I must go across the stormy sea."

THE DEVIL CARRYING OFF THE FARMER'S SCOLDING WIFE.

Songs

BILLY BOY. "Can she bake a pone of bread?" "Can she milk a muley cow?"

FROGGY WENT A-COURTING. "He rode down to Miss Mousie's door." "Oh what will the wedding supper be?" "Kee- me- O! Ky-me-O! Up jumped Johnny Jinkle, here came Penny Winkle, up stepped Nip Cat hit him with a brick bat!" "Sing song kitty, won't you kimey O!"

THE PAPER OF PINS. "—and that's the way our love begins." "I'll give to you . . . a little lap dog . . . a dress of red . . . the key of my chest that you may have money at your request . . ." etc.

"I'll be sixteen next Sunday."

"Soldier, soldier, won't you marry me?"

"This old man came over the sea—" "My mother told me to let him in." "—with his old gray beard a-shakin'."

"Come let us sing." "What shall we sing?" "I'll sing you one." "What is your one?" "One is one and all alone—" "Twelve are the twelve apostles, eleven are the eleven that went to heaven—" "Two of them are the lily white babes."

"The cuckoo is a pretty bird, she sings as she flies."

"To see the waters gliding, hear the nightingales sing."

"Come all you fair young ladies—" "Never place your affections on a green-growing tree."

And all "lonesome songs," "foolish songs," "kids' songs," comic songs dealing with old times, songs making fun of womankind, songs about foolish man or boy. Folk songs (*i.e.* not ballads) are usually lyric and not strictly narrative.

232

II. Folk Traditions, Rarely Recorded

Dramatic Dialogues

Any play or dialogue entitled: OLD DUMB SHOW, GUISERS, GEEZERS, WAITS, WASSAILERS, SAINT GEORGE AND THE DRAGON, CHRISTMAS PLAY, SOULERS, SOUL CAKE-ERS, SWORD DANCERS, PACE EGGERS, GUIZARDS, PLOW BOYS, JOHNNY JACK, ROBIN HOOD PLAY, THE CHRISTMAS BOYS, TEPTEERERS, MORRIS MEN, or any other play or ceremony that was (or still is) performed by a group of boys or men at Christmas time, or in the Spring, or at any other fixed seasonal time.

Any play-acting that includes such characters as: "Old Father Christmas" "Little Jack Finney," "The Fool," "Tom Fool," "Little Devil Dout," "The Turkish Knight," "Bold Slasher," "The Doctor," "Old Doctor Ball," "Old Dirty Bet," "Betsy," "The King," "Pickle Herring," or "King Alfred"; or any play-acting done with masks and absurd costumes, and, perhaps, one man dressed as a woman.

III. Tales, Known to Exist, but Not Fully Reported

1. Why bluejays *"take sand to Hell"* on Good Friday—"and when all the sand there is is in Hell, it'll be the end of the world."
2. Why *"Job's turkey"* was so poor. "Poor as Job's turkey—and it had to lean against the fence to gobble!"
3. KING JOHN AND OLD BUCHANAN. KING JOHN AND HIS FOOL.
4. Tales about animals who act like humans: fox, bear, wolf, rabbit, etc., but *as told by Anglo-American folk,* and totally unconnected with "Uncle Remus" or any other Negro tradition.
5. LITTLE NIPPY—A boy who outwitted a giant a number of times. "Hey, little Nippy! Are you ever comin' this way again?"

233

6. Jack threw his ax at ducks swimming on the pond. While Jack was under the water trying to get his ax back his clothes were stolen, and Jack "had to beat his way back home" in that condition!—"and all sorts of things happened."
7. THE LOST SILVER MINE.
8. Someone who tries to imitate a witch, and gets into trouble.
9. The boy who had never seen a woman.
10. The boy who couldn't do anything without asking his mother.
11. Two friends swear never to part. One dies and the other goes with him.
12. Any additional information, or variations, on the whole, or any part of any of the tales given in this book.

IV. Songs and Ballads Known to Exist, but Not Fully Reported

Songs

1. The words for dance tunes, "jig songs"—GIVE THE FIDDLER A DRAM, ARKANSAS TRAVELLER and the dialogue that usually goes with this; THE MISSISSIPPI SAWYER, THE GIRL I LEFT BEHIND ME, THE FORK-ED DEER, THE IRISH WASHERWOMAN, etc.
2. THE FOGGY DEW: One different from the version recently recorded and now so well known.
3. Number songs: "I will sing you one. What is your one?" etc. "The first day of Christmas . . ." etc. THE BLESSINGS OF MARY, THE SEVEN JOYS OF MARY.
4. Songs about the cuckoo, or the nightingale.
5. "Where are you going, my good old man? . . . my honey, my love?"

Ballads

6. YOUNG CAROLINE OF EDINBORO TOWN: ". . . she lies asleep within the deep, small fishes watch around."

7. "What blood is this on your knife, my son?" Or "on your shirt sleeve?" The "Edward Ballad."
8. THE GREENWOOD SIDE: "Babes, Oh babes, if you were mine——"
9. Any song about Robin Hood. These are invaluable! Only a small handful have, thus far, been discovered as known by word-of-mouth in America.
10. THE DEATH OF QUEEN JANE: "The flower of England will flourish no more."
11. FAIR ANNIE: "She took her flute all in her hand and up her bower she ran. She fluted East, she fluted West, she fluted loud and shrill. She wished her sons were seven greyhounds and her a wolf on the hill."
12. Any variant of the songs and ballads given in this book.

7. Suggested Further Reading

The books listed below relate particularly to the traditions presented in this book.

COLLECTIONS OF TRADITIONAL TALES:

Joseph Jacobs, *English Fairy Tales*, 1895. (Dover reprint, 1967.)
——*More English Fairy Tales*, G. P. Putnam's Sons, New York and London. (Dover reprint, 1967.)
——*Celtic Fairy Tales*, G. P. Putnam's Sons. (Dover reprint, 1968.)
——*More Celtic Fairy Tales*, G. P. Putnam's Sons. (Dover reprint, 1968.)
William Butler Yeats, *Irish Fairy & Folk Tales*, Modern Library; Boni & Liveright, New York.
Richard Chase, *The Jack Tales*, Houghton Mifflin Co., Boston, 1943. (Contains 18 Anglo-American tales from North Carolina and Virginia.)
——*Grandfather Tales*, Houghton Mifflin Co., Boston, 1948. (Contains 24 Anglo-American tales from Virginia, Kentucky, and North Carolina.)
Joel Chandler Harris, *The Complete Uncle Remus* (edited by Richard Chase), Houghton Mifflin Co., Boston, 1955.
Zora Neale Hurston, *Mules and Men* (Florida Negro folklore), J. B. Lippincott, Philadelphia, 1935.
Leonard W. Roberts, *South from Hell-fer-Sartin*, University of Kentucky Press, Lexington, 1955. (Kentucky mountain folk tales.)
Henri Pourrat, *Treasury of French Tales* (translated from the French by Mary Mian), Houghton Mifflin Co., Boston, 1954.
E. E. Gardner, *Folklore from The Schoharie Hills*, University of Michigan, Ann Arbor, 1937.
Percy MacKaye, *Tall Tales of The Kentucky Mountains*, George H. Doran Co., New York, 1926.
Richard Chase, *Jack and The Three Sillies* (single-tale picture-book), Houghton Miffllin Co., Boston, 1950.
——*Wicked John and The Devil* (single-tale picture-book), Houghton Mifflin Co., Boston, 1951.

COLLECTIONS OF SONGS AND BALLADS:

Cecil J. Sharp, *English Folk Songs from the Southern Appalachians*, edited by Maud Karpeles), 2 vols., Oxford University Press, London, 1932. Reissued 1954.
——*One Hundred English Folk Songs* (with piano settings), Oliver Ditson Co., Philadelphia, 1916.
Francis James Child, *English and Scottish Popular Ballads* (edited by Helen Child Sargent and George Lyman Kittredge), Cambridge Edition, Houghton Mifflin Co., Boston, 1932. (Dover reprint, 1965.)

236

John Powell, *Five Virginian Folk Songs* (for baritone voice and piano), J. Fischer and Brothers, New York, 1938.

Cecil J. Sharp, *American and English Folk Songs* (collected in the Southern Appalachian Mountains, with piano settings), 1st series, Schirmer, New York and Boston, 1918.

——*Folk Songs of English Origin* (collected in Southern Appalachian Mountains, with piano settings), 2nd series, Novello & Co., London; The H. W. Gray Co., New York, 1921.

Evelyn Kendrick Wells, *The Ballad Tree* (British and American ballads; their folklore, verse, and music, together with sixty traditional ballads and their tunes), The Ronald Press Co., New York, 1950. (This is the standard book on the genuine folk ballad, its Old World background, and its living uses. It also contains a full bibliography on the whole field of Anglo-American folk traditions.)

Schirmer's *American Folk Song Series*. In 25 sets. G. Schirmer, Inc., New York.

Set 1.—*Folk Songs from the Kentucky Highlands*, Combs & Mixson.

Set 3.—*Mountain Songs of North Carolina*, Bartholomew.

Set 10.—*Songs from the Hills of Vermont*, Sturgis & Hughes.

Set 15.—*Beech Mountain (N. C.) Folk Songs & Ballads*, Matteson & Henry.

Set 21.—*American-English Folk Songs*, Cecil J. Sharp.

Set 22.—*American-English Folk Ballads*, Cecil J. Sharp.

John A. and Alan Lomax, *American Ballads and Folk Songs*, The Macmillan Co., New York, 1934.

——*Our Singing Country*, The Macmillan Co., 1938.

——*Folk Song: U. S. A.*, Duell Sloan & Pearce, New York, 1948.

Olive Dame Campbell, R. Chase, Marie Marvel, *Songs of All Time* (a 62-page booklet), The Council of Southern Mountain Workers, Berea College, Berea, Kentucky.

The Frank C. Brown Collection of North Carolina Folklore, General Editor, Newman I. White, 5 vols. (tunes to be published in vol. 6.), Duke University Press, Durham, N. C., 1952.

Mary O. Eddy, *Ballads and Songs From Ohio* (with tunes), J. J. Augustin, New York, 1939.

Reed Smith & Hilton Rufty, *American Anthology of Old World Ballads*, J. Fischer & Brothers, New York, 1937. (25 ballads with piano settings, explanatory notes on texts and tunes, and bibliography.)

Jean Ritchie, *A Garland of Mountain Song* (songs from the Ritchie family of Viper, Ky., with piano settings), Broadcast Music, Inc., New York, 1953.

——*Swapping Song Book* (21 songs, with piano settings), Oxford University Press, New York, 1952.

——*Singing Family of the Cumberlands* (words and music for 42 songs), Oxford University Press, New York, 1954.

Arthur Kyle Davis, *Traditional Ballads of Virginia*, Harvard University Press, 1929. (Mostly texts.)

Cecil J. Sharp, *17 Nursery Songs from the Southern Appalachians*, The H. W. Gray Co., New York.

The Oxford Book of Light Verse (edited by W. H. Auden), Oxford University Press, London, 1938. (Texts for many American and English folk songs, ballads, singing games, and carols. No tunes.)

COLLECTIONS OF CAROLS AND FOLK HYMNS:

The Oxford Book of Carols (edited by Percy Deamer, Ralph Vaughan Williams, and Martin Shaw), Oxford University Press, 1928. (A full collection of Christmas carols, spring carols, and general carols, traditional texts and tunes, and ancient texts to composed tunes; all with arrangements for piano, for four voices, and for organ.)

Twelve Folk Hymns (edited by John Powell, Annabel Morris Buchanan, and Hilton Rufty), J. Fischer & Brothers, New York, 1934. (Set for four voices.)

Annabel Morris Buchanan, *Folk Hymns of America*, J. Fischer & Brothers, New York, 1938. (50 traditional sacred songs set for four voices, or voice and piano; with notes on origins, modes, shape-notes.)

George Pullen Jackson, *White Spirituals in the Southern Uplands*, University of North Carolina Press, 1933. (Dover reprint, 1965.)
——*Spiritual Folk Songs of Early America*, 1937. (Dover reprint, 1964.)
——*Down East Spirituals & Others*, J. J. Augustin, New York, 1939.
——*White and Negro Spirituals*, J. J. Augustin, New York, 1943.

COLLECTIONS OF SINGING GAMES, COUNTRY DANCES, SQUARE DANCES:

Douglas and Helen Kennedy, *Square Dances of America*, printed for the English Folk Dance and Song Society, by Novello & Co., Ltd., obtainable from The Country Dance Society, New York. (Calls and directions for 36 figures and 18 tunes, 4 with piano arrangements.)

Country Dances of Today. Book 1.

Country Dances of Today. Book 2. (Selection of easy figure-dances from America and England. There are four 10-inch records, and one 12-inch record, to accompany eleven of these dances.) Obtainable from The Country Dance Society, New York.

American Folk Dances. (10 country dances, 25 square dance figures, and 9 tunes.) Obtainable from the Cooperative Recreation Service, Delaware, O.

Cecil J. Sharp, *The English Country Dance* (Graded series, 8 vols.), The H. W. Gray Co., New York.
——*The Country Dance Book.* (6 parts. Tunes, with piano accompaniments are issued separately. Part 5 is a full account of "The Kentucky Square Dance.")

Alice Bertha Gomme, *Traditional Singing Games of England, Scotland, and Ireland*, 2 vols., London, David Nutt, 1894. (A scholar's book, with full historical background of each game.) (Dover reprint, 1964.)

William Wells Newell, *Games and Songs of American Children*, Harper & Brothers, New York, 1903. (Dover reprint, 1963.)

Richard Chase, *Hullabaloo, and Other Singing Folk Games*, Houghton Mifflin Co., Boston, 1949. (18 singing games for grades 1 through 7, with six piano settings by Hilton Rufty. Illustrated by Joshua Tolford.) (Reprinted by Dover as *Singing Games and Playparty Games*, 1967).

Douglas Kennedy, *England's Dances*, G. Bell & Sons, Ltd., London, 1949. (A book on the background of traditional dances: both the social and ritual uses of country dances, sword dances, morris dances, etc., but not a handbook of figures.)

Douglas and Helen Kennedy, *Walking on Air*. (An introduction to the technique of dancing country dances and American square dances.) Obtainable from The English Folk Dance and Song Society, Cecil Sharp House, 2 Regent's Park Road, London N.W., 1, England. (A pamphlet on how to get the best individual and social pleasure out of country dancing.)

Twelve Traditional Country Dances (with piano arrangements by Ralph Vaughan Williams), Novello & Co. for The English Folk Dance & Song Society; The Country Dance Society, New York.

Five Popular Country Dances (with piano settings by Arnold Foster), Oxford Press for The English Folk Dance & Song Society. Obtainable from The Country Dance Society, New York.

Raymond Smith, *Square Dance Handbook*, Obtainable from author at 1038 Cedar Hill, Dallas, Tex. (About 50 Western style four-couple square dance figures, with full directions and calls. No music.)

MAGAZINES AND QUARTERLIES ON FOLK TRADITIONS:

The Journal of American Folklore. University of Pennsylvania, Philadelphia 4, Penn. (Carries folk traditions of all nationalities, races, tribes, regions, and languages of North America. In publication since 1888. Lists all American folklore societies and publications.)

The Southern Folklore Quarterly. The University of Florida, Gainesville, Florida. (In co-operation with The Southeastern Folklore Society.)

The Country Dancer. Organ of The Country Dance Society, 31 Union Square West, New York 3, N. Y.

English Dance and Song. The magazine of The English Folk Dance and Song Society, Cecil Sharp House, 2 Regent's Park Road, London N.W., 1, England.

Mountain Life and Work. Council of Southern Mountain Workers, Berea College, Berea, Ky. (Each issue contains "folk tales for telling," and "folk songs for singing.")

PAPERBOUND BOOKS:

The Burl Ives Song Book. Ballantine Books, New York, 1953. (Contains about 40 traditional songs with their tunes.)

A Treasury of Folk Song. By Sylvia & John Kolb. Bantam Books, New York, 1948. (Contains about 30 traditional songs with their tunes.)

Pocket Treasury of American Folklore (edited by Ben A. Botkin), Pocket Books, Inc., New York, 1950. (Contains 1 Jack Tale, a Maryland version of "Wicked John and The Devil," other tales, songs—with their tunes—playparty games, etc.)

One important book on the whole subject of English folk music, its nature, its origins, its evolution, and its uses in the present day both for popular enjoyment and for creative musicians in America and in England is: Ralph Vaughan Williams, *National Music*, Oxford University Press, New York, 1934. Unfortunately this book is out of print, but might be found in college or university libraries.

8. Title Index

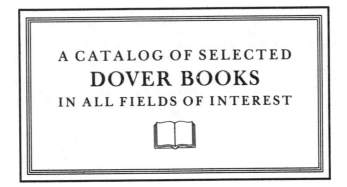

A CATALOG OF SELECTED
DOVER BOOKS
IN ALL FIELDS OF INTEREST

A CATALOG OF SELECTED DOVER
BOOKS IN ALL FIELDS OF INTEREST

DRAWINGS OF REMBRANDT, edited by Seymour Slive. Updated Lippmann, Hofstede de Groot edition, with definitive scholarly apparatus. All portraits, biblical sketches, landscapes, nudes. Oriental figures, classical studies, together with selection of work by followers. 550 illustrations. Total of 630pp. 9⅛ × 12¼.
21485-0, 21486-9 Pa., Two-vol. set $25.00

GHOST AND HORROR STORIES OF AMBROSE BIERCE, Ambrose Bierce. 24 tales vividly imagined, strangely prophetic, and decades ahead of their time in technical skill: "The Damned Thing," "An Inhabitant of Carcosa," "The Eyes of the Panther," "Moxon's Master," and 20 more. 199pp. 5⅜ × 8½. 20767-6 Pa. $3.95

ETHICAL WRITINGS OF MAIMONIDES, Maimonides. Most significant ethical works of great medieval sage, newly translated for utmost precision, readability. Laws Concerning Character Traits, Eight Chapters, more. 192pp. 5⅜ × 8½.
24522-5 Pa. $4.50

THE EXPLORATION OF THE COLORADO RIVER AND ITS CANYONS, J. W. Powell. Full text of Powell's 1,000-mile expedition down the fabled Colorado in 1869. Superb account of terrain, geology, vegetation, Indians, famine, mutiny, treacherous rapids, mighty canyons, during exploration of last unknown part of continental U.S. 400pp. 5⅜ × 8½. 20094-9 Pa. $6.95

HISTORY OF PHILOSOPHY, Julián Marías. Clearest one-volume history on the market. Every major philosopher and dozens of others, to Existentialism and later. 505pp. 5⅜ × 8½. 21739-6 Pa. $8.50

ALL ABOUT LIGHTNING, Martin A. Uman. Highly readable non-technical survey of nature and causes of lightning, thunderstorms, ball lightning, St. Elmo's Fire, much more. Illustrated. 192pp. 5⅜ × 8½. 25237-X Pa. $5.95

SAILING ALONE AROUND THE WORLD, Captain Joshua Slocum. First man to sail around the world, alone, in small boat. One of great feats of seamanship told in delightful manner. 67 illustrations. 294pp. 5⅜ × 8½. 20326-3 Pa. $4.95

LETTERS AND NOTES ON THE MANNERS, CUSTOMS AND CONDITIONS OF THE NORTH AMERICAN INDIANS, George Catlin. Classic account of life among Plains Indians: ceremonies, hunt, warfare, etc. 312 plates. 572pp. of text. 6⅛ × 9¼. 22118-0, 22119-9 Pa. Two-vol. set $15.90

ALASKA: The Harriman Expedition, 1899, John Burroughs, John Muir, et al. Informative, engrossing accounts of two-month, 9,000-mile expedition. Native peoples, wildlife, forests, geography, salmon industry, glaciers, more. Profusely illustrated. 240 black-and-white line drawings. 124 black-and-white photographs. 3 maps. Index. 576pp. 5⅜ × 8½. 25109-8 Pa. $11.95

HOW TO WRITE, Gertrude Stein. Gertrude Stein claimed anyone could understand her unconventional writing—here are clues to help. Fascinating improvisations, language experiments, explanations illuminate Stein's craft and the art of writing. Total of 414pp. 4⅝ × 6⅜. 23144-5 Pa. $5.95

ADVENTURES AT SEA IN THE GREAT AGE OF SAIL: Five Firsthand Narratives, edited by Elliot Snow. Rare true accounts of exploration, whaling, shipwreck, fierce natives, trade, shipboard life, more. 33 illustrations. Introduction. 353pp. 5⅜ × 8½. 25177-2 Pa. $7.95

THE HERBAL OR GENERAL HISTORY OF PLANTS, John Gerard. Classic descriptions of about 2,850 plants—with over 2,700 illustrations—includes Latin and English names, physical descriptions, varieties, time and place of growth, more. 2,706 illustrations. xlv + 1,678pp. 8½ × 12¼. 23147-X Cloth. $75.00

DOROTHY AND THE WIZARD IN OZ, L. Frank Baum. Dorothy and the Wizard visit the center of the Earth, where people are vegetables, glass houses grow and Oz characters reappear. Classic sequel to *Wizard of Oz*. 256pp. 5⅜ × 8. 24714-7 Pa. $4.95

SONGS OF EXPERIENCE: Facsimile Reproduction with 26 Plates in Full Color, William Blake. This facsimile of Blake's original "Illuminated Book" reproduces 26 full-color plates from a rare 1826 edition. Includes "The Tyger," "London," "Holy Thursday," and other immortal poems. 26 color plates. Printed text of poems. 48pp. 5¼ × 7. 24636-1 Pa. $3.50

SONGS OF INNOCENCE, William Blake. The first and most popular of Blake's famous "Illuminated Books," in a facsimile edition reproducing all 31 brightly colored plates. Additional printed text of each poem. 64pp. 5¼ × 7. 22764-2 Pa. $3.50

PRECIOUS STONES, Max Bauer. Classic, thorough study of diamonds, rubies, emeralds, garnets, etc.: physical character, occurrence, properties, use, similar topics. 20 plates, 8 in color. 94 figures. 659pp. 6⅛ × 9¼. 21910-0, 21911-9 Pa., Two-vol. set $15.90

ENCYCLOPEDIA OF VICTORIAN NEEDLEWORK, S. F. A. Caulfeild and Blanche Saward. Full, precise descriptions of stitches, techniques for dozens of needlecrafts—most exhaustive reference of its kind. Over 800 figures. Total of 679pp. 8⅜ × 11. Two volumes. Vol. 1 22800-2 Pa. $11.95
Vol. 2 22801-0 Pa. $11.95

THE MARVELOUS LAND OF OZ, L. Frank Baum. Second Oz book, the Scarecrow and Tin Woodman are back with hero named Tip, Oz magic. 136 illustrations. 287pp. 5⅜ × 8½. 20692-0 Pa. $5.95

WILD FOWL DECOYS, Joel Barber. Basic book on the subject, by foremost authority and collector. Reveals history of decoy making and rigging, place in American culture, different kinds of decoys, how to make them, and how to use them. 140 plates. 156pp. 7⅞ × 10¾. 20011-6 Pa. $8.95

HISTORY OF LACE, Mrs. Bury Palliser. Definitive, profusely illustrated chronicle of lace from earliest times to late 19th century. Laces of Italy, Greece, England, France, Belgium, etc. Landmark of needlework scholarship. 266 illustrations. 672pp. 6⅛ × 9¼. 24742-2 Pa. $14.95

ILLUSTRATED GUIDE TO SHAKER FURNITURE, Robert Meader. All furniture and appurtenances, with much on unknown local styles. 235 photos. 146pp. 9 × 12. 22819-3 Pa. $7.95

WHALE SHIPS AND WHALING: A Pictorial Survey, George Francis Dow. Over 200 vintage engravings, drawings, photographs of barks, brigs, cutters, other vessels. Also harpoons, lances, whaling guns, many other artifacts. Comprehensive text by foremost authority. 207 black-and-white illustrations. 288pp. 6 × 9. 24808-9 Pa. $8.95

THE BERTRAMS, Anthony Trollope. Powerful portrayal of blind self-will and thwarted ambition includes one of Trollope's most heartrending love stories. 497pp. 5⅜ × 8½. 25119-5 Pa. $8.95

ADVENTURES WITH A HAND LENS, Richard Headstrom. Clearly written guide to observing and studying flowers and grasses, fish scales, moth and insect wings, egg cases, buds, feathers, seeds, leaf scars, moss, molds, ferns, common crystals, etc.—all with an ordinary, inexpensive magnifying glass. 209 exact line drawings aid in your discoveries. 220pp. 5⅜ × 8½. 23330-8 Pa. $4.50

RODIN ON ART AND ARTISTS, Auguste Rodin. Great sculptor's candid, wide-ranging comments on meaning of art; great artists; relation of sculpture to poetry, painting, music; philosophy of life, more. 76 superb black-and-white illustrations of Rodin's sculpture, drawings and prints. 119pp. 8⅜ × 11¼. 24487-3 Pa. $6.95

FIFTY CLASSIC FRENCH FILMS, 1912–1982: A Pictorial Record, Anthony Slide. Memorable stills from Grand Illusion, Beauty and the Beast, Hiroshima, Mon Amour, many more. Credits, plot synopses, reviews, etc. 160pp. 8¼ × 11. 25256-6 Pa. $11.95

THE PRINCIPLES OF PSYCHOLOGY, William James. Famous long course complete, unabridged. Stream of thought, time perception, memory, experimental methods; great work decades ahead of its time. 94 figures. 1,391pp. 5⅜ × 8½. 20381-6, 20382-4 Pa., Two-vol. set $19.90

BODIES IN A BOOKSHOP, R. T. Campbell. Challenging mystery of blackmail and murder with ingenious plot and superbly drawn characters. In the best tradition of British suspense fiction. 192pp. 5⅜ × 8½. 24720-1 Pa. $3.95

CALLAS: PORTRAIT OF A PRIMA DONNA, George Jellinek. Renowned commentator on the musical scene chronicles incredible career and life of the most controversial, fascinating, influential operatic personality of our time. 64 black-and-white photographs. 416pp. 5⅜ × 8¼. 25047-4 Pa. $7.95

GEOMETRY, RELATIVITY AND THE FOURTH DIMENSION, Rudolph Rucker. Exposition of fourth dimension, concepts of relativity as Flatland characters continue adventures. Popular, easily followed yet accurate, profound. 141 illustrations. 133pp. 5⅜ × 8½. 23400-2 Pa. $3.50

HOUSEHOLD STORIES BY THE BROTHERS GRIMM, with pictures by Walter Crane. 53 classic stories—Rumpelstiltskin, Rapunzel, Hansel and Gretel, the Fisherman and his Wife, Snow White, Tom Thumb, Sleeping Beauty, Cinderella, and so much more—lavishly illustrated with original 19th century drawings. 114 illustrations. x + 269pp. 5⅜ × 8½. 21080-4 Pa. $4.50

SUNDIALS, Albert Waugh. Far and away the best, most thorough coverage of ideas, mathematics concerned, types, construction, adjusting anywhere. Over 100 illustrations. 230pp. 5⅜ × 8½. 22947-5 Pa. $4.50

PICTURE HISTORY OF THE NORMANDIE: With 190 Illustrations, Frank O. Braynard. Full story of legendary French ocean liner: Art Deco interiors, design innovations, furnishings, celebrities, maiden voyage, tragic fire, much more. Extensive text. 144pp. 8⅜ × 11¾. 25257-4 Pa. $9.95

THE FIRST AMERICAN COOKBOOK: A Facsimile of "American Cookery," 1796, Amelia Simmons. Facsimile of the first American-written cookbook published in the United States contains authentic recipes for colonial favorites—pumpkin pudding, winter squash pudding, spruce beer, Indian slapjacks, and more. Introductory Essay and Glossary of colonial cooking terms. 80pp. 5⅜ × 8½. 24710-4 Pa. $3.50

101 PUZZLES IN THOUGHT AND LOGIC, C. R. Wylie, Jr. Solve murders and robberies, find out which fishermen are liars, how a blind man could possibly identify a color—purely by your own reasoning! 107pp. 5⅜ × 8½. 20367-0 Pa. $2.50

THE BOOK OF WORLD-FAMOUS MUSIC—CLASSICAL, POPULAR AND FOLK, James J. Fuld. Revised and enlarged republication of landmark work in musico-bibliography. Full information about nearly 1,000 songs and compositions including first lines of music and lyrics. New supplement. Index. 800pp. 5⅜ × 8¼. 24857-7 Pa. $14.95

ANTHROPOLOGY AND MODERN LIFE, Franz Boas. Great anthropologist's classic treatise on race and culture. Introduction by Ruth Bunzel. Only inexpensive paperback edition. 255pp. 5⅜ × 8½. 25245-0 Pa. $5.95

THE TALE OF PETER RABBIT, Beatrix Potter. The inimitable Peter's terrifying adventure in Mr. McGregor's garden, with all 27 wonderful, full-color Potter illustrations. 55pp. 4¼ × 5½. (Available in U.S. only) 22827-4 Pa. $1.75

THREE PROPHETIC SCIENCE FICTION NOVELS, H. G. Wells. *When the Sleeper Wakes, A Story of the Days to Come* and *The Time Machine* (full version). 335pp. 5⅜ × 8½. (Available in U.S. only) 20605-X Pa. $5.95

APICIUS COOKERY AND DINING IN IMPERIAL ROME, edited and translated by Joseph Dommers Vehling. Oldest known cookbook in existence offers readers a clear picture of what foods Romans ate, how they prepared them, etc. 49 illustrations. 301pp. 6⅛ × 9¼. 23563-7 Pa. $6.50

SHAKESPEARE LEXICON AND QUOTATION DICTIONARY, Alexander Schmidt. Full definitions, locations, shades of meaning of every word in plays and poems. More than 50,000 exact quotations. 1,485pp. 6½ × 9¼. 22726-X, 22727-8 Pa., Two-vol. set $27.90

THE WORLD'S GREAT SPEECHES, edited by Lewis Copeland and Lawrence W. Lamm. Vast collection of 278 speeches from Greeks to 1970. Powerful and effective models; unique look at history. 842pp. 5⅜ × 8½. 20468-5 Pa. $11.95

CATALOG OF DOVER BOOKS

THE BLUE FAIRY BOOK, Andrew Lang. The first, most famous collection, with many familiar tales: Little Red Riding Hood, Aladdin and the Wonderful Lamp, Puss in Boots, Sleeping Beauty, Hansel and Gretel, Rumpelstiltskin; 37 in all. 138 illustrations. 390pp. 5⅜ × 8½.   21437-0 Pa. $5.95

THE STORY OF THE CHAMPIONS OF THE ROUND TABLE, Howard Pyle. Sir Launcelot, Sir Tristram and Sir Percival in spirited adventures of love and triumph retold in Pyle's inimitable style. 50 drawings, 31 full-page. xviii + 329pp. 6½ × 9¼.   21883-X Pa. $6.95

AUDUBON AND HIS JOURNALS, Maria Audubon. Unmatched two-volume portrait of the great artist, naturalist and author contains his journals, an excellent biography by his granddaughter, expert annotations by the noted ornithologist, Dr. Elliott Coues, and 37 superb illustrations. Total of 1,200pp. 5⅜ × 8.
Vol. I 25143-8 Pa. $8.95
Vol. II 25144-6 Pa. $8.95

GREAT DINOSAUR HUNTERS AND THEIR DISCOVERIES, Edwin H. Colbert. Fascinating, lavishly illustrated chronicle of dinosaur research, 1820's to 1960. Achievements of Cope, Marsh, Brown, Buckland, Mantell, Huxley, many others. 384pp. 5¼ × 8¼.   24701-5 Pa. $6.95

THE TASTEMAKERS, Russell Lynes. Informal, illustrated social history of American taste 1850's–1950's. First popularized categories Highbrow, Lowbrow, Middlebrow. 129 illustrations. New (1979) afterword. 384pp. 6 × 9.
23993-4 Pa. $6.95

DOUBLE CROSS PURPOSES, Ronald A. Knox. A treasure hunt in the Scottish Highlands, an old map, unidentified corpse, surprise discoveries keep reader guessing in this cleverly intricate tale of financial skullduggery. 2 black-and-white maps. 320pp. 5⅜ × 8½. (Available in U.S. only)   25032-6 Pa. $5.95

AUTHENTIC VICTORIAN DECORATION AND ORNAMENTATION IN FULL COLOR: 46 Plates from "Studies in Design," Christopher Dresser. Superb full-color lithographs reproduced from rare original portfolio of a major Victorian designer. 48pp. 9¼ × 12¼.   25083-0 Pa. $7.95

PRIMITIVE ART, Franz Boas. Remains the best text ever prepared on subject, thoroughly discussing Indian, African, Asian, Australian, and, especially, Northern American primitive art. Over 950 illustrations show ceramics, masks, totem poles, weapons, textiles, paintings, much more. 376pp. 5⅜ × 8. 20025-6 Pa. $6.95

SIDELIGHTS ON RELATIVITY, Albert Einstein. Unabridged republication of two lectures delivered by the great physicist in 1920–21. *Ether and Relativity* and *Geometry and Experience*. Elegant ideas in non-mathematical form, accessible to intelligent layman. vi + 56pp. 5⅜ × 8½.   24511-X Pa. $2.95

THE WIT AND HUMOR OF OSCAR WILDE, edited by Alvin Redman. More than 1,000 ripostes, paradoxes, wisecracks: Work is the curse of the drinking classes, I can resist everything except temptation, etc. 258pp. 5⅜ × 8½.   20602-5 Pa. $4.50

ADVENTURES WITH A MICROSCOPE, Richard Headstrom. 59 adventures with clothing fibers, protozoa, ferns and lichens, roots and leaves, much more. 142 illustrations. 232pp. 5⅜ × 8½.   23471-1 Pa. $3.95

CATALOG OF DOVER BOOKS

PLANTS OF THE BIBLE, Harold N. Moldenke and Alma L. Moldenke. Standard reference to all 230 plants mentioned in Scriptures. Latin name, biblical reference, uses, modern identity, much more. Unsurpassed encyclopedic resource for scholars, botanists, nature lovers, students of Bible. Bibliography. Indexes. 123 black-and-white illustrations. 384pp. 6 × 9. 25069-5 Pa. $8.95

FAMOUS AMERICAN WOMEN: A Biographical Dictionary from Colonial Times to the Present, Robert McHenry, ed. From Pocahontas to Rosa Parks, 1,035 distinguished American women documented in separate biographical entries. Accurate, up-to-date data, numerous categories, spans 400 years. Indices. 493pp. 6½ × 9¼. 24523-3 Pa. $9.95

THE FABULOUS INTERIORS OF THE GREAT OCEAN LINERS IN HISTORIC PHOTOGRAPHS, William H. Miller, Jr. Some 200 superb photographs capture exquisite interiors of world's great "floating palaces"—1890's to 1980's: *Titanic, Ile de France, Queen Elizabeth, United States, Europa*, more. Approx. 200 black-and-white photographs. Captions. Text. Introduction. 160pp. 8⅜ × 11¼. 24756-2 Pa. $9.95

THE GREAT LUXURY LINERS, 1927–1954: A Photographic Record, William H. Miller, Jr. Nostalgic tribute to heyday of ocean liners. 186 photos of Ile de France, Normandie, Leviathan, Queen Elizabeth, United States, many others. Interior and exterior views. Introduction. Captions. 160pp. 9 × 12. 24056-8 Pa. $9.95

A NATURAL HISTORY OF THE DUCKS, John Charles Phillips. Great landmark of ornithology offers complete detailed coverage of nearly 200 species and subspecies of ducks: gadwall, sheldrake, merganser, pintail, many more. 74 full-color plates, 102 black-and-white. Bibliography. Total of 1,920pp. 8⅜ × 11¼. 25141-1, 25142-X Cloth. Two-vol. set $100.00

THE SEAWEED HANDBOOK: An Illustrated Guide to Seaweeds from North Carolina to Canada, Thomas F. Lee. Concise reference covers 78 species. Scientific and common names, habitat, distribution, more. Finding keys for easy identification. 224pp. 5⅜ × 8½. 25215-9 Pa. $5.95

THE TEN BOOKS OF ARCHITECTURE: The 1755 Leoni Edition, Leon Battista Alberti. Rare classic helped introduce the glories of ancient architecture to the Renaissance. 68 black-and-white plates. 336pp. 8⅜ × 11¼. 25239-6 Pa. $14.95

MISS MACKENZIE, Anthony Trollope. Minor masterpieces by Victorian master unmasks many truths about life in 19th-century England. First inexpensive edition in years. 392pp. 5⅜ × 8½. 25201-9 Pa. $7.95

THE RIME OF THE ANCIENT MARINER, Gustave Doré, Samuel Taylor Coleridge. Dramatic engravings considered by many to be his greatest work. The terrifying space of the open sea, the storms and whirlpools of an unknown ocean, the ice of Antarctica, more—all rendered in a powerful, chilling manner. Full text. 38 plates. 77pp. 9¼ × 12. 22305-1 Pa. $4.95

THE EXPEDITIONS OF ZEBULON MONTGOMERY PIKE, Zebulon Montgomery Pike. Fascinating first-hand accounts (1805–6) of exploration of Mississippi River, Indian wars, capture by Spanish dragoons, much more. 1,088pp. 5⅜ × 8½. 25254-X, 25255-8 Pa. Two-vol. set $23.90

A CONCISE HISTORY OF PHOTOGRAPHY: Third Revised Edition, Helmut Gernsheim. Best one-volume history—camera obscura, photochemistry, daguerreotypes, evolution of cameras, film, more. Also artistic aspects—landscape, portraits, fine art, etc. 281 black-and-white photographs. 26 in color. 176pp. 8⅜ × 11¼. 25128-4 Pa. $12.95

THE DORÉ BIBLE ILLUSTRATIONS, Gustave Doré. 241 detailed plates from the Bible: the Creation scenes, Adam and Eve, Flood, Babylon, battle sequences, life of Jesus, etc. Each plate is accompanied by the verses from the King James version of the Bible. 241pp. 9 × 12. 23004-X Pa. $8.95

HUGGER-MUGGER IN THE LOUVRE, Elliot Paul. Second Homer Evans mystery-comedy. Theft at the Louvre involves sleuth in hilarious, madcap caper. "A knockout."—Books. 336pp. 5⅜ × 8½. 25185-3 Pa. $5.95

FLATLAND, E. A. Abbott. Intriguing and enormously popular science-fiction classic explores the complexities of trying to survive as a two-dimensional being in a three-dimensional world. Amusingly illustrated by the author. 16 illustrations. 103pp. 5⅜ × 8½. 20001-9 Pa. $2.25

THE HISTORY OF THE LEWIS AND CLARK EXPEDITION, Meriwether Lewis and William Clark, edited by Elliott Coues. Classic edition of Lewis and Clark's day-by-day journals that later became the basis for U.S. claims to Oregon and the West. Accurate and invaluable geographical, botanical, biological, meteorological and anthropological material. Total of 1,508pp. 5⅜ × 8½. 21268-8, 21269-6, 21270-X Pa. Three-vol. set $25.50

LANGUAGE, TRUTH AND LOGIC, Alfred J. Ayer. Famous, clear introduction to Vienna, Cambridge schools of Logical Positivism. Role of philosophy, elimination of metaphysics, nature of analysis, etc. 160pp. 5⅜ × 8½. (Available in U.S. and Canada only) 20010-8 Pa. $2.95

MATHEMATICS FOR THE NONMATHEMATICIAN, Morris Kline. Detailed, college-level treatment of mathematics in cultural and historical context, with numerous exercises. For liberal arts students. Preface. Recommended Reading Lists. Tables. Index. Numerous black-and-white figures. xvi + 641pp. 5⅜ × 8½. 24823-2 Pa. $11.95

28 SCIENCE FICTION STORIES, H. G. Wells. Novels, *Star Begotten* and *Men Like Gods*, plus 26 short stories: "Empire of the Ants," "A Story of the Stone Age," "The Stolen Bacillus," "In the Abyss," etc. 915pp. 5⅜ × 8½. (Available in U.S. only) 20265-8 Cloth. $10.95

HANDBOOK OF PICTORIAL SYMBOLS, Rudolph Modley. 3,250 signs and symbols, many systems in full; official or heavy commercial use. Arranged by subject. Most in Pictorial Archive series. 143pp. 8⅛ × 11. 23357-X Pa. $5.95

INCIDENTS OF TRAVEL IN YUCATAN, John L. Stephens. Classic (1843) exploration of jungles of Yucatan, looking for evidences of Maya civilization. Travel adventures, Mexican and Indian culture, etc. Total of 669pp. 5⅜ × 8½. 20926-1, 20927-X Pa., Two-vol. set $9.90

DEGAS: An Intimate Portrait, Ambroise Vollard. Charming, anecdotal memoir by famous art dealer of one of the greatest 19th-century French painters. 14 black-and-white illustrations. Introduction by Harold L. Van Doren. 96pp. 5⅜ × 8½.
25131-4 Pa. $3.95

PERSONAL NARRATIVE OF A PILGRIMAGE TO ALMANDINAH AND MECCAH, Richard Burton. Great travel classic by remarkably colorful personality. Burton, disguised as a Moroccan, visited sacred shrines of Islam, narrowly escaping death. 47 illustrations. 959pp. 5⅜ × 8½. 21217-3, 21218-1 Pa., Two-vol. set $17.90

PHRASE AND WORD ORIGINS, A. H. Holt. Entertaining, reliable, modern study of more than 1,200 colorful words, phrases, origins and histories. Much unexpected information. 254pp. 5⅜ × 8½. 20758-7 Pa. $5.95

THE RED THUMB MARK, R. Austin Freeman. In this first Dr. Thorndyke case, the great scientific detective draws fascinating conclusions from the nature of a single fingerprint. Exciting story, authentic science. 320pp. 5⅜ × 8½. (Available in U.S. only) 25210-8 Pa. $5.95

AN EGYPTIAN HIEROGLYPHIC DICTIONARY, E. A. Wallis Budge. Monumental work containing about 25,000 words or terms that occur in texts ranging from 3000 B.C. to 600 A.D. Each entry consists of a transliteration of the word, the word in hieroglyphs, and the meaning in English. 1,314pp. 6⅜ × 10.
23615-3, 23616-1 Pa., Two-vol. set $27.90

THE COMPLEAT STRATEGYST: Being a Primer on the Theory of Games of Strategy, J. D. Williams. Highly entertaining classic describes, with many illustrated examples, how to select best strategies in conflict situations. Prefaces. Appendices. xvi + 268pp. 5⅜ × 8½. 25101-2 Pa. $5.95

THE ROAD TO OZ, L. Frank Baum. Dorothy meets the Shaggy Man, little Button-Bright and the Rainbow's beautiful daughter in this delightful trip to the magical Land of Oz. 272pp. 5⅜ × 8. 25208-6 Pa. $4.95

POINT AND LINE TO PLANE, Wassily Kandinsky. Seminal exposition of role of point, line, other elements in non-objective painting. Essential to understanding 20th-century art. 127 illustrations. 192pp. 6½ × 9¼. 23808-3 Pa. $4.50

LADY ANNA, Anthony Trollope. Moving chronicle of Countess Lovel's bitter struggle to win for herself and daughter Anna their rightful rank and fortune—perhaps at cost of sanity itself. 384pp. 5⅜ × 8½. 24669-8 Pa. $6.95

EGYPTIAN MAGIC, E. A. Wallis Budge. Sums up all that is known about magic in Ancient Egypt: the role of magic in controlling the gods, powerful amulets that warded off evil spirits, scarabs of immortality, use of wax images, formulas and spells, the secret name, much more. 253pp. 5⅜ × 8½. 22681-6 Pa. $4.50

THE DANCE OF SIVA, Ananda Coomaraswamy. Preeminent authority unfolds the vast metaphysic of India: the revelation of her art, conception of the universe, social organization, etc. 27 reproductions of art masterpieces. 192pp. 5⅜ × 8½.
24817-8 Pa. $5.95

CATALOG OF DOVER BOOKS

CHRISTMAS CUSTOMS AND TRADITIONS, Clement A. Miles. Origin, evolution, significance of religious, secular practices. Caroling, gifts, yule logs, much more. Full, scholarly yet fascinating; non-sectarian. 400pp. 5⅜ × 8½.
23354-5 Pa. $6.50

THE HUMAN FIGURE IN MOTION, Eadweard Muybridge. More than 4,500 stopped-action photos, in action series, showing undraped men, women, children jumping, lying down, throwing, sitting, wrestling, carrying, etc. 390pp. 7⅞ × 10⅝.
20204-6 Cloth. $19.95

THE MAN WHO WAS THURSDAY, Gilbert Keith Chesterton. Witty, fast-paced novel about a club of anarchists in turn-of-the-century London. Brilliant social, religious, philosophical speculations. 128pp. 5⅜ × 8½.
25121-7 Pa. $3.95

A CEZANNE SKETCHBOOK: Figures, Portraits, Landscapes and Still Lifes, Paul Cezanne. Great artist experiments with tonal effects, light, mass, other qualities in over 100 drawings. A revealing view of developing master painter, precursor of Cubism. 102 black-and-white illustrations. 144pp. 8¾ × 6⅝.
24790-2 Pa. $5.95

AN ENCYCLOPEDIA OF BATTLES: Accounts of Over 1,560 Battles from 1479 B.C. to the Present, David Eggenberger. Presents essential details of every major battle in recorded history, from the first battle of Megiddo in 1479 B.C. to Grenada in 1984. List of Battle Maps. New Appendix covering the years 1967–1984. Index. 99 illustrations. 544pp. 6½ × 9¼.
24913-1 Pa. $14.95

AN ETYMOLOGICAL DICTIONARY OF MODERN ENGLISH, Ernest Weekley. Richest, fullest work, by foremost British lexicographer. Detailed word histories. Inexhaustible. Total of 856pp. 6½ × 9¼.
21873-2, 21874-0 Pa., Two-vol. set $17.00

WEBSTER'S AMERICAN MILITARY BIOGRAPHIES, edited by Robert McHenry. Over 1,000 figures who shaped 3 centuries of American military history. Detailed biographies of Nathan Hale, Douglas MacArthur, Mary Hallaren, others. Chronologies of engagements, more. Introduction. Addenda. 1,033 entries in alphabetical order. xi + 548pp. 6½ × 9¼. (Available in U.S. only)
24758-9 Pa. $11.95

LIFE IN ANCIENT EGYPT, Adolf Erman. Detailed older account, with much not in more recent books: domestic life, religion, magic, medicine, commerce, and whatever else needed for complete picture. Many illustrations. 597pp. 5⅜ × 8½.
22632-8 Pa. $8.95

HISTORIC COSTUME IN PICTURES, Braun & Schneider. Over 1,450 costumed figures shown, covering a wide variety of peoples: kings, emperors, nobles, priests, servants, soldiers, scholars, townsfolk, peasants, merchants, courtiers, cavaliers, and more. 256pp. 8⅜ × 11¼.
23150-X Pa. $7.95

THE NOTEBOOKS OF LEONARDO DA VINCI, edited by J. P. Richter. Extracts from manuscripts reveal great genius; on painting, sculpture, anatomy, sciences, geography, etc. Both Italian and English. 186 ms. pages reproduced, plus 500 additional drawings, including studies for *Last Supper*, *Sforza* monument, etc. 860pp. 7⅞ × 10¾. (Available in U.S. only) 22572-0, 22573-9 Pa., Two-vol. set $25.90

THE ART NOUVEAU STYLE BOOK OF ALPHONSE MUCHA: All 72 Plates from "Documents Decoratifs" in Original Color, Alphonse Mucha. Rare copyright-free design portfolio by high priest of Art Nouveau. Jewelry, wallpaper, stained glass, furniture, figure studies, plant and animal motifs, etc. Only complete one-volume edition. 80pp. 9⅜ × 12¼. 24044-4 Pa. $8.95

ANIMALS: 1,419 COPYRIGHT-FREE ILLUSTRATIONS OF MAMMALS, BIRDS, FISH, INSECTS, ETC., edited by Jim Harter. Clear wood engravings present, in extremely lifelike poses, over 1,000 species of animals. One of the most extensive pictorial sourcebooks of its kind. Captions. Index. 284pp. 9 × 12. 23766-4 Pa. $9.95

OBELISTS FLY HIGH, C. Daly King. Masterpiece of American detective fiction, long out of print, involves murder on a 1935 transcontinental flight—"a very thrilling story"—NY Times. Unabridged and unaltered republication of the edition published by William Collins Sons & Co. Ltd., London, 1935. 288pp. 5⅜ × 8½. (Available in U.S. only) 25036-9 Pa. $4.95

VICTORIAN AND EDWARDIAN FASHION: A Photographic Survey, Alison Gernsheim. First fashion history completely illustrated by contemporary photographs. Full text plus 235 photos, 1840–1914, in which many celebrities appear. 240pp. 6½ × 9¼. 24205-6 Pa. $6.00

THE ART OF THE FRENCH ILLUSTRATED BOOK, 1700–1914, Gordon N. Ray. Over 630 superb book illustrations by Fragonard, Delacroix, Daumier, Doré, Grandville, Manet, Mucha, Steinlen, Toulouse-Lautrec and many others. Preface. Introduction. 633 halftones. Indices of artists, authors & titles, binders and provenances. Appendices. Bibliography. 608pp. 8⅜ × 11¼. 25086-5 Pa. $24.95

THE WONDERFUL WIZARD OF OZ, L. Frank Baum. Facsimile in full color of America's finest children's classic. 143 illustrations by W. W. Denslow. 267pp. 5⅜ × 8½. 20691-2 Pa. $5.95

FRONTIERS OF MODERN PHYSICS: New Perspectives on Cosmology, Relativity, Black Holes and Extraterrestrial Intelligence, Tony Rothman, et al. For the intelligent layman. Subjects include: cosmological models of the universe; black holes; the neutrino; the search for extraterrestrial intelligence. Introduction. 46 black-and-white illustrations. 192pp. 5⅜ × 8½. 24587-X Pa. $6.95

THE FRIENDLY STARS, Martha Evans Martin & Donald Howard Menzel. Classic text marshalls the stars together in an engaging, non-technical survey, presenting them as sources of beauty in night sky. 23 illustrations. Foreword. 2 star charts. Index. 147pp. 5⅜ × 8½. 21099-5 Pa. $3.50

FADS AND FALLACIES IN THE NAME OF SCIENCE, Martin Gardner. Fair, witty appraisal of cranks, quacks, and quackeries of science and pseudoscience: hollow earth, Velikovsky, orgone energy, Dianetics, flying saucers, Bridey Murphy, food and medical fads, etc. Revised, expanded In the Name of Science. "A very able and even-tempered presentation."—The New Yorker. 363pp. 5⅜ × 8. 20394-8 Pa. $6.50

ANCIENT EGYPT: ITS CULTURE AND HISTORY, J. E Manchip White. From pre-dynastics through Ptolemies: society, history, political structure, religion, daily life, literature, cultural heritage. 48 plates. 217pp. 5⅜ × 8½. 22548-8 Pa. $4.95

SIR HARRY HOTSPUR OF HUMBLETHWAITE, Anthony Trollope. Incisive, unconventional psychological study of a conflict between a wealthy baronet, his idealistic daughter, and their scapegrace cousin. The 1870 novel in its first inexpensive edition in years. 250pp. 5⅜ × 8½. 24953-0 Pa. $5.95

LASERS AND HOLOGRAPHY, Winston E. Kock. Sound introduction to burgeoning field, expanded (1981) for second edition. Wave patterns, coherence, lasers, diffraction, zone plates, properties of holograms, recent advances. 84 illustrations. 160pp. 5⅜ × 8¼. (Except in United Kingdom) 24041-X Pa. $3.50

INTRODUCTION TO ARTIFICIAL INTELLIGENCE: SECOND, EN-LARGED EDITION, Philip C. Jackson, Jr. Comprehensive survey of artificial intelligence—the study of how machines (computers) can be made to act intelligently. Includes introductory and advanced material. Extensive notes updating the main text. 132 black-and-white illustrations. 512pp. 5⅜ × 8½. 24864-X Pa. $8.95

HISTORY OF INDIAN AND INDONESIAN ART, Ananda K. Coomaraswamy. Over 400 illustrations illuminate classic study of Indian art from earliest Harappa finds to early 20th century. Provides philosophical, religious and social insights. 304pp. 6⅜ × 9⅜. 25005-9 Pa. $8.95

THE GOLEM, Gustav Meyrink. Most famous supernatural novel in modern European literature, set in Ghetto of Old Prague around 1890. Compelling story of mystical experiences, strange transformations, profound terror. 13 black-and-white illustrations. 224pp. 5⅜ × 8½. (Available in U.S. only) 25025-3 Pa. $5.95

ARMADALE, Wilkie Collins. Third great mystery novel by the author of *The Woman in White* and *The Moonstone*. Original magazine version with 40 illustrations. 597pp. 5⅜ × 8½. 23429-0 Pa. $9.95

PICTORIAL ENCYCLOPEDIA OF HISTORIC ARCHITECTURAL PLANS, DETAILS AND ELEMENTS: With 1,880 Line Drawings of Arches, Domes, Doorways, Facades, Gables, Windows, etc., John Theodore Haneman. Sourcebook of inspiration for architects, designers, others. Bibliography. Captions. 141pp. 9 × 12. 24605-1 Pa. $6.95

BENCHLEY LOST AND FOUND, Robert Benchley. Finest humor from early 30's, about pet peeves, child psychologists, post office and others. Mostly unavailable elsewhere. 73 illustrations by Peter Arno and others. 183pp. 5⅜ × 8½. 22410-4 Pa. $3.95

ERTÉ GRAPHICS, Erté. Collection of striking color graphics: *Seasons, Alphabet, Numerals, Aces* and *Precious Stones*. 50 plates, including 4 on covers. 48pp. 9⅜ × 12¼. 23580-7 Pa. $6.95

THE JOURNAL OF HENRY D. THOREAU, edited by Bradford Torrey, F. H. Allen. Complete reprinting of 14 volumes, 1837–61, over two million words; the sourcebooks for *Walden*, etc. Definitive. All original sketches, plus 75 photographs. 1,804pp. 8½ × 12¼. 20312-3, 20313-1 Cloth., Two-vol. set $80.00

CASTLES: THEIR CONSTRUCTION AND HISTORY, Sidney Toy. Traces castle development from ancient roots. Nearly 200 photographs and drawings illustrate moats, keeps, baileys, many other features. Caernarvon, Dover Castles, Hadrian's Wall, Tower of London, dozens more. 256pp. 5⅜ × 8¼. 24898-4 Pa. $5.95

CATALOG OF DOVER BOOKS

AMERICAN CLIPPER SHIPS: 1833–1858, Octavius T. Howe & Frederick C. Matthews. Fully-illustrated, encyclopedic review of 352 clipper ships from the period of America's greatest maritime supremacy. Introduction. 109 halftones. 5 black-and-white line illustrations. Index. Total of 928pp. 5⅜ × 8½.
25115-2, 25116-0 Pa., Two-vol. set $17.90

TOWARDS A NEW ARCHITECTURE, Le Corbusier. Pioneering manifesto by great architect, near legendary founder of "International School." Technical and aesthetic theories, views on industry, economics, relation of form to function, "mass-production spirit," much more. Profusely illustrated. Unabridged translation of 13th French edition. Introduction by Frederick Etchells. 320pp. 6⅛ × 9¼. (Available in U.S. only)
25023-7 Pa. $8.95

THE BOOK OF KELLS, edited by Blanche Cirker. Inexpensive collection of 32 full-color, full-page plates from the greatest illuminated manuscript of the Middle Ages, painstakingly reproduced from rare facsimile edition. Publisher's Note. Captions. 32pp. 9⅜ × 12¼.
24345-1 Pa. $4.95

BEST SCIENCE FICTION STORIES OF H. G. WELLS, H. G. Wells. Full novel *The Invisible Man*, plus 17 short stories: "The Crystal Egg," "Aepyornis Island," "The Strange Orchid," etc. 303pp. 5⅜ × 8½. (Available in U.S. only)
21531-8 Pa. $4.95

AMERICAN SAILING SHIPS: Their Plans and History, Charles G. Davis. Photos, construction details of schooners, frigates, clippers, other sailcraft of 18th to early 20th centuries—plus entertaining discourse on design, rigging, nautical lore, much more. 137 black-and-white illustrations. 240pp. 6⅛ × 9¼.
24658-2 Pa. $5.95

ENTERTAINING MATHEMATICAL PUZZLES, Martin Gardner. Selection of author's favorite conundrums involving arithmetic, money, speed, etc., with lively commentary. Complete solutions. 112pp. 5⅜ × 8½.
25211-6 Pa. $2.95

THE WILL TO BELIEVE, HUMAN IMMORTALITY, William James. Two books bound together. Effect of irrational on logical, and arguments for human immortality. 402pp. 5⅜ × 8½.
20291-7 Pa. $7.50

THE HAUNTED MONASTERY and THE CHINESE MAZE MURDERS, Robert Van Gulik. 2 full novels by Van Gulik continue adventures of Judge Dee and his companions. An evil Taoist monastery, seemingly supernatural events; overgrown topiary maze that hides strange crimes. Set in 7th-century China. 27 illustrations. 328pp. 5⅜ × 8½.
23502-5 Pa. $5.95

CELEBRATED CASES OF JUDGE DEE (DEE GOONG AN), translated by Robert Van Gulik. Authentic 18th-century Chinese detective novel; Dee and associates solve three interlocked cases. Led to Van Gulik's own stories with same characters. Extensive introduction. 9 illustrations. 237pp. 5⅜ × 8½.
23337-5 Pa. $4.95

Prices subject to change without notice.

Available at your book dealer or write for free catalog to Dept. GI, Dover Publications, Inc., 31 East 2nd St., Mineola, N.Y. 11501. Dover publishes more than 175 books each year on science, elementary and advanced mathematics, biology, music, art, literary history, social sciences and other areas.